Master Stress:
Tame Your Inner Monster

A My Guide

Rebecca Richmond

Cambridge, England

First published in Great Britain 2015
by My Guide
The Studio
High Green
Great Shelford
Cambridge CB22 5EG

www.januspublishing.co.uk
www.cambridge-media.com

British Library Cataloguing-in-Publication Data
A catalogue record for this book is available from the British Library

Book cover image designed by Daniela Frongia, Cais Arts

ISBN-13: 978-1-910141-03-8

Printed and bound in the UK by PublishPoint
from KnowledgePoint Limited, Reading

Dedication

For Ian and Rose,

who make my life special.

Legal Disclaimer

By purchasing and reading this book you agree that you understand that the author is an individual who is sharing with you her personal knowledge and experience of managing stress. You accept that she is not a doctor, licensed medical practitioner, nutritionist, dietician or trained to advise on diet and exercise.

The author is not suggesting that you use the information in this book as a substitute for professional or medical advice and she is by no means telling you what to do. The text reflects only the measures that she personally took to reduce the effects of her own stress. Therefore, you accept that she is not suggesting that you change your diet, either by adding or subtracting foods and/ or liquids.

Neither is the author implying or suggesting that you stop taking any prescribed medication. Indeed, she strongly recommends that you check with the medical specialist to whom you have been referred or that you seek advice from your GP, hospital or a qualified medical professional before making amendments to your diet, undertaking an exercise regime, changing your existing regime or engaging in alternative or complementary therapies.

This book is not intended to diagnose or treat any ailments and the author is not attempting to prescribe medical treatment or cures for any medical conditions, diagnosed or otherwise. Neither the author nor the publisher, My Guide, accept responsibility for any loss or injury resulting from the use of any information contained herein.

Master Stress: Tame Your Inner Monster – part of the *My Guide* series – is for information purposes only. It reflects the author's personal journey and her personal beliefs. By adopting, imitating or following any of the processes described by the author, you are doing so of your own accord and at your own risk.

The author strongly recommends that if you are concerned about the effects of stress on either your mental or physical well-being that you consult a qualified doctor. This book is no substitute for professional advice.

Contents

Children

Chapter Thirteen – Work Stress   213

Preface

Hakuna Matata (There are no worries)

Timon and Pumbaa

'I'm stressed' is a phrase that is commonly used and it generally signifies unpleasant feelings. But the reality is that how we each feel about and react to stress is as individual as we are.

One thing that everyone has in common is that excessive stress reduces the ability to enjoy life. However, the human race appears to have accepted being stressed out as the norm. Thankfully, just because everyone else around us appears stressed, that does not mean we have to accept it as a normal way to live our lives.

Our bodies are able to cope with short periods of intense pressure. However, long-term exposure to stress and the stress response – also known as the fight or flight response – can cause damage to health and well-being.

For much of my life I was either afraid or stressed. It is my belief that this constant state of feeling stressed and my response to it almost resulted in my paying the ultimate price – my life. As a child raised in poverty, with the added strains, fears and shame that came from being abused, life wasn't easy. Hindsight is a wonderful thing, but I now know that the choices I made as an adult and the pressures I piled on myself – through my career, relationships, insecurities and lack of self-esteem – resulted in overwhelming levels of stress for nearly two decades. Looking back, I think I only managed to keep my sanity through sheer determination.

☺ Although some might think I'm not exactly sane! Just kidding.

Throughout my life I have always been very health conscious, but despite looking after my health and body, and having a healthy

1

lifestyle, I still developed debilitating and life-threatening conditions: fibromyalgia, CFS (Chronic Fatigue Syndrome), a pancreatic tumour and a malignant melanoma. In case you are wondering, no, I have never been a sun worshipper. It is my opinion that these conditions were the direct result of my body reacting to prolonged and extreme stress.

As a coach, for over a decade I have been working to reduce stress in both my life and those of my clients. Stress is the plague of the twenty-first century and it is reaching epidemic proportions. The irony is that many people suffering from stress have become so used to the feeling that they may not even realise that they have been experiencing the effects of stress for many years. Often, it is only when it has reached a level where it manifests in the form of broken relationships, addictions, depression or ill health that they feel compelled to take action to stop the tidal wave of stress from blighting their lives.

Within this guide you will gain a real understanding of what stress means for you and what your triggers are. You will also learn how to reduce the stress you are experiencing, control your reaction to challenges in life and develop the ability to relax completely. In the final chapters you will discover how to live life in a way that is more fulfilling and enjoyable, as well as less stressful.

Things to look out for in this guide:

1. Notes to self – at the end of each chapter, these inspirational notes are designed to remind you what you should be doing to decrease the stress in your life. Copy them out and put them somewhere where you can read them every day.

2. Smiley faces – these have been added because I like them and they remind me not to take life too seriously. ☺

3. Quotes – at the beginning of each chapter and within the text you will find quotations relating to stress or life in general. They are not there just to fill a space – some will make you smile, others will inspire you and hopefully they will all help you realise that you are not alone in this stress-filled world.

4. Stories or poems – these are an important part of this guide and should not be skipped. Stories have been used as a teaching tool for thousands of years. However, you should

not allow yourself to become stressed trying to overanalyse the meaning behind them – your unconscious mind will do that for you.

You cannot wave a magic wand to eliminate all the stress in your life. But by using the processes described in this guide and by being prepared to accept a new way of thinking and behaving, you can:

- minimise the bad stress in your life
- manage the remaining stress
- learn to use stress to your advantage
- develop ways to relax quickly and easily

You will need to acquire a notebook or set up a notes file on your computer or tablet, because over the coming weeks I will be your personal coach. As such, I will be asking you to think about yourself and your life, probably in more detail and in ways you never have before.

If you have already begun giving yourself reasons not to participate in this coaching process fully or have decided to read through the guide quickly, it is unlikely you will get the results you desire.

Managing stress is a lifelong commitment and I certainly have not perfected stress management in my own life. Like everyone else, I am a work in progress, but I have come a long way.

When I was writing this book my husband made a decision that resulted in me breaking many of my own rules, placing me under considerable stress for a period of about six months. But as we worked through the challenges, achieved our goal and came out the other side smiling, I realised that I was perfectly equipped to write a book on stress management.

☺ I am a normal person who will always have challenges to face.

I am committed to helping you reduce the stress in your life and manage the stress that does come along. I challenge you now to make the same commitment to yourself. Now it is your turn, so when you are ready, let us move on and begin your journey to a better life ... ☺

Chapter One – Simply Stress

We all live with the objective of being happy; our lives are
all different and yet the same.

Anne Frank

Introduction

You may have been suffering from stress for so long that you have forgotten what it feels like *not* to be stressed. Ironically, for many it is only when they relax that they realise they have been stressed.

Maybe you long for the freedom you feel while on holiday or at weekends before the Sunday-night dread sets in. Or perhaps for the first few minutes in the morning you glimpse that lovely feeling of peace before stress swamps you. Whatever your motivation for wanting to deal with the stress you are experiencing, some remarkable benefits are within your grasp.

By dealing with the stress in your life you will undoubtedly enjoy life more, feel more energetic, be healthier and maybe even live longer. If these aren't enough to convince you, then you are not thinking clearly, which is one of the effects of stress – so keep reading. ☺

External events may cause you to feel under pressure, but the stress you feel comes from inside you. As the pressure builds your inner 'Stress Monster' begins to wake and when it does, it wreaks havoc with your life, damaging your mind, body and spirit. It may attack when least expected and overwhelm you within minutes. Or it could begin by disturbing your peace of mind in small ways, gradually gaining in strength until it is out of control. However, when it is misbehaving, learning to understand your inner monster gives you a firm foundation from which to master it. The monster may always be by your side, but if it is behaving and walking to heel then that is fine, because not all stress is bad – as you will discover as you read on.

5

In simple terms, stress is the feeling of being placed under too much emotional or mental pressure. Pressures of everyday life such as work, relationships and money can turn into stress. Once you are feeling stressed it can:

- affect how you feel
- reduce your ability to make rational decisions
- change your behaviour
- generally have a negative effect on your life

This makes it difficult to sort out any challenges you are facing.

People have different ways of reacting to situations, so what one person might find stressful another might be unaffected by. Others might even find it exciting or motivating. Only you will know if you need to take action and, most importantly, if you are ready to take control of your life.

Give your stress wings and let it fly away.

Terri Guillemets

Why You Need *Some* Stress in Your Life

Right now, you might feel that you want to eliminate *all* stress from your life. However, it is important to understand from the start that it is *not* possible for you to go through life experiencing no stress at all.

Not all stress is bad and some short-term stress – for example, what you feel before an important job presentation, test, interview or sporting event – may even give you the extra energy you need to perform at your best. If you did manage to achieve a completely stress-free existence, you would not be living life to your full potential. Indeed, you would be missing out on the enjoyment that comes from a sense of achievement and handling challenges well.

There is a Tibetan prayer that actually asks for challenges:

Grant that I may be given appropriate difficulties and suffering on this journey so that my heart may be truly awakened.

Although I would not consciously invite difficulties into my life, I definitely agree that they are an opportunity for growth.

Automatic Stress Response

Stress is not just an emotional reaction or in the mind. It actually causes a physical reaction commonly known as the 'fight or flight' response, which was first described by American physiologist Walter Cannon in 1932. The SNS – sympathetic nervous system – governs fight or flight. When working correctly it gives you focus, energy, strength and increased alertness. In life-threatening emergency situations, such as escaping from a house fire, the fight or flight response can be crucial to your survival.

But if you frequently find yourself in situations you find stressful, your fight or flight response can become overactive, until you perceive potential threats everywhere. This is why work-related stress can have an adverse affect on your health.

When you feel threatened or trapped, or perceive a significant threat to your existence, your body releases hormones to prepare for either a fight to the death or a desperate flight from a superior adversary. In the modern world, an example of this heightened response would be a car accident, where it triggered you to slam on the brakes to avoid a collision. However, on most occasions the threat you feel is not life-threatening but imagined.

Whenever you experience something that is frustrating, unexpected or worrying, the fight or flight response can be triggered. This has physical effects on the body, which begin with adrenaline being released into the blood stream. The result is a number of changes in your body to prepare you to take action, including:

Physical Reaction	Symptoms
Muscles tense, ready for action – fight or flight	Muscle aches
Body cools itself	Sweating, blushing
Heart beats faster to get blood and oxygen to the muscles	Palpitations
Saliva production reduced	Mouth becomes dry
Breathing becomes fast and shallow, supplying more oxygen to the muscles	Chest pain, palpitations, tingling, feeling faint or dizzy

Physical Reaction	Symptoms
Blood temporarily diverted away from the stomach	Churning sensation, nausea, indigestion
Muscles of anus and bladder relax	Urge to urinate/defecate

Once the threat (real or perceived) has passed, the PNS – parasympathetic nervous system, which operates the body's natural rest-and-recuperation process – should enable stress hormone levels to return to normal. However, if you are constantly under stress, stress hormones will remain in your body, leading to the symptoms of stress – see later.

Prior to learning how to manage stress better I was constantly on the alert for problems. The downside of this – apart from the negative effects to my health – was that being stressed about what might occur meant I was constantly looking for problems. I would perceive them even when they didn't exist. I also believed that situations were far worse than they really were. Now, I have faith in my ability to deal with things if they arise. Because of this, challenges arise far less frequently and I no longer suffer the negative effects of unnecessary stress.

☺ Which is better for me and everyone around me.

Natural Predisposition

Research has shown that some people are naturally more prone to stress than others. These people are known as 'Type A' personalities. They tend to be more competitive and impatient. They are also more likely to set themselves deadlines and tight schedules than 'Type B' personalities, who are more relaxed and generally laid-back.

Find out if you are a 'Type A' personality by seeing if some the following traits apply to you:

Are you:

- determined to get things finished?
- always in a hurry?
- never late for appointments?

- fiercely competitive?
- unable to listen patiently, often interrupting and finishing other people's sentences?
- impatient and unable to wait?
- needing for everything to be perfect?
- bottling things up, holding feelings in?
- quick and breathless in speech?
- seldom completely content with work or home life?
- lacking in social interests or activities?

In comparison, a 'Type B' personality is the type of person who is:

- not bothered if they leave things unfinished
- calm and unhurried about appointments
- not particularly competitive
- able to listen and let others speak
- never in a hurry, even when busy
- generally easy-going
- unperturbed if things are imperfect
- slow and deliberate in speech
- generally satisfied with their lot
- socially active

  ☺ If you have discovered you are a type-A personality in every way, don't freak out on me – there *are* things you can do to avoid potentially stressful situations. You can even choose to adopt some type-B personality traits.

If you have a natural predisposition to stress, this guide will help you learn to spot the signs of stress early on, so you can take action to stop it getting out of control.

Your Stress Symptoms

There is an old saying that: *'A journey of a thousand miles begins with a single step'*. While this is very true, before you begin any journey, you need to know where you are starting from. It is the same with achieving goals in that in order to achieve your goal – which in your case is to reduce and manage stress – you have to be clear what your starting point is.

By understanding where you are right now, you will be able to measure your progress. So let us begin by looking at how stress manifests itself in your life.

Symptoms of stress can be broken down into four areas:

1. Cognitive symptoms
These affect your ability to carry out normal mental processes such as learning, judgement, reasoning and problem-solving. Symptoms include:

- an inability to concentrate
- memory problems
- negative perception
- anxiety and constant worrying
- racing thoughts from an overactive mind

Feeling stressed is difficult enough to cope with on its own, but when it reaches the stage where you are experiencing cognitive symptoms, it can affect every area of your life. The symptoms in themselves are very likely to increase your stress levels. For example, if you are suffering from stress at work and you perceive everything negatively, coping with your work situation will be even more difficult.

2. Behavioural symptoms
Behaviour is the way in which you conduct yourself, how you respond to situations, stimulus or circumstances, and the manner in which you act towards others. Behavioural symptoms of stress are unhelpful and in some cases harmful. They include:

- sleeping too much
- insomnia
- nervous habits such as nail-biting, overeating and teeth-grinding
- isolating yourself from other people

- procrastinating or neglecting responsibilities
- using drugs (including prescription medication), alcohol or cigarettes to relax

Stress is often displayed through behaviour and whilst biting your nails might not be harmful to you, your loved ones or society, some other behaviours are. If you can't relax after a day at work without half a bottle of wine, or you feel you can't cope being around other people, then it is a clear signal that you need to take action to reduce your feelings of stress.

3. Emotional symptoms

Emotions are the feelings you experience at any given time, including joy, sorrow, love and hate. Your mental state arises spontaneously rather than through conscious thought and is often accompanied by physiological changes. Emotional symptoms of stress relate to inappropriate or frequent negative emotions and they include the following:

- general unhappiness or depression
- short temper or irritability
- frequent mood swings
- a feeling of overwhelm
- agitation and an inability to relax or remain still
- a sense of loneliness and isolation

It is perfectly natural to experience negative emotions in certain circumstances. However, when you are stressed, these negative feelings become part of everyday life, which can pose a real problem.

4. Physical symptoms

Physical symptoms affect the body rather than the mind. They can be caused by many conditions or illnesses; therefore, if you are suffering from physical symptoms, *you should always seek a diagnosis from your doctor or medical provider to rule out other conditions*. Stress can cause many physical symptoms, including:

- chest pain

- a feeling of tightness in the chest
- a rapid heartbeat
- sweating
- loss of libido
- diarrhoea
- constipation
- irritable bowel syndrome
- muscle tension
- loss of appetite
- nausea
- dizziness
- headaches
- aches and pains
- exhaustion
- frequent coughs and colds

Every day, millions of people take medication for symptoms related to stress, without tackling the cause. However, once we understand the fight or flight response described earlier, it is easy to see why it will eventually affect our health. In addition, if we have another condition or illness, its symptoms may be aggravated by stress.

Review the lists of stress symptoms and acknowledge the ones that are affecting you.

☺ It is okay to admit you are stressed – there is only me listening.

Superhero Syndrome

Society seems to foster the belief that we all have to be superheroes. This makes it difficult for people to admit that stress is having a negative effect on their well-being and happiness.

We live in a have-it-all, be-everything world. Men are expected to be strong and to have the ability to handle everything life throws at them without complaint. They have to provide for a family, work longer hours than ever, help out around the house, be a hands-on dad, yet still find the time to hit the gym and get a six-pack. And all this before rushing home to keep the romance alive in the relationship and offer support to their partner, in any way she/he needs.

☺ Not easy while they are changing nappies and putting the dishwasher on …

Women, on the other hand, are regarded as less worthy if they are not doing a good imitation of being superwoman, both in the workplace and at home. Despite the fact that men are doing more than ever these days, women are generally still expected to run the home without objection, be the ideal mother, be active on the PTA, help with homework/school projects and provide a taxi service. Not only that, but they also need to ensure their little angels are perfect, with everything they could possibly need, whilst making sure they attend the right after-school clubs and classes. Not forgetting the need to be a sex goddess and a supportive wife, of course. Whilst at work they are expected to be focused only on the job, proving they can 'hack it', travel anywhere and work all the hours God sent!

Okay, I mustn't rant, but the things I have mentioned are just a few of the demands we all pile on ourselves. And I didn't even mention the extra pressures of looking after ageing relatives, not having enough money or being a single parent …

☺ Had to stop myself there; I was about to rant again!

Although it is unrealistic to expect you to drop some of your responsibilities to reduce stress, as you will learn in later chapters, you can still be successful in all areas of your life whilst enjoying yourself – you just need to drop the superhero cape.

How Stressed are You?

Often, people only notice the physical effects of stress when they reach the stage where they are experiencing the symptoms listed earlier. But if they notice the early warning signs of stress as it is increasing, it is easier to bring it under control.

Over the next week, actively observe your reactions to uncomfortable situations. Each time you realise you are reacting badly and beginning to feel stressed, make a note of it so that you become familiar with the signs. When you start this exercise, you will notice that you are unconsciously doing or experiencing some or all of the following:

- tightness in your calf or thigh muscles
- hunching your shoulders
- pursing your lips
- curling your toes
- tension in your arms
- tightness in your chest
- a sick or churning feeling in your stomach
- headaches
- biting your nails
- fiddling with something
- rapid breathing
- or another reaction that you recognise occurs as stress increases

The level of stress you feel will vary depending on the situation you are in. Think of it like a scale marked zero to ten, zero being a state where you feel completely relaxed and ten being a state of complete overwhelm. Depending on the circumstances, you might spend much of your day at around four or five, peaking at nine or ten in difficult situations. Devise your own scale in order to measure how stressed you are feeling; for example:

10 incredibly stressed and unable to cope any longer

8 very stressed, with tightness in your chest and rapid breathing

6 moderately stressed, to the degree where you can feel your muscles tensing

3 slightly stressed, where it could even be excitement about a presentation or meeting

0 no feeling of stress at all, where your shoulders are relaxed and you don't feel like biting your nails, etc.

Perform a quick scan of your body several times a day. By doing the scan at various times, including when you are not feeling stressed, you will be able to establish a benchmark that you can use as a comparison in stressful situations.

The stress scale may be simple, but it is a very effective way of gauging how you are feeling. The following table has been devised in order to help you measure your stress levels (I have completed the first one to get you started):

Stress Rating	Situations	Thoughts	Stress Symptoms
4	Just managed to catch the train on time	Hope it's not delayed; can't afford to be late for this meeting	Shoulders slightly hunched; chest feels tight

Life's Big Stresses

No matter how hard we try, we cannot isolate ourselves from obstacles and problems, as they are a natural part of life. Although being problem-free makes us happy, changing our reaction to problems and altering beliefs that prevent us from being happy with our current situation is the best way to reduce stress when issues arise – which they will …

It is well recognised that for many people certain life events and changes will trigger stress. Therefore, if you have experienced one or more of the following in the past twelve months, it is quite likely you will be more prone to stress than you otherwise would be:

- death of a partner or close family member/friend
- partner or close family member suffering from serious illness
- personal health problems

- job loss/new job
- serious debt
- strained relationships
- divorce or separation
- problems at work
- job promotion
- demanding financial commitments
- legal issues
- serious fallout with a close friend, work colleague, neighbour or family member
- term of imprisonment
- major alterations in working life or patterns
- significant change in living conditions/arrangements
- organising a wedding
- pregnancy or birth of a child
- change in spiritual habits

It is important to note that not everyone will find these events stressful and that all of life's events affect different people in different ways.

Stress is not just about the situations you encounter, but how you perceive them, the thoughts that follow and your subsequent reactions. Each event, just like you, is unique. Therefore, regardless of how anyone else might feel about your situation, you need to use the information provided in this book in order to manage the feelings of stress and get your life back on a more even track.

Identify and Rate Your Stress Triggers

One of the wonderful things about human beings is how unique we all are. It is this uniqueness that dictates how we react to situations differently. It also determines why a situation can make one person run for the hills, whereas another may view it as an exciting challenge or at most a minor inconvenience.

Just as we all find different things amusing or funny, we all find different situations stressful. Thankfully, how stressful we find a particular situation is down to our perception of it and therefore it can be changed.

We will cover this in the next chapter, but for now it is only important to recognise what your stress triggers are.

Stress triggers generally fall into the following categories:

1. Change
Some people thrive on change but for others it can be immensely stressful, particularly when related to a key area of their lives.

2. Work
There can be a number of reasons why the workplace can cause stress, including our own beliefs. But it may also be down to external factors that can contribute to the anxiety felt by an increasing number of people. Workplace stress is covered in greater detail in Chapter Thirteen.

3. Financial
Financial stress is probably the one that causes the most problems in relationships. Although being rich does not eliminate all stress and money cannot bring happiness, there is no doubt that a lack of sufficient money to meet perceived needs is for many the cause of a great deal of anxiety. Dealing with financial stress often requires practical and internal changes, covered in Chapter Seven.

4. Chemical
Although people often use them to relax, introducing chemicals into our system can put our bodies under stress. Chemicals include alcohol, nicotine, caffeine and tranquillisers.

5. Decision-making
This can be a source of major stress, especially when it is perceived as having a large impact on someone's life.

6. Emotional or Internal
These stressors are very individual and are caused by internal thought processes and beliefs. Certain personality traits – including perfectionism, pessimism and suspiciousness – can also distort both our way of thinking and our perception of others.

7. Environmental

Often we do not pay much attention to our environment, until there is an issue such as excessive noise, pollution, lack of space, too much heat or cold, or even clutter, which can then result in stress.

8. Family

Problems and changes in relationships, bereavement, parenting and 'empty-nest' syndrome can all be a source of stress in the family unit.

9. Illness

When faced with our own mortality through a life-threatening illness, it naturally triggers the stress response, as can chronic illness.

10. Phobias

Anyone who has a phobia can attest to the fact that situations we are extremely afraid of, such as spiders, flying in airplanes or being confined in tight spaces, are stress triggers.

11. Physical

This can include situations where we put our bodies under too much pressure; for example, working for prolonged periods with insufficient rest, over-exercising or continual deprivation of healthy food.

12. Social

Any interaction with others, including public speaking, can be perceived by individuals as unpleasant, uncomfortable or even frightening.

13. Media

The TV, radio, newspapers and even magazines frequently run stories of distress, disasters, wars and suffering. This type of information can be extremely stressful if it causes anxiety for those involved or concerns about the welfare of those we care about.

Realising how many stress triggers you have can be stressful in itself, but don't despair. Regardless of your particular triggers, it is your thoughts about a situation that cause the stress. The more you think about what has already or what could go wrong in the future, the more stressed you will feel.

We all have the same fears, but there is no doubt that we all feel some of them more acutely than others. Sadly, these fears can be crippling, in turn causing anxiety.

Make a list of all the stress triggers and rate them from zero to five in accordance with how you feel about them, zero being that you are unaffected by it at all and five being a major stress trigger.

Apologies if you thought identifying all the areas in your life that stress you out was bad enough, because in the next chapter we are going to take a look at your fears ...

☺ Stick with me – it is an important part of the process. After all, how can you address a problem if you don't know that the problem really is?

Self-awareness is a vital step to this new way of living. Learning to understand stress and your individual stress triggers is just the first step, so keep reading.

The Doe

A doe, blind in one eye, feared grazing in the open. Her worry was that a hunter would approach her from the side where her sight had gone.

She devised a plan so she could feel safer and only grazed near to the edge of the cliff, ensuring her good eye was constantly focused on the land, with her bad eye facing out to sea.

Anticipating no danger from the sea, she felt assured of being alerted to any threat to her safety should hunters approach by land.

It was a calm, sunny day when a ship sailed by. The captain, taking successful aim, claimed fresh meat for his crew ...

Notes to Self

- Stress is not a weakness or a lack of something within me. I can learn to control stress and change the way I think, feel and behave in any situation.
- Where I am today is a measure of my past and does not determine the future. As long as I take positive action, I can improve my life.
- Not all stress is bad and it should not be eliminated altogether.

Take Action

- Acknowledge your stress symptoms.
- Find your motivation to overcome stress.
- Adopt some type-B personality traits.
- Gain an understanding of where you are now and where you want to be in a year.
- Notice your reaction to uncomfortable or stressful situations and make a note of them so that you become familiar with the signs.
- Measure your stress levels on the stress scale.
- Identify your stress triggers.
- Pin the 'Notes to Self' somewhere where you can see them every day.

Chapter Two – You Have the Power to Start Changing Today

The time to relax is when you don't have time for it.

Attributed to both Jim Goodwin and Sydney J. Harris

Introduction

If you are feeling stressed it is because you believe you are in a situation you don't have the capacity to deal with. This inevitably takes away your freedom and leads to a feeling of being trapped. After all, if you weren't feeling trapped, you would just walk away from the situation that is making you feel unhappy.

Whether or not your reasons for holding on to your current situation are valid is not important at this stage. First, we are going to focus on the immense amount of untapped power you have within you right now by exploring the two ways we make sense of our world: consciously and unconsciously.

The Conscious Mind

The conscious mind is where decision-making takes place and is the part of our thinking we are conscious or aware of. Whilst some people are proficient at multitasking, it is not as effective as we might think. This is because we can only consciously handle very limited pieces of information at any one time.

The Unconscious Mind

The unconscious mind is able to handle many things simultaneously and efficiently. Although we are not consciously aware of it all, it receives and processes millions of messages every second via our senses: sight, smell, hearing, taste and touch. It contains all of our memories and even represses some painful ones. The reason we can do certain tasks with little or no attention is that we become unconsciously skilled at it. This can include both useful tasks like tying shoelaces and less helpful ones like making ourselves feel depressed or stressed.

When we are asleep, our conscious mind continues to help us process what has happened during the day through dreaming. This is the reason we can wake up with the solution to a problem we had not been able to resolve the previous day.

Most importantly, the unconscious mind operates our bodies, carrying out numerous tasks simultaneously and even ensuring we continue to function whilst we are asleep.

☺ A woman saw a little old man sitting on his porch.

'You look so happy. What's your secret?' she asked.

'I never exercise, I eat fatty food, I drink a bottle of whisky a night and I smoke forty cigarettes a day,' he said.

'Wow! that's amazing,' the woman said. 'How old are you?'

'Twenty-five,' he said.

Perception

In order to be able to perceive something, it must first be understood by our minds. To clarify what perception is, it is the process of becoming aware of or conscious of something. The way in which people perceive things and make sense of the world around them is completely individual and is centred around our beliefs, values and even our mood at any given moment. Examples of this are:

- Person A believes that all forms of stealing are wrong.
- Person B believes it is okay as long as it is only from companies, not individuals.
- Person C also believes that it is wrong to steal from companies but that it is okay to copy DVDs and download music illegally.
- Person D believes it is every man for himself and you can take what you like regardless of who owns it or its value.

- Person E believes fraudulent insurance or benefit claims and tax avoidance definitely do not count as stealing

Our current mood alters our perception, which is why if we are feeling stressed even little things like having to queue in the bank can send stress levels through the roof. Days where we feel like everything is wrong without good reason for feeling that way are a direct result of our internal processing that day.

If you are already experiencing feelings of stress, you will automatically and unconsciously view every event with more anxiety, suspicion and nervousness, which is likely to cause you to overreact.

Perception is an individual's personal opinion or viewpoint about a particular event. It is not the external events themselves that lead directly to an emotional reaction. It is our beliefs, values and thoughts about what has occurred that create the emotion about the event.

There is no doubt that some events are unpleasant, painful, inconvenient, disruptive, etc. But the thoughts we have about the events can magnify or reduce the magnitude of the events in our minds and therefore have a direct effect on our stress levels.

I love the old story of the young woman who wrote to her parents from university. It has been adapted many times over the years, but this is my version:

Dear Mum and Dad,

I'm so sorry I haven't been in touch, but a lot has been happening and I didn't want to worry you. I'll tell you everything now, but you need to sit down before you carry on reading.

There was a bad fire in the university dorms and I had to jump from the second storey. Although I fractured my skull and suffered burns, I'm recovering well and the doctors say that eventually I'll be able to live a normal life.

Thankfully Spike, a Hell's Angel, was riding past as I jumped and he went to the hospital with me. He was great and visited me every day. As the dormitory has burnt down, I've been crashing at his squat. It's not as bad as you might think and even though the others take drugs, Spike is against all that. I know you'll love him as much as I do.

Although he doesn't have a job, he's ambitious and has asked me to run a burger van with him in Australia. I know it's on the other side of the world, but you've always wanted to travel and I'm sure you'll come and see me often.

So I've decided to quit university. It seems so pointless now as we're getting married in a few weeks, before the pregnancy shows. Yes, I'm pregnant – and I know how much you'll enjoy being grandparents.

Well, now I've brought you fully up to date, I hope you aren't too disappointed, because actually I want to tell you that there was no dormitory fire, I wasn't injured, I wasn't admitted to hospital, I'm not pregnant, I'm not getting married, I'm not quitting university and I don't know anyone called Spike.

However, I've failed my statistics module and have to re-sit this summer. I wanted to help you keep it in perspective so gave you the worst-case scenario first.

Your ever-loving daughter

Take Another's Viewpoint

The information and exercises throughout this manual will help you gain control of your emotions and become more objective about your perception. To get you started, a quick tip is to practise perceiving events from another's viewpoint.

Ask yourself how a more relaxed, confident, positive or optimistic version of you might react to an event you find stressful.

If you realise you are reacting badly to events because of your emotional state or even out of habit, don't reproach or criticise yourself about it. The purpose is to become self-aware and recognise that the way you see situations is not unquestionable reality, merely your perception.

Beliefs and Values

Our model of the world is unique to us and is formed around our personal beliefs and values. Most of us think of our beliefs as facts, overlooking the reality that they are just one perspective and that another person will view the situation differently.

If you want to discover what someone's beliefs are, simply chat to them for a while. As you will discover, almost everything we say is a belief. Which is why a person's opinion of how we should behave and live our lives will differ greatly from person to person.

During childhood we were constantly learning and developing. Beliefs and values start in childhood and continue to develop over our lifetime. A belief starts with a thought and then as events occur, we decide if the events prove or disprove the theory. Problems occur once an unhelpful or incorrect belief has formed. In such cases, over time we will unconsciously seek evidence to support it, until it becomes a conviction. Convictions are extremely strong beliefs that can evoke strong emotional reactions if challenged.

People who are most significant in our lives – including parents, siblings and peers – can greatly influence our beliefs and values. However, some form as a result of experiences we have encountered. Either way, it is often possible to pinpoint how they developed.

When my clients have a belief that is adversely affecting their lives, they often find it easier to change that belief once they have identified the source.

> ☺ However, identifying the source of your beliefs and values is not fundamental to being able to change them, so no stressing about it!

Power of beliefs

Beliefs are the starting point from which we make all decisions. When we feel threatened in some way beliefs provide certainty, which make us feel more secure, even if it is in a negative way. If, for example, we believe that people are always looking to take advantage of us, this will greatly influence how we react to and treat others.

Not all beliefs will be incorrect or increase stress levels, but it is worth finding out which ones are holding you back or causing you problems.

Limiting beliefs

We all have limiting beliefs and in many ways they can keep us safe and prevent us from taking irresponsible risks. But it is a great shame if your beliefs hold you back from fulfilling your full potential or finding happiness. Examples might be:

- I am no good at studying
- I will never be able to trust men again
- I am unable to change
- people like me cannot become rich

People generally back up their limiting beliefs with negative reasoning – in effect justifying their belief – but often without real evidence.

If you have the limiting belief that you will never be able to do your job without being stressed, you should address that immediately. You may have given yourself reasons like:

- stress gives me the edge to perform better
- stress is just part of the job
- I have been stressed the entire time I have worked here so it won't change now
- everyone who works here is stressed

These statements may all be true to some degree, but the fact is that there will be someone in a role very similar to you who finds it exciting not stressful.

Likewise, no one can *make* you stressed, no matter how much they try – unless you allow it to happen. Use the Limiting Belief Buster (coming up) and start consciously choosing what you believe. Each day that you make small changes you will gradually move forward, until you are in a much better frame of mind to enjoy life.

Limiting Belief Buster (part one)

There are two types of limiting or negative beliefs I want you to address. The first are any negative beliefs you have about yourself.

Finish these statements:

- The biggest limiting beliefs I have about myself are …

- The one that has held me back the most is …
- The limiting belief that makes me most stressed is …
- I developed this belief as a result of …
- Because of these beliefs my life has been …
- These beliefs have stopped me …

Just in case finishing those statements has led you to feel stressed or fed up, let's establish some ground rules:

1. Remember: beliefs are not facts.
2. You are no one's opinion of you, not even your own.
3. If you choose to, you *can* change your beliefs.
4. If you feel these beliefs were dumped on you by someone else, forgive both them and yourself for taking them on board.

You can then start to free yourself from the limiting beliefs that have held you back in the past:

1. For each limiting belief you identified, write down the opposite of that belief – the polar view or what you would prefer to believe instead. Right now it may feel like a lie, but if you consciously start to seek out evidence to support your new belief gradually, over time, you will realise your beliefs can change.
2. List the personality traits that you admire in people you know or those you have observed in people in the public eye. Decide which ones you want to adopt in your own life and then write out the following, listing how you feel: The personality traits that I am choosing to show to the world from today are patience, tolerance, generosity …
3. Consider what things you would like people to say about you; for example: He is patient and understanding.
4. Make a list of things you like about your own personality. Include things you only show occasionally but would like to exhibit more.
5. Commit to displaying at least one of your desired personality traits every day. You will fall back into old habits at some point, so be patient with yourself. Just remember to start

each day focused on displaying your chosen characteristics and at the end of each day, recognise your successes.

Limiting Belief Buster (part two)

We all face challenging situations from time to time, but there are occasions when it is our beliefs that are the real issue, not the situation. When faced with a situation that is making you feel negative and stressed, ask yourself the following questions:

- What are my beliefs about this situation?
- How are these beliefs affecting how I feel about what is happening or the people involved?
- Is there an alternative belief that will help me react to or handle this situation better?
- How can I respect the other person's beliefs and work with them to resolve the situation, even though their beliefs differ from mine?

Your Internal Processing

In order to ensure our conscious mind is not overloaded by the deluge of information that is constantly flooding in, it simultaneously filters the information by deleting, distorting and generalising it:

1. Deletion

Information your unconscious mind does not regard as relevant at that precise moment is deleted from your awareness so it can bring to your attention what is regarded as important or relevant. For example, you are not always consciously aware of the clothes on your body, or the fact that you are breathing – that is, of course, unless your clothes are uncomfortable or there is something unusual about the way you are breathing.

☺ Deleting information is why someone can be apparently oblivious to the dirty dishes stacked up in the kitchen, an overflowing ironing basket or the pile of things on the stairs waiting to be taken up.

The mind deletes information that does not fit in with your beliefs. Using the example above, if you believe dirty dishes and piles of ironing are unimportant and not your responsibility, you may fail to be aware of them consciously.

Because we tend to fear the unknown, we are always on the lookout to prove what is known to us, even if it brings negativity and stress. For example, if you believe that some dislikes you, you will regard their actions from this perspective. So when they do something that could be regarded as nice, you may automatically disregard this information.

2. Distortion
Beliefs and values are stored in the unconscious mind, which will unconsciously seek out information that supports those beliefs. If one of your beliefs is that a colleague dislikes you, when they offer to assist you in a project you might assume they have negative reasons for doing so.

3. Generalising
The mind generalises information it receives. This is useful when dealing with similar objects or situations, in that it means you do not have to start from scratch. For example, when you come to a door you can open it instantly without having to work out how it opens. Consider the following example of how the mind might generalise in a negative way:

If you are told you are getting a new line manager at work, rather than feeling positive about it or open-minded, you instantly think things like:

- he will probably be as bad as the last one
- he won't understand the job
- the last boss probably told him I am incompetent
- things won't get any better

rather than thinking:

- great, this a new person and a new opportunity
- perhaps this will be my opportunity to achieve a promotion
- maybe he will have ideas to address the problems we face in the department

The mind labels things and stores information in groups, including beliefs and memories. This speeds up the processing of information and helps you to recover it from your memory. However, if negative beliefs are causing you to assume that every time you have a relationship it will end badly, it can prevent you from finding happiness.

Whenever you experience something new, the brain has to decide how to categorise it and where to store it for future reference. It does so by finding a group of previous experiences that are similar.

If you are feeling negative or stressed, you will find that you are automatically on the alert for problems. In such situations, your unconscious mind may well delete and distort positive information, instead generalising situations as being negative.

Cause and Effect

If you frequently believe that someone or something is to blame for the things that go wrong in your life, you are living at the effect side of life. The same applies if you believe that you have little or no control over the events in your life. When you feel like this you give your power away and become a victim of circumstances. But if you are able to accept that generally things in life occur as a result of conscious or unconscious decisions you make, it is empowering and enables you to feel in control of your own destiny.

Blaming yourself for unpleasant things that happen is unhelpful and will only increase your stress levels. Instead, accept that you can only do your best with the internal and external resources available to you at the time.

If you are feeling trapped by circumstances, it is a good indicator that you are allowing yourself to be a victim. How often do you think you have no choice with regard to a particular situation?

Remember: we always have a choice. But it may be that the choices available to us are perceived as at least as unpleasant as or even more so than the action, or non-action, we are choosing to take presently.

In the majority of situations there are usually alternatives that have been overlooked or dismissed, through the automatic processes described earlier of deletion, distortion and generalisation.

Moving from effect to cause

Over the coming months I want to help you move away from the effect towards the cause side of life. You can do this by consciously using a questioning process whenever you feel trapped or in a situation that is not of your choosing.

So if you experience a situation where you feel trapped, rather than viewing those feelings as acceptable – or an unpleasant but understandable part of your situation – instead I want you to question your beliefs about the situation by asking the following questions:

- What conscious or unconscious decisions have I made that have led to my current situation?
- What decisions can I make that will allow me to move on or away from my current situation?

It is common to feel that there is nothing that can be done about a situation – either that or we feel so confused that we don't know what to do and therefore take no action. What few people fail to realise is that taking no action is in itself a decision – a decision to stay exactly as we are.

Which of my thoughts allow me to feel trapped?

Whether we realise it or not, we all experience thoughts that stop us from taking action to change the situation we are finding unpleasant. Usually, these thoughts revolve around the perception that even though the situation is unpleasant, the consequences of taking action may be worse.

Despite not knowing what the outcome of any action we take might be, the fear of the unknown (which we will look at in more detail later) may be sufficient to paralyse us.

Consider how valid this thought is:

How do we know the things we fear will actually happen?

Often, our worries about a situation have very little evidence to support them, yet we allow them to steer our future and cause stress and fear. So what thoughts could we choose that would allow us to feel more in control?

Even recognising that we are choosing to stay in our current unpleasant situation will help us feel more in control. Consider this next question:

What are we avoiding by choosing to stay in our current situation?

It is important to understand that even though we may not enjoy our present circumstances, if we avoid action we are still choosing to accept them. Which leads us to this question:

How would we choose to feel about this situation?

This is a key question because if we are not feeling the way we want to about a certain situation then we are giving away our control. What this means is that in effect, we are operating on autopilot in accordance with our past programming. In other words we are reacting to a situation in the way we have learnt to, not the way we want to. It is therefore our perception of a situation that alters how we feel about it.

This is often the case with my clients when they allow themselves to feel trapped in a job or a relationship. They produce a stream of reasons why they have not made changes to their situation and as a result have felt trapped for many years.

Although there is no *one* solution that fits all situations, the following generally holds true: Once they accept that they *can choose* to take action or they *can choose* to change the way they feel about the situation, they begin to feel less trapped. For example:

Rita had remained in a job for five years and complained she was bored and underpaid. Her rationale for not leaving was:

- There were no other jobs; although other than a glance at the Thursday-night job section in the local paper she had not actually looked.
- The location of her current job meant she could take her son to school on the way to work; this was her main priority.

- She refused to ask for new or different tasks to do as she believed they would 'just pile extra work on her and she was stressed enough'.

By conducting an intensive search for alternate employment she discovered that there were in fact suitable alternatives available. These included working flexi-time at a local customer service centre of a large organisation. By accepting that she did have a choice she felt less trapped and began to focus on the positives of working for her current employer:

- Being able to take her son to school.
- How helpful and understanding they were if she ever needed time off.

Eventually she spoke to her manager about how she was feeling and to her surprise, he was extremely supportive. After changes to her duties she decided to stay in her current role.

Not all situations are as easy to resolve as Rita's, but the principle remains the same:

1. Never discount options you have not fully explored.
2. Don't allow yourself to assume the worst will happen if you make changes to your situation.
3. If you decide not to change your situation, acknowledge that you are doing so because there is some advantage to keep the situation as is. Instead, focus on the positive aspects.

Sometimes we find ourselves in situations that frankly we feel we hate. But when there are others involved, our love or feelings for them can prevent us from changing the status quo. This can lead to us resenting the person or people we are trying to protect, as our desire not to harm them forms a wall around us like a fortress of barbed wire. *However*, by protecting those we love and care about we are also protecting ourselves. Let me explain further.

A common reason – although less so these days – for staying in a bad relationship is to protect the children involved. However, the reason parents want to protect their children is because the thought of seeing them distressed or causing them emotional harm goes against their beliefs and would be too painful to contemplate. So in effect they are also protecting themselves from the possibility of experiencing these feelings.

> *Wrinkles should merely indicate where the smiles have been.*
>
> Mark Twain

I Think, Therefore I am (Nature or Nurture?)

By the time we reach adulthood, most of us firmly believe we have become the person we are going to be for the rest of our lives. We start to recognise personality traits in ourselves and usually dislike the ways in which we are like our parents.

None of us enters the world fully equipped with the knowledge we need in order to live a happy and fulfilled life. As with our eye or hair colour, some of our behaviours, likes and dislikes will be inherited genetically. However, many behaviours are learnt.

From an early age we learn from those around us. If people we spend most time with have attitudes and behaviours that make their lives difficult, in turn they will teach these ways to us. It is not that they wish to cause us harm, but because they know no better.

Some people feel they have no control over their thinking or behaviour. They make statements like: 'It's the way I am ...' But the fact is that we can all change both our behaviours *and* the way we think.

Once we accept how our brain processes information, we can begin to question the thoughts that cause us to feel stressed or unhappy.

Positive Versus Negative

Being negative is second nature for most people. Often, they don't even realise that they regard everything negatively. They simply assume that how they see a situation or person – as bad or negative – is correct.

Resolve today to become a Pollyanna. For those of you who don't know, Pollyanna was a character from the bestselling 1913 novel of the same name by Eleanor H. Porter. Put briefly, her positive and sunny attitude transformed the lives of those around her. Amazingly, for some the term Pollyanna has become a derogatory phrase to describe people who are regarded as *too* optimistic and positive!

☺ Great attitude! Let's all be negative and pessimistic – that's sure to make life better!

How negative are you?

Very negative people tend to be cynical and stressed, often becoming depressed. They lose their enthusiasm and energy for life, have difficulty trusting others and believe people will exploit them. Resigned to a life of getting by, coping and licking their emotional wounds, they often forget what it is like to feel positive. If they continue in this mode they are at risk of becoming isolated and lonely, alienating people around them, becoming withdrawn from life.

People with negative tendencies are often lethargic and bored. Generally their life is stuck in a safe place, but secretly they feel that life is passing them by. If they are a people-pleaser, they still see things negatively but will change their opinions based on the opinions of those around them.

The positive among us see the world as interesting and full of possibilities. We have a positive, flexible and energetic attitude to everything we do. We spend our time enjoying life and work, valuing ourselves, our time, our freedom and that of others. We actively seek ways to challenge and improve our lives, and we know how to enjoy ourselves.

If you want to reduce the stress in your life you need to develop a Pollyanna attitude. The following exercise, whilst it is incredibly challenging, is one of the most powerful and enlightening I have ever experienced:

Negativity boycott

Every feeling you have, including stress, is linked to the internal thoughts and images you make in your mind. So I want you to commit to having only positive thoughts for seven consecutive days! Believe me, this is not easy, as negative thoughts come into our minds with alarming frequency. I still find this challenging, but it is why I recognise its importance. Although it is hard, it is simple.

Every time you notice you have had a negative thought, stop your thought process immediately and begin your seven-day challenge again. Many of you will be lucky if you manage an hour in the beginning, but you were born happy and positive, and can learn to block out the negativity.

> *In Scotland, there is no such thing as bad weather – only the wrong clothes.*

> *Billy Connolly*

Believe in Your Ability to Overcome Stress

Your ability to overcome stress will depend on two things: being determined and having the right belief. Determination comes from motivation. Therefore, in order to be sufficiently motivated you need to be very clear about what your motivation is for learning to manage and reduce your stress levels.

My determination to manage stress is fuelled by my firm belief that stress damages health and may even cause cancer; therefore, given my medical history, it is one of my top priorities. But where does overcoming stress come in your list of priorities? If you are struggling to answer that question, start by asking yourself the following:

- What problems has stress caused in my life so far?
- What might the cost to my life be if I don't learn to manage stress?
- How does my being stressed affect my family and my relationships?
- How is stress affecting my health and well-being?
- In what way will my life be better if I overcome stress?
- What will I be able to achieve or do if I learn to manage stress effectively?

The answers to these questions will help you identify the cost to you in terms of the quality of your life and general sense of well-being, which should be your motivation to overcome stress.

Based on your findings, how determined are you to learn to manage stress, on a scale of one to ten – one being only slightly motivated and ten being absolutely determined to succeed, no matter what?

If you score below five, continue exploring your reasons for overcoming stress until you come up with something that really motivates you.

> *Many of life's failures are people who did not realise how close they were to success when they gave up.*
>
> *Thomas Edison*

Believe you *can* reduce your stress levels

Top athletes use visualisations to improve their performance because it is much easier to create or achieve something if one can see an image of it. The footballer who scores the winning goal will have visualised himself doing so many times before.

It is so much easier to make things happen if you believe strongly that it will. In order to increase your belief that you *can* reduce your stress levels, do the following exercises every day:

Determination visualisation

Visualise yourself stress-free and relaxed:

a) Imagine you are looking through your own eyes rather than looking at yourself:

- What do you see?
- What do you hear?
- What are you doing?
- How does it feel?

b) Make the image vivid and appealing to you.

c) Run the movie in your mind several times and enjoy the feelings associated with it.

Determination enhancer

a) Recall any negative suggestions that you or anyone else has given you in the past that suggest you cannot overcome stress.

b) Hear yourself or them say it in a voice you do not trust or believe – make it sound silly like Mickey Mouse or sexy like

Marilyn Monroe. Choose whatever tone makes you smile and will hold the least power over you.

c) Next, promise yourself in a confident manner that you *can* learn to manage stress.

d) Then reflect back on the times when you have got through difficult or challenging situations. Remember how good it felt and how you grew as a result of the experience.

e) Focus on one of those times and visualise it:

- What did you see?
- What did you hear?
- How did it feel?

f) Notice where you had this feeling in your body.

g) Give it a positive colour. Whatever instinctively pops into your mind is fine.

h) Imagine the colour glowing brightly inside you.

i) Promise yourself once again that you will manage your stress and achieve the life you want.

j) Say it with determination.

Practise these exercises often until you can recall your vision and immediately invoke positive feelings of determination. Once you are able to recall these positive images at will, do so at any time you feel your motivation and determination waning.

The Little Frog Who Did Not Give Up

The farmer's wife was in need of rest having been up all night helping with lambing, so she placed the bucket of cream she was holding by the door of the cowshed. Having gone inside for a much-needed cup of tea, she fell into a deep sleep.

Meanwhile, in the farmyard, two inquisitive little frogs named Ben and Bob hopped onto the edge of the pail to see what was inside. Ben leaned too far and fell in, while Bob gasped in dismay, sure his brother would die. But the little frog shouted from within: 'Do not despair, Brother, for I will find a way out.'

First, Ben tried swimming down to the bottom of the bucket. But once he touched the bottom, he discovered it was too far for him to jump out. He could find no way out from the side, either. While he tried with all his might to push against the side of the pail and tip it over, it was all to no avail.

Sadly, Bob decided he could watch no longer, so he hopped off the edge of the bucket and went home to mourn the loss of his little brother.

But the determined little frog just kept on swimming, convinced he would come up with an idea. Either that, or the farmer's wife would return and save him.

For hours he swam and swam, until eventually his feet had a soft yellow substance to stand on – he had made butter out of the cream. Realising he had enough for a foothold, he positioned himself and jumped clean out of the bucket!

Notes to Self

- My beliefs and behaviours have been learnt and therefore *can* be changed.
- My perception of a situation is a result of internal processing. I am in charge of my feelings and emotions.
- I can control how I react to events.
- My determination to reduce stress in my life will be given the priority it deserves.

Take Action

- Consider how your perception is affecting how you judge situations.
- Practise focusing on one task at a time.
- Question the beliefs and values you currently have that are negatively affecting your life or causing you stress.
- Free yourself of limiting beliefs that are keeping you trapped in stressful situations.
- Take responsibility for your own life.
- Boycott negativity – become a Pollyanna.
- Change your belief about becoming stress-free using the technique in this chapter.
- Use the determination visualisation daily.

Chapter Three – Powerful Relaxation Techniques

No one can get inner peace by pouncing on it.

Harry Emerson Fosdick

Introduction

When you are stressed, it is very difficult to relax for any great length of time. In fact, you may never truly relax. Throughout this guide, you will be learning ways to reduce the stress in your life. Since it is impossible to eliminate all stress forever, you need strategies to enable you to relax, no matter what is currently happening in your life.

There are many techniques available that have been bringing relief to stressed people for centuries, yet very few people understand or use them. In this chapter, I explain them simply and provide practical exercises that you can start using straight away.

Find the Time

To function at its best, your body needs to find a balance between activity and periods of rest in order to recuperate. Without this balance, you will suffer from the effects of stress. Individuals who continually rush around are susceptible to viruses the minute they stop or unwind for a holiday or a break. So if you think you cannot afford to spend time indulging in relaxation activities, you are wrong – in fact, you cannot afford not to.

Many of us have a tendency to cram our lives with activities and obligations. Taking even a few minutes each day to do nothing or recharge your batteries will help you to release the pressure before it builds up. Stop being afraid of admitting that you cannot handle everything, because the more you take on, the more you will be given. In turn, this will have a direct effect on how stressed you feel.

The Dalai Lama has been reported as saying that on very busy days, he doubled the time he spent meditating. In many ways, it is like going to the gym, but without all the effort and perspiration. Whilst we may often feel we don't have enough time for the gym, when we do go, we feel more awake, energised, happier and more in control of life. As a result, we actually achieve more.

NOTE OF CAUTION:

All meditations and relaxation practices should only be done when and where it is safe to do so.

Benefits of Meditation

Meditation is broadly classified under mind–body medicine. In short, it is a simple and safe technique for bringing about a sense of calm and balance to your physical, emotional and mental state. More and more people are finding that through mediation, they can reduce stress.

There are many different kinds of meditation. Some are designed to produce altered states of awareness and others are intended to promote relaxation. In its various forms meditation has been used to promote wellness for thousands of years.

We can all benefit from taking time to relax and to be at one with ourselves rather than being focused on the world around us – particularly our problems. I had become an expert at ignoring my inner needs and being stressed.

☺ Meditation is such a lovely feeling that you may get hooked on the practice, the relaxation and the happiness it brings into your life!

Don't place too much importance on doing it right, as anyone can meditate. Forget the idea that you have to make your mind go blank – the intention is to slow your mind and focus on the meditation practice, not the million and one things you normally stress about. If you feel you need help there are pre-recorded sessions available that you may wish to try. But I suggest you begin meditating by starting with some simple exercises.

Meditation – step one

1. Select a simple object to focus on.
2. Focus on the shape, colour, taste, sound and texture, moving it around in your hand as you do so.
3. When you are able to focus on the object for two minutes, move on to step two.

Meditation – step two

1. Take a deep breath in and hold for a count of five.
2. Exhale, making a slight 'harr' sound as you do so.
3. Imagine a golden thread connecting you to the sky, whilst continuing to breathe deeply.
4. Whilst enjoying the feeling of the controlled breathing, repeat the following affirmations in your mind:

   - the energy of the sun flows through me
   - I am at peace
   - my mind is relaxed
   - I am enjoying the sense of calm I feel

5. As other thoughts drift into your mind, allow them to float out again.
6. Continue this exercise for several minutes.

Practise steps one and two three times a day for a week, then move on to step three.

Seven-minute meditation to your sanctuary – step three

Brief, twice-daily meditations of seven minutes are very effective, but you may prefer to do it once or even three times a day. Experiment to determine what fits in best with your schedule and to establish what feels right for you:

1. Sit in a straight-backed chair.
2. Sit slightly forward, so your spine isn't quite touching the back of the chair; if you are unable to do so, lean back against the chair.
3. Ensure that your feet are flat on the floor.

4. Close your eyes.

5. Allow your thoughts to slow, drop your shoulders and relax as you follow these simple steps:

   a) Bring your attention to your breath; notice how it happens without any effort.

   b) Slow the pace of your breathing slightly; notice the temperature of the breath as it enters your nostrils.

   c) Breathe in deeply, counting to five.

   d) Breathe out slowly, counting to five.

   e) Continue in this way breathing in and out through the nose.

   f) Count backwards slowly from ten to one.

   g) Become aware of your feet touching the floor.

   h) Feel a sense of connection to the earth, solid and reliable beneath your feet.

   i) Visualise strolling down a gentle slope to your special place, perhaps an idyllic beach or a beautiful garden – anywhere that you feel very safe – knowing that with each step you are getting closer to a state of relaxation.

   j) If other thoughts come into your head, gently brush them away – this is your time, your place.

   k) Enjoy walking around your safe haven until a state of calm and quiet is reached.

   l) Remain there a little longer until you feel able to leave, taking the good feelings with you.

   m) When you feel ready, walk slowly back up the slope, still focusing on the good feelings you have achieved.

   n) When you reach the top of the path, slowly count up from one to ten and then open your eyes.

   o) Avoid using an alarm to end your relaxation session. If you are concerned about keeping to a set time, play some gentle music that lasts for seven minutes, so that you know when it is time to end your session.

p) Finish by affirming that your mind knows how to achieve this relaxed state. It can return you to your sanctuary whenever you need to and when it is safe to do so.

Being present – thirty-minute practice – step four

Unless your mind is fully occupied with what is happening at any particular moment, you will tend to find that you spend your time focusing on the past or the future. This practice is about staying in the moment and bringing your attention back to yourself rather than focusing on worrying thoughts. Accepting the moment and yourself as you are right now can bring a sense of calm that remains with you after the session.

If you spend your time trying to run away from problems you can actually increase your stress levels. Rather than struggling to get away from experiences you find difficult, practise being with them.

Likewise, the pleasure you get from enjoyable experiences can be lessened by focusing on not wanting it to end rather than emerging yourself fully in the moment.

Being present during pleasurable experiences sounds easy, but many people spoil the experience by worrying that it won't last, thereby diluting the pleasure they are feeling.

There are four aspects to this next meditation technique: body, breath, sounds and thoughts:

1. Sit up straight but relaxed on the floor and cross your legs so your hips are higher than your knees. There are special cushions (a zafu) and stools (seiza bench) designed for meditation practice, but a folded blanket will do.

2. If you cannot sit on the floor for whatever reason, sit on a straight-backed chair, with your feet flat on the floor. If your feet don't reach the floor, use a cushion to raise them. Adopt an upright and dignified posture, with your spine slightly away from the back of the chair where possible.

3. Rest your hands on your thighs, palms facing up.

4. Close your eyes or soft focus your gaze on the floor a metre in front of you.

5. Begin by sitting in this posture for a few minutes with your attention focused on your breath.

6. Notice it as it enters and leaves your body.

7. Don't try to change it – just be aware of it, allowing the breath and you to be just as you are.

8. Accept that your mind will wander, because that is entirely natural. Each time you notice it has wandered, escort it back to your breath.

9. Next, become aware of any sounds, either in the room, outside or even coming from you, such as the sound of your breathing.

10. Don't label them – simply become aware.

11. Continue in this way for a few minutes.

12. Remember: if your mind wanders simply escort it back to any sounds, without judgment or emotion.

13. Now become aware of your body and notice any sensations such as warmth, relaxation or even discomfort.

14. Don't make judgements or try to label them.

15. If you are experiencing discomfort, imagine breathing into it, so your breath enters your body and you imagine it flowing to the point of the discomfort.

16. Next, notice your thoughts as they arise. Be curious about them.

17. Don't dwell on them, judge them or attach any significance to them – just allow them to drift in to your mind and out again.

18. Bring your focus back to your body.

19. Scan your body and ascertain any feelings.

20. If you feel any discomfort from sitting, for example, breathe into it.

21. Imagine your breath going into the discomfort and back out again.

22. Notice the sensation of where your body touches the chair or cushion.

23. Don't try to change anything, simply become aware.

24. After a few minutes move your attention away from all of the sensations in your body and focus on your breathing again.

25. Become absorbed in each breath.

26. Continue in this way for about twenty-five minutes, rotating between noticing your breath, hearing any sounds, any thoughts you might have and the sensations in your body.

27. Simply be curious and accept everything as it is right now.

28. Finally, spend five minutes focusing on your breath before slowly bringing your attention back into the room.

29. When you begin meditating it can be difficult to judge how much time has passed. If you finish before thirty minutes that is fine – you will get better at timing your session as time goes along. If you are concerned about overrunning it will make it more difficult to relax, so you may find it easier to set a timer with a gentle bell to signal when thirty minutes is up.

What you can expect to experience

Few people are privileged enough to experience the enriching state of meditation. As a result, they miss out on immense mental and physical benefits. There is a false conception that meditating involves sitting for hours humming cross-legged when in fact just a few minutes a day can be beneficial.

The most important thing about all of the meditation practices in this chapter is to remember that it is not about having a completely blank mind. Many people make the mistake of trying to stop thinking and then become frustrated when they cannot achieve this. Don't try to get rid of your thoughts – it won't work. When meditating, you may experience emotions that come to the surface. Acknowledge the emotions without analysing them, then return your mind to your meditation.

The purpose of these meditation practices is to take a few moments for yourself. It gives you the chance to be in the present moment, accepting it as it is without trying to change anything. It is about creating a place where you can enjoy a quiet inner sanctuary within your own mind.

Breathing

Our bodies are made up of trillions of cells, all needing a constant supply of oxygen to keep them healthy. As air enters our lungs it is picked up by our red blood cells and carried to the rest of the cells in our bodies.

We never really think about breathing because it happens naturally, all by itself. When people are stressed or anxious their breathing tends to be shallow. This means they are not using their full lung capacity and therefore they won't be taking in as much oxygen as they could be.

☺ There were times when I was so stressed and busy that if breathing had not happened automatically, I felt I would not have had time to do it!

Benefits of breathing exercises

For a long time I experienced chest pains when stressed and would hold my breath for a few seconds, mistakenly thinking this would help. My doctor told me it was a result of my being tense and therefore tightening my chest muscles. He advised me to learn to relax. Despite trying really hard, the pain only really disappeared when I exercised. In the morning I would feel relaxed for the first two minutes, but then the tightness would return.

Breathing exercises can be called conscious, intentional or transformational breathing, but essentially they are the same thing. Conscious breathing is believed to release the energy that can become trapped in your body after mental, emotional or physical trauma. Regardless of your beliefs about whether or not this is true, I am sure you will find breathing exercises very beneficial.

Conscious breathing has been used in disciplines as diverse as kung fu, ta'i chi, yoga, Christian monasticism and Kabbalah for centuries. It is an excellent way to release stress, allowing you to develop inner peace, health and vitality.

Breathing consciously

There are lots of books available on the subject if you want to study further, but this very simple exercise is the one I practise:

1. Start by paying attention to your breath.
2. Notice the speed and where in your chest you are breathing from.
3. Continue in this way for a few minutes.
4. Now turn your focus on each inhalation.

5. Notice any feelings and sensations of breath flowing into your body.
6. Actively feel the breath entering your body.
7. Notice the places in your torso that move with each inhalation.
8. Next, pay attention to the quality of each exhalation.
9. Notice the sensations as the breath leaves your body.
10. Focus on the temperature of the air leaving your nostrils.
11. Observe how your shoulders drop slightly and your torso moves.
12. Close your eyes and continue to pay close attention to the ebb and flow of each breath.
13. Enjoy the feeling of breathing consciously for a few more moments.

The great thing about conscious breathing is that it can be done anytime, anywhere. It is also a very effective way to calm both your mind and your body.

The Present Moment

Most of us are never fully present in the moment. Instead, part of our attention is diverted either to the past or the future. We spend so much of our time being preoccupied with what has gone before or what may or may not happen that we are rarely completely alive. Although being present in the moment can take practice, particularly in today's chaotic world, the benefits can be huge, including the ability to:

• live life with a calmer, more relaxed awareness
• achieve greater enjoyment and appreciation of daily life
• overcome any limitations that you have placed on yourself
• stop allowing yourself to be negatively affected by the actions of others
• live your life intentionally rather than surviving it
• stop reactive thoughts and actions

If you reminisce about past happy events or daydream about future plans, it can be very pleasant. But if you find yourself mulling over negative events or worrying about the future, it can cause a significant amount of stress.

Most of us rarely stop and think about the fact that the only moment that actually exists is the present. But we should do, because the past is just a memory and the future is simply imagined. This doesn't mean we should deny the past, suppress memories or ignore the future. It is simply a case of accepting that when yesterday was happening it was the present moment, which is now nothing more than a memory, and when tomorrow arrives it will also be the present moment. While there is no getting away from the fact that minds wander, the important thing is that we bring our attention back to the present.

Animals always live in the present moment. They immerse themselves fully in whatever it is they are doing at any given moment. If you witness an animal stalking its prey, you will be witnessing 100 per cent focus.

First-class athletes have perfected this present-moment technique, referred to as being in 'the zone'. And we all operate more effectively and achieve more when fully focused on the task in hand. It is certainly worth the effort, given the added bonus that we can achieve more enjoyment and satisfaction when fully focused on a task.

Simple ways to be in the moment

1. Exercise One

a) When chatting to someone, take the time to listen to what they are saying.

b) Listen to their words, the tonality and the speed of their voice.

c) Notice their body language.

d) Don't anticipate what they are going to say or plan what you will say next.

e) Simply be fully focused – see if they notice being *really* listened to.

2. Exercise Two

a) Be completely present for just a few minutes whilst carrying out a routine task like showering, vacuuming or brushing your teeth.

b) Make sure it is something you don't really have to think about, where your unconscious mind has taken over the job.

c) Focus on the process with all your senses.

d) When you notice your attention wandering, simply escort it back to the task in hand.

3. Exercise three

Only ever do this exercise when it is completely safe to do so. Choose three times every day to bring your attention inward. It is best to select three set times to do this practise until you are proficient at it. You can then use this technique at any point when you are in danger of becoming focused on anxious thoughts or your stress levels are rising:

a) The first step is to acknowledge where your thoughts are at this particular moment.

b) Recognise that you are thinking about things other than the present moment.

c) Bring your attention inwards and focus on your breathing for fifteen to twenty breaths.

d) Next, allow your awareness to expand to your entire body.

e) Notice any sensations.

f) Become aware of how your body, mind and spirit feel at this precise moment.

g) Continue to breathe calmly.

h) As you sense the life inside you, enjoy this feeling.

i) Allow yourself to feel comforted in the knowledge that you can use this technique to help you come back to the present moment at any time.

Living most of your life focused on the present actually makes it easier to plan for the future. This is because you will be more relaxed and therefore have a clearer mind from which to make decisions.

4. Exercise Four

The pleasure from eating can be greatly increased by being fully focused and you will find that you tend to eat less. Use all of your five senses: sight, hearing, smell, touch and taste.

a) Choose one meal a day – not breakfast if you have to get off to work, etc.

b) If you eat lunch alone and normally tend to eat it quickly, this would be an excellent time to practise this exercise.

c) Work out roughly how long it would normally take you to eat it and aim to triple that time.

d) Ensure that you get as much enjoyment out of each mouthful as possible by chewing properly and focusing on the taste and texture.

☺ If you do this correctly you should taste and enjoy your food more. Conversely, you may find you have been eating things you don't even like that much.

Deep Relaxation

When was the last time you felt completely relaxed and free from tension? Our stress is carried not only in our minds, but also in our bodies and most people need to relax more. The benefits are immense, so take the time to do this next exercise:

Relaxation practice

The purpose of this next exercise is to learn to relax your body. Muscle tension and stress go hand in hand. You may be so used to feeling tense that you no longer realise that you are actually tensing your body. This prolonged tensing of the muscles can result in numerous symptoms including headaches, neck pain, stomach cramps and muscle spasms.

Relaxing your muscles is an excellent way to release muscle tension and achieve a more restful state. All you need to do is follow these simple steps and with practice, it will be possible to achieve a wonderful relaxed state:

1. Find a quiet place, preferably where you have some degree of privacy.
2. Sit or lie in a comfortable position and close your eyes.
3. Tense the muscles in your hands by clenching your fists.
4. Notice the tension in your hands and lower arms.

5. Maintain the tension as you bend your arms and then flex your biceps.

6. Hold the tension for six to seven seconds, but don't tense too tightly as this may strain the muscles.

7. If you feel pain, release the tension slightly.

8. Next, release the tension completely. Allow the muscles to relax and go limp and say in a calm, relaxed voice: 'My hands and arms are relaxed'.

9. Notice the difference in how your hand and arm feel now compared to beforehand.

10. Next, move on to other parts of your body, always releasing the tension before moving on to another part of the body:

    a) Tighten the muscles in your thighs by squeezing your thighs together.

    b) Tighten your calf muscles.

    c) Curl your toes as tightly as you can.

    d) Bend your ankles toward your body to tense your feet.

    e) Tighten your hip and buttock muscles.

    f) Arch your back off the floor or chair.

    g) Tighten your stomach muscles by drawing your belly in towards your spine.

    h) Shrug your shoulders up to your ears.

    i) Wrinkle your forehead, by trying to make your eyebrows touch your hairline rather than frowning.

    j) Close your eyes and squeeze them shut as tightly as you can.

    k) Draw the centres of your mouth back and grimace, to tense your lips, cheeks and jaw.

11. Each time you release the tension in a particular part of your body, tell yourself that you are relaxing the muscles and releasing the tension in that part of the body.

12. Notice the difference in how it felt before, during and after it was tensed.

As with all relaxation practices, it is important that you are patient with yourself. Each time you do the relaxation practice, your experience will be different. Your only aim is to take a short time each day to relax fully.

Meditation and relaxation are often put at the bottom of our to-do lists. It is common to think that when one has a busy lifestyle there is no time to stop, be still and relax. You may be thinking that you don't have time to do all these relaxation therapies and meditations. Perhaps you feel that by finding time for them your work, etc., will suffer. This isn't actually the case. In fact, life in the fast lane can be counterproductive. In reality if you are relaxed, you will be more productive and thereby achieve far more each day than you ever thought possible.

Practical Ways to Reduce Stress

As much as we might like the idea of creating ourselves a stress-free life and becoming entranced in a Zen-like state, where we meditate frequently and handle everything perfectly, life has a way of keeping us running around. In fact, despite their best intentions for creating a lifestyle free of stress, many people only succeed in creating more stress than their minds and bodies can handle.

The good news is that there *are* practical ways to reduce stress without spending lots of money, learning new skills or even leaving the house. Let us now take a look at some ideas for helping you to relax that can be built into your life on a daily basis. The goal here is to open up space in your day so that you can recharge and reinvigorate both your mind and body for the next merry-go-round of activity.

This can be achieved by taking a little time each day to unwind and enjoy a relaxing activity. It can be one that either absorbs your attention, taking your mind off the things that cause you stress, or one that helps you relax in other ways. Here are some of the ones I recommend:

- reading
- soaking in a warm bath
- socialising or chatting to a friend
- puzzles, crosswords and games
- exercise – swimming, aerobics, dance, football, cricket, walking

- grooming or stroking a pet
- hobbies – painting, sewing, woodwork, playing an instrument or computer games, etc.
- writing songs, poems, stories, articles, a book or even a diary
- listening to music
- meditation and relaxation techniques
- watching a good film
- watching the world go by

1. Reading

Reading a good book is absorbing, because as you are reading you will be focusing on the words, interpreting their meaning and forming pictures in your mind of the scene that the author is describing.

2. Bathing

The key here is to enjoy a relaxing bath, not lie there in the tub feeling unhappy while worrying about things. Add lots of bubbles, aromatic oil, a rubber duck or a plastic boat – if that's your preference.☺ Listening to relaxing music, reading, or focusing on pleasant thoughts or visualisations can also enhance the experience.

3. Socialising or chatting to a friend

Socialising is the way many people choose to relax and unwind. Whether it be a night out dancing, going for afternoon tea, chatting over a round of golf or simply talking to a friend on the phone, socialising is a vital part of maintaining happiness. However you choose to socialise, ensure you don't spend the time talking about your worries or other people's. Whilst it is very helpful to talk about your problems and bottling things up is never a good idea, constantly going over the same old issues is only going to reinforce them.

4. Puzzles, crosswords and games

These are an excellent way to help you relax while keeping the brain active at the same time. If you are focused fully on the puzzle or game, it means you are not thinking about things that cause you anxiety. If you prefer to play against someone else and there is no one available, games like Scrabble, Tetris or Boggle which can be played on a tablet or hand-held device are similar to playing against someone else and are great fun.

5. Exercise

Exercise is good for your mind, body and spirit and it can be enjoyable. If you are averse to the idea of exercise, find something physical that you don't regard as exercise like dancing, gardening or walking the dog. You don't need a dog to go walking – all you need to do is take yourself off somewhere pleasant and safe, and just stroll for fifteen to twenty minutes. Use all of your senses to take in your surroundings.

6. Grooming or stroking a pet

Animals are extremely responsive to affection and attention, and it is good for us, too. Stroking a pet has been shown to slow the heart rate, lower blood pressure and release tension in muscles. It may even release endorphins – the body's natural painkiller and stress-reducer.

7. Hobbies

There are so many hobbies to choose from and not all of them are expensive. Try a few different ones – there are no rules that say you can only have one hobby. I have lots and indulge in whichever one takes my fancy at the time.

8. Music

I have several play lists of really happy songs that are guaranteed to lighten my mood. The only guideline here is to choose music that makes you feel happy and not something that metaphorically catapults you back to sad or unpleasant times.

9. Meditation and relaxation techniques

There is lots of help in this book to get you started on meditation and relaxation techniques. If you are not already using them – why not?

10. Watching a good film

Television is an enjoyable pastime and although watching endless hours of television to block out the reality of life is definitely not advised, watching great films, series dramas or comedies can be both absorbing and entertaining.

11. Watching the world go by

This one is for when you are running around doing errands or racing through your to-do list. Sometimes it feels like the whole world is racing around like a movie that has been sped up, leaving no time to enjoy life. When you are feeling like life is passing you by, take a break and go to the local cafe or coffee shop. Choose a pleasant seat and simply watch the world go by. Notice how people rush past, hardly aware of their surroundings. Breathe slowly and enjoy the experience of just sitting, then imagine freezing the world for a minute in a snapshot. Visualise everyone stopping what they are doing and becoming still. Continue to breathe slowly as you imagine the world is stationary. After a few minutes, slowly allow everyone to begin to move again in your mind's eye, only slower and happier in their lives.

Not using the techniques in this chapter in order to relax is a conscious choice to accept and live life the way you are currently feeling – stressed. Not all of the techniques will suit you, but you can experiment with them and decide which ones you are going to build into your routine so they become part of your life or come up with some ideas of your own.

> *The mark of a successful man is one that has spent an entire day on the bank of a river without feeling guilty about it.*

> *Author Unknown*

The Man and the Fly

A fly kept buzzing around and landing on the head of a bald man, finally landing and biting him on the pate. Becoming irritated, the man resolved to splat the fly, but he only succeeded in giving himself a heavy slap on the head.

Escaping, the fly said mockingly: 'You who have wished to revenge the prick of a tiny insect, even with death, see what you have done to yourself to add insult to injury.'

The bald man replied, 'I can easily make peace with myself, because I know there was no intention to hurt. But you, an ill-favoured and contemptible insect, I wish that I could have killed you even if I had incurred a heavier penalty.'

Notes to Self

- No matter what is currently going on in my life, I can always bring my attention back to my breath and inner self in order to relax.
- I have the ability to change my thought process and improve my life.
- The present moment is a gift.

Take Action

- Practise all the meditation exercises.
- Select the meditation practice which suits you best and use it daily.
- Focus on ten minutes of conscious breathing per day.
- Carry out the present-moment exercise three times a day.
- Once a day, take some time to carry out the relaxation exercise.
- Try out the practical ways to reduce stress and choose the ones that work for you.

Chapter Four – Stop Stressful Thoughts

The greatest weapon against stress is our ability to choose one thought over another.

William James

Introduction

Have you ever noticed how stressed you become when you are caught up in a cycle of negative thinking? How you become absorbed in the details of whatever it is that is making you anxious?

The majority of the stress you feel on a daily basis comes directly from the thoughts you have. In fact, there is a direct correlation between negative thoughts and stress.

If you are to reduce the stress you feel, you need to start by recognising the signs that your stress levels are rising. You then need to make a conscious choice to manage your thoughts before they get out of hand.

Fear is not real. The only place that fear can exist is in our thoughts of the future. It is a product of our imagination, causing us to fear things that do not at present and may not ever exist. That is near insanity. Do not misunderstand me, danger is very real, but fear is a choice.

Will Smith in the film After Earth

Feeling afraid is extremely unpleasant for a reason – it is the brain's way of telling us to take action to change the situation. Fear is part of the survival instinct in that we fear things that will harm or kill us. But sometimes fear can be felt about other things that are not life-threatening but unpleasant.

Fear can direct and control so many aspects of our lives that it can paralyse us and stop us from moving forward. When we perceive that we are under threat – real or otherwise – our bodies respond by adopting the fight or flight mode. So if we are constantly fearful or stressed it will eventually have an effect on our health. To combat fear, the best strategy is to train ourselves to bring our attention back to the present.

> *I have been through some terrible things in my life, some of which actually happened.*
>
> Mark Twain

The Ten Most Common Fears

The main fears we all have include:

1. Loss of freedom

This does not necessarily refer to incarceration. Most of us may not think about it every day, but the fear of losing control over one's life is something that occurs to us all at some point. Whether it starts early within childhood, adolescence or later when we consider the commitment of marriage, being controlled makes most of us feel uncomfortable. For many of us work represents loss of freedom and that is sufficient to cause work-related stress.

2. The unknown

Our conscious mind tells us that in order to move forward safely we must know what lies ahead. This is because we feel that if we know what is around the corner, we can be in control and deal with the situation. The more control we feel we have in any given situation, the greater we believe our influence will be over the outcome.

3. Pain

The intensity of physical pain is purely subjective.

☺ I always find it amusing when medical professionals ask people to rate the pain they feel from one to five – five being the worst (agony) – and they are sat calmly in their chair stating that it is a five.

This is because we can only gauge things from what we have personally experienced.

Apart from a few exceptions, most of us are intolerant to and therefore afraid of pain. Fear of pain can also be linked to loss of freedom, as a great deal of physical pain can result in loss of mobility and therefore control over one's life.

The fear of emotional pain that we believe will result from loss or hurt, etc., for some can be far greater than the fear of physical pain and can cause significant stress.

4. Disappointment

There are two areas to this fear: feeling disappointed with yourself and disappointing others. Most of us as children will have experienced the awful feeling that comes from being told we have disappointed our parents. The hurt that is felt at that moment can stay with us for many years. The fear of suffering from disappointment of some kind is often the reason we avoid the unknown, feel stressed and fail to do things or take opportunities that may present themselves.

5. Extreme poverty

Poverty is defined as having insufficient resources to meet the human needs of shelter, food and warmth. However, the media use this fear to their advantage and advertising makes people feel that they need far greater material wealth in order to be happy and stress-free than is actually necessary. No one should live in poverty, but poverty doesn't necessarily equate to happiness – I know several unhappy multimillionaires.

☺ As a child we would sit of an evening wrapped in coats and newspapers to keep warm. Not an ideal situation, but I was happy in the security that being with my mum and sisters gave me.

6. Loneliness

The dreadful feeling of emptiness that is caused by feeling alone doesn't always come from a lack of human interaction. Sometimes, the loneliest people are those who are in unhappy relationships. Yet, they remain in the relationship rather than face the fear of being alone.

Feeling that no one cares what happens to you and having no one to share your joys, fears or thoughts can be very stressful. This fear has evolved from one of our earliest survival instincts.

At the primeval level we fear loneliness, because survival is more likely as part of a group. In the modern world we often fear that for our actions to be meaningful or important, someone has to witness or notice them. If you make a groundbreaking discovery but no one ever learns about it, will it still count?

☺ Just recently whilst away with my husband on business I went for a 17-mile walk and visited a pottery studio to paint a vase whilst he was at a meeting. I had a wonderful day, even though I was without company and by myself for twelve hours. This was because I was alone – not lonely.

7. Ridicule

No one enjoys being criticised or made fun of. In short, this fear comes from concern that we might project a bad image of ourselves to others. The explosion of social media has increased this fear for many people. If we 'put ourselves out there' and bring public attention to ourselves, people could be laughing at us on the other side of the world within minutes. We are at the mercy of other people's opinions!

The fear of ridicule never really leaves us and even people who actively seek media attention generally don't like being in the spotlight for negative reasons.

☺ Remember: other people's opinions are just that – opinions, not fact.

8. Rejection

People tend to copy the actions of others in order to avoid dealing with rejection from society, friends, colleagues and family. A great deal of stress can be caused by trying to live a life that we feel is conforming to normal behaviour, in an attempt to try to fit in. Another part of the fear of rejection relates to relationships. Being afraid to love or seek out new friendships or relationships can leave people feeling lonely, unhappy and stressed, yet they suffer these feelings rather than face the risk of rejection.

9. Death

For all the right reasons this tends to be fear number one. Despite the fact that we all know that one day it comes to us all, when we are functioning normally, our most basic survival instinct tells us to hang on to life. Fear of death is also linked to the fear of the unknown, as we have no way of knowing what death actually means. It is for this reason that people with strong religious beliefs tend to fear death less, as they believe they know what comes next.

Despite death being the number one fear, it is not the main fear we worry about on a daily basis – our stress is caused by all the other fears we believe will affect our happiness.

Back in 2007 I was diagnosed with a pancreatic tumour, had a pancreatectomy – which is a massive operation – contracted MRSA, developed peritonitis and was diagnosed with a malignant melanoma all in the space of eight months.

☺ Yes, I have nine lives.

Thankfully, I had already learnt to handle stress well, which allowed me to deal with these events with a calmness I would never previously have believed I was capable of. Since then, this period of my life helps me to keep things in perspective. I certainly hope you don't have to face thoughts of your own mortality for a very long time, but I would ask you to consider this: if you were faced with the situation I was, how many of the current things you worry and stress about would really matter?

10. Failure

We all do or don't do things in order to avoid failure. Failure and success are very subjective, as they are based purely on a person's perspective and therefore never the same for two people. This fear is also linked to others in the form of disappointment, ridicule and rejection.

The fact is that you have only really failed when you fail to learn. With every piece of information you receive, if you choose to learn from it, it can be used to evaluate whether or not your actions are taking you nearer to or further away from your goals. High achievers realise that success comes from failure. Every time you make a mistake, you are being given the opportunity to learn and improve.

I have learnt more from my failures than my successes.

Richard Branson

Success and failure are relative. What is failure to one might be a great success to another. People often forget to take into account the circumstances, such as the starting point, or the individual challenges faced in relation to achieving a goal. This was brought home to me in a way I will never forget when I watched a documentary called *The Boy Whose Skin Fell Off*. It was an incredibly frank, humbling and moving film about Jonny Kennedy (1966–2003), an extraordinary man with a terrible condition – Dystrophic Epidermolysis Bullosa (EB) – which meant his skin fell off at the slightest touch. If you watch it, be warned – you will cry buckets, unless you are not a very nice person – only joking. ☺

Identify and rate your fears

Go through the list of fears and rate them on a scale of 1 to 5, with 5 being an extremely powerful fear that affects your everyday life and causes you great stress, and 1 being a very mild fear that only occurs occasionally with the minimum intensity of feeling.

Just as with recognising your stress triggers, identifying the fears that cause you the most stress and that hold you back is just the first but vital step towards overcoming them. Throughout the remaining chapters you will discover information that will help you transform the way you think and feel, which in turn will diminish your fears.

We often worry about things that never happen. Unfortunately, we do not have a crystal ball and therefore have no way of knowing what the future holds. Even if something unpleasant does happen, though, it is just possible that it is that particular event that may ultimately lead to greater happiness in the future ...

Given that we have no way of knowing what the future holds, the best way to be happy is to learn to live from moment to moment. This means learning to manage our thoughts so we can enjoy today, whilst still achieving our goals.

Problem Resolution

If people are prone to stressful thoughts, when faced with a problem it is common for them to become trapped in a negative thought loop, without ever coming to a solution to their problem. They might find themselves:

- Reliving the event or conversation, looking at every detail of it for evidence that their beliefs are correct, generally resulting in more negative feelings and stress.
- Agonising about the negative things that might happen in the future.
- Rehearsing difficult or unpleasant conversations in their head.
- Imagining conversations where they stand up for themselves, yet knowing deep down they will never actually have the conversation.

They also ask questions which will inevitably make them feel less powerful. For example:

- Why has this happened to me?
- How did it go so wrong?
- Why did I let this happen?
- What have I done to deserve this?

If this is the type of question you ask yourself, your unconscious mind will go off looking for answers to these questions. It will then come back with responses that, in accordance with your beliefs, explain how you reached your current situation. These will invariably fuel your belief that you are a victim of circumstances outside your control. It is very unlikely that the information gained is going to move you forward to where you wish to be. The key to problem resolution is to ask the right sort of questions.

Asking great questions

How quickly and easily we overcome issues, resolve problems and achieve things is largely related to the type of questions we ask. Take look at these next questions:

- How can I move on from this point to improve my life?

- Which of my beliefs are causing me to feel negatively about this set of circumstances?
- In what ways am I not trapped or stuck?
- What is there in this situation that will help me live a happier life or move me forward towards my goal?
- How can I enjoy the process of achieving what I desire?
- What positive learning can I take from this experience?
- What steps can I take to improve my situation?
- What steps am I prepared to take to get the results I want?
- What am I willing to stop doing to achieve my desired results?

Unlike the first set of questions, the answer to these will help you see the benefits and advantages of your situation, so you can move forward to a resolution of any problems.

The following very simple techniques can be highly effective at enabling you to come up with creative ways to solve challenges:

1. Imagine it is solved

Simply imagine a point in the future when the problem has already been successfully resolved, then ask yourself the following questions:

- What happened to solve this problem?
- What actions did I take?

Take a note of any insights and ideas that come from the process.

2. A more resourceful you

Next, imagine how a more resourceful you, someone you admire or your hero/heroine would resolve this issue. Once you are clear how they would handle the situation, you know it is actually possible to do so and can act on any appropriate insights.

3. Brainstorm

Write down as many ways as you can think of to solve the problem. Even if you think they are impractical, it does not matter at this stage. The idea is to free your imagination and creativity. Once you have a list you can then go back through the options to see which ones you can act on.

Taking the initiative

If you frequently find yourself not taking action to resolve your problems and instead you repeatedly have thoughts like:

- Yes, but ...
- It's not fair.
- I have no choice.
- If only ...

accept the fact that this type of thinking will get you nowhere. If anything, it will actually increase your stress levels and even make you feel depressed. Instead, take decisive action. Make a list of all the problems or injustices that constantly cause you stress, then for each one write down all the possible steps you can take to change things, and take action.

For example, if your friend expects immediate attention every time she phones and never takes into consideration what you are doing, you could:

1. Phone her today and explain how you feel.
2. Next time she rings, simply say, 'Sorry, I don't have time to speak right now.'
3. Buy an answerphone or use caller display and only take calls when it is convenient.

Using this example to illustrate my next point, no doubt you will not have taken any of these actions because of fears (based on the list I shared earlier) of repercussions. If this is the case, at the very least acknowledge that you are not trapped in this situation. You are simply choosing not to take action, which is still a choice – no action is a decision to accept the situation as it is and its consequences.

The next time you find yourself in a situation where you are unhappy, ask the right questions to inspire you to move your life in a positive direction and change the way you feel. It is a great place to start transforming your life and reducing your stress levels.

Change of Focus

As a society we tend to focus on what we do not have or on what is wrong in our lives or the world in general. This leads to feelings of discontentment and stress. Ironically, the quickest way to get what you want in life and to reduce stress is to learn to be happy with where you are, what you have and who you are at this moment in time. Focusing on the good things in life and noticing the extraordinary or wonderful, even if they only last a moment, is something people with a positive and happy disposition do naturally.

Thankfully, it is a skill we can all learn. That does not mean that we cannot desire or strive for change. It is simply about appreciating and feeling genuine gratitude for the good things that we have in our lives right now. By focusing on this we have less time for thoughts that lead to stress.

Look for the Extraordinary in the Ordinary Things in Life

It is very easy to find fault with things, especially if one thing is not how you want it, at which point everything in your life can appear to be wrong. If you look for faults in almost anything you will find them – career, spouse, family, friends or the world in general.

But once you choose to start appreciating the good things life has to offer and begin to notice the amazing and extraordinary all around you, life can look a whole lot better. When was the last time you really appreciated the small things that can bring a smile to your face, like your child's laughter or the beauty of nature, for example?

Sometimes it is the little things that can transform your day into something special, but you have to take a moment to notice and appreciate them. If after looking for some special moments in your day you are still convinced there aren't any, then perhaps it is time to make small changes in your routine to allow them to happen. Examples of small things that can briefly raise your spirits that you can incorporate into your day include:

- buying yourself some flowers
- jogging somewhere pleasant
- browsing around some antique shops or flea markets
- eating an ice cream on a bench in the park

- chatting to the person serving you in the supermarket
- going for a bike ride
- dancing like no one is watching
- watching the rain while you are cosy inside
- having a coffee or cake in your favourite cafe
- visiting a historic house or public garden
- going for walk on a beach or by a river – have a paddle if it's not too cold and it is safe to do so
- playing a game of tennis or badminton just for fun
- taking up a new activity like ice-skating, snooker, pool, yoga, an art class, bingo, joining a choir, birdwatching, dance lessons, learning a language
- reading to your children and watching their expression
- chatting to a friend or family member on Skype or FaceTime

You will have your own ideas of what is extraordinary and/or special, but whatever it is, enjoy it and appreciate it.

Gratitude list

Whenever I first ask clients to do this, often their first reaction is that they don't have much to be grateful for. One client of mine was young and healthy. She had her own home, a career, a loving family and lots of friends, but she only put three things on her list for which she was grateful:

- her cat
- her new car
- cheese

Now even though I can appreciate the delights of cheese, I was very concerned that my client had completely disregarded the wonderful things she had been blessed with. She was not overlooking them because she was a horrible person. It was simply that she had become so used to having them that she had stopped appreciating what she did have to be happy about. At the time she was also so overwhelmed by what she felt was wrong in her life – the lack of a loving boyfriend, the need to lose weight, etc. – that it was obliterating any pleasure that she could have experienced from things she did have.

There are so many things to be grateful for even when times are difficult or stressful. If you can't think of any at the moment, use the following list to start you off:

- things in nature you enjoy – animals, trees, plants
- good health or aspects of your health that are good
- skills and talents you possess
- past enjoyable experiences
- your family and friends
- the weather and seasons
- music
- the ability to hear, see and taste
- hobbies and pastimes you enjoy
- your job or career
- films, plays and TV shows you like watching
- foods you love

Once you have covered these topics you should be on a roll. When you are writing your list don't just write things down. Really think about the pleasure they bring into your life and connect with the emotion of gratitude.

Whenever you notice you are focusing on what is wrong in your life, stop and change the focus of your thinking by concentrating on what is good or right in your life. The more you focus on these aspects – instead of what is missing or wrong – the happier and less stressed you will feel.

Forget About Perfection

I am not suggesting that you no longer maintain high standards. I am simply asking that you recognise that an obsession with being perfect can lead to a great deal of disappointment, frustration and stress. If instead of celebrating your successes and achievements you look at what was not quite perfect, you will reduce the sense of satisfaction that accompanies achievement.

The same applies to events, special occasions and in fact any would-be pleasant experience. By focusing on the aspects that are not quite right, instead of focusing on what was good or great, you will diminish any pleasure that could be derived from the situation.

☺ Stop trying to be perfect and instead be a great example of a good human being.

I increased the level of stress in my life by being a perfectionist, by trying to control everything in my life and by being really hard on myself when I could not meet my own exacting standards.

☺ I am still focused and I have high standards, but these days I am kinder to myself – most of the time, but this is definitely a work-in-progress area for me.

Stop Worry in its Tracks

If you lie awake at night agonising over decisions that need to be made or going over past decisions, rethinking every angle to make sure you got it right, it is time to stop worry in its tracks. You can do this by changing the inbuilt pattern of worrying and accepting the negative thoughts. Next time you notice that you are worrying about a situation, begin to question yourself logically:

1. What can one truly be certain about in life?
2. Am I predicting bad things because I am uncertain about the outcome?
3. How is worrying about this actually helping me?

Take a few moments to consider how much time you spend worrying. If you are unaware as to the extent that worrying is blighting your life, carry a notepad around and each time you catch yourself worrying, jot down the time of day and the thoughts you are having. This will help you build a clear picture of the severity of your worrying and give you an insight into how this will be raising your stress levels.

Do worrying thoughts enter your head rarely? Or do you worry several times a day? If the latter is the case, you need to take action now. There are several things you can do:

1. Write about your worries

As your worries occur, write them down on the left-hand side of a piece of paper. Then on the right-hand side, write down the answers to the following:

a) How realistic is this particular worry?

b) What are the chances of it actually occurring?

c) If it does happen, what will you do to handle it?

d) What can you do to mitigate the chances of it happening?

e) What advice would you give a friend with the same problem?

Once you have done this, exaggerate the problem until it becomes so ridiculous that it makes you feel like laughing.

Recognise what you can control and what you can't. For things you cannot control, trust that a power outside yourself will only bring things into your life that you can cope with.

2. Schedule a time for your worries

Some people feel that worrying is an essential part of controlling what happens in their life, in that they need to think things through in order to feel secure. As long as there are no errors in your thinking there is nothing wrong with thinking about things, as long as it is not consuming your day

Start by scheduling a short time each day, say fifteen minutes, and perhaps even a particular place where you do your worrying. Somewhere that you can sit down to analyse your worries as described in step one. If worrying thoughts come into your mind at other times, refuse to dwell on them by using the techniques I am sharing with you.

☺ Some people advocate wearing an elastic band on their wrist and snapping it against their skin when they notice themselves worrying – tough love.

3. Stop the negative dialogue!

If I have to spend time in the company of negative people, who talk constantly about how bad everything is and what could go wrong, I begin to feel drained and experience the need to escape from their company. But if the negative person is your inner self there is no escape …

The way you talk to yourself has an effect on both your emotional state and your performance. If you are bombarding yourself all the time with negative internal dialogue, you will be significantly increasing your stress levels and bringing your mood down. Thoughts that will increase stress include:

- I can't handle this
- I can't cope any more
- everything is ruined
- I never have enough time
- nobody else has to put up with as much as me
- trust me to mess things up
- my whole life is a mess
- I know things will go wrong again
- it's all just too much

This type of thinking serves no useful purpose and will definitely increase stress levels. However, the following type of thoughts will help you to feel calm and in control:

a) I have the resources I need to deal with this challenge
b) some areas of my life are still good
c) this situation will be resolved if I remain calm and focused

Thought Distraction

Sometimes we just need to distract ourselves from stressful thoughts for a few minutes, by breaking the thought pattern and regaining our composure. At this point we can then assess the situation by asking what action we can take, rather than just going over and over it, allowing ourselves to feel trapped. Stop your thoughts spiralling into a negative tornado by:

1. Bringing your attention to your breathing.
2. Doing a seven-minute meditation like the one in this book.

The following couple of exercises will help you retrain your inner voice:

1. Control your inner voice

Whenever you find yourself running a negative script in your mind, break the pattern by:

- humming or singing a few lines of a cheerful song

- telling your inner voice to shut up – literally tell yourself to '*Shut up!*', either in your head or out loud
- recalling a pleasant memory
- thinking about something positive for a few moments

After you have done this you should proceed with the rest of your day.

Repeat this process every time you notice your negative inner voice taking over. The good news is that it is possible to alter the sound of your negative inner voice:

- Notice the tone of your inner voice. Is it harsh, intimidating or sarcastic? Does it sound familiar – like anyone you know?
- Focus on the tone and begin to alter it. Make it whatever will hold the least power over you; for example, fast and squeaky like a cartoon character or sexy and sultry.

2. Choose your words carefully

Consider these words: must, should, have to, need to, got to. Insert them into the following sentences:

- I xxxxx to see my mother on Saturday.
- I xxxxx to book our holiday tomorrow.
- I xxxxx to pick the children up from school.
- I xxxxx to go to the gym on Saturday mornings.

When you add the words I have given into these sentences, they automatically take on a negative feel and apply unnecessary pressure.

While there will always be things we don't particularly enjoy, like putting the rubbish out, many people get into the habit of making everything an obligation. This automatically increases pressure and causes stress, as we become weighed down by all the things we *have* to do.

Hopefully, you want to visit your mother, collect your children from school or book a holiday. If you are like me, you will even love going to the gym. Become aware of the words you are using and substitute negative ones that add unnecessary pressure for more positive ones that accurately reflect how you feel:

- I prefer to go to the gym on Saturday mornings.
- I want to visit my mother on Sunday.
- I am going to pick the children up today.

It may not feel like you have a choice, but you do. Although you may not realise it, everything you do in life is a choice. You can even choose to stay in bed and never get up again. Deciding not to get up will have consequences, but if you are prepared to accept them it is still a choice open to you – although I would definitely not recommend it. It is important to recognise that life is all about choices, because when you feel like you have no choice, you feel powerless and trapped, which in turn leads to stress.

Every day we have thousands of thoughts and it is estimated that we may have as many as 50,000. Some of these are nonsense and for those who tend to dwell on the past or the future, a large proportion of these – perhaps even as high as 80 per cent – may even be negative.

You may have heard the expression 'monkey mind', which refers to a Chinese metaphor for a mind that cannot be at rest that jumps from one thought to another. Your mind is in monkey-mind mode when it is engaged with the thoughts passing through it, rather than being present in the moment.

This concept can be confusing to grasp at first, but right now it is a good example. As you are reading this text, along with absorbing the words, there will be other thoughts occurring at the same time. This happens as you interpret concepts and ideas. For instance, maybe words of agreement or judgement of what you are reading will be passing through your mind subconsciously. As you are reading this text it may even be that other completely unrelated thoughts pop into your head. Perhaps you are thinking about something you have to do later, something that has annoyed you or what to have for lunch. As your thoughts jump from one thing to another, that is your monkey mind jumping from one branch to the next, unable to focus on one thing for very long and rarely still.

If you spend the majority of the time like this, it can feel like your thoughts are controlling you, rather than you being in control of them. When your thoughts flit from one unrelated thought to another, whilst performing another task that is totally unrelated, it can be difficult to gain clarity.

There are many techniques throughout this guide that will help you reduce troubling thoughts, and improve your ability to focus on the present moment and the task in hand. But if you find your Monkey Mind jumping around out of control, simply close your eyes and concentrate on your breathing for a few moments.

Unhelpful thought paths

As part of managing your stress levels, you need to become aware of how many of these are focused on the present, as that is what is real and important. This means actively noticing your thoughts. Once you have a greater awareness of your thoughts, you can deal with the negative or unhelpful ones.

By controlling your thought processes you will have the ability to control your emotional responses. The following are examples of negative or unhelpful thinking, with an alternative more positive thought. Stop:

1. Labelling yourself with negative names – I'm a fool, I'm stupid, etc. Be kinder to yourself if you have made a mistake. Accept that it is simply that – a mistake.
2. Filtering out all the positives – ignoring all the things that have gone well and instead focusing on what went wrong. Switch your focus by making a list of what went well.
3. Using 'all or nothing' reasoning; for example, unless everything is perfect or exactly as planned or desired it is unacceptable. Be prepared to be flexible, and adjust your plans and attitudes as required.
4. Emotional reasoning – I am feeling worried, therefore something must be wrong. Recognise that you don't have a sixth sense and that your negative thoughts do not signal the arrival of challenges.
5. Assuming that someone is completely bad if they do something you regard as wrong or hurtful. Like you, they will

have good and bad traits. For example, if someone appears aloof when introduced, it may be that they are uncomfortable meeting new people.

6. Jumping to conclusions without evidence – I know it will go wrong. Rather than simply assuming the worst, look for evidence as to why things may go well and take steps to mitigate any genuine risks you foresee.

7. Being unrealistic. Accept that appointments overrun, public transport is subject to delays and children act up occasionally.

8. Always expecting the worst – my husband is late so therefore he is having an affair.

9. Spoiling the good times. Even when things are going well, people who are skilled at being stressed find reasons to worry by playing the what-if game. Instead, live in the moment and enjoy what you have right now. For example, if you meet a new man or woman, don't assume it is moving too fast or it will inevitably go wrong. Instead, enjoy the situation. Stop your mind from running a negative what-if script:

   • What if they go off me?
   • What if I allow myself to fall in love and get hurt?
   • What if their family or friends don't like me?

   ☺ Of course, all of the above could happen, but it is also possible that the relationship will flourish and just like a Disney movie, everyone will live happily ever after – it does happen. So celebrate your future instead of agonising over it.

10. Generalising – I was really stressed today, therefore I'm not improving. If you are likely to adopt this attitude, keep a diary and write down the improvements made each day. If you start to feel negatively about your progress, you can look back and see just how well you are doing and how far you have come.

11. Mind reading – deciding what someone thinks based on their actions. There could be a dozen reasons for someone acting

in the way they did, as there are usually circumstances in their life you know nothing about.

12. Agonising over the past or worrying about the future. You cannot change the past and do not know what will happen in the future, so live in the present. People can develop poor thinking habits, taking a difficult or bad situation and making it much worse by assuming the worst. For example, if someone is unwell, they assume it will be fatal, without receiving a medical diagnosis. Or they assume that the loss of a job will mean it is impossible to find another, thereby resulting in the loss of one's home, without having evidence to suggest this. If your thoughts begin to take you along this negative path, simply bring your attention back to the present moment.

13. Judging yourself based on what others think. You should assess yourself and your behaviour based on your own beliefs and strive to be the best person you can be.

14. Making every situation a catastrophe. As the old saying goes, don't make a mountain out of a molehill. Small things go wrong or not as planned all the time without it meaning that things are spoilt.

15. Talking yourself into a frenzy with thoughts like: I can't take any more, I can't cope. The fact is you *are* coping and will have done so on many other occasions. You will also have grown stronger as a result. Remind yourself of these times.

You may not be aware of your negative thoughts, so if this is the case, keep a diary for week and make a note of any negative thoughts and how they made you feel, both physically and emotionally. Then use questioning techniques to remove their power as described earlier.

The best way to deal with negative thoughts is to think the situation through calmly. Ask yourself if there is any evidence to support negative prophesies. Then work through each thought, contradicting it.

Whether you think you can or you think you can't, you're probably right!

Henry Ford

Controlling Your Emotions

Challenging times are a part of life, but if you can control your emotions in situations that would previously have caused you stress, you will feel calm and handle them with more ease.

Practise the following two exercises at times when you are not feeling anxious or stressed. This will mean that when the need arises you are able to use what you have learned to your advantage, in that you will already know how to do them effectively:

1. Calming visualisation:

a) Sit up straight in a comfortable position.

b) Imagine a golden thread running up your spine, out of the top of your head and all the way up to the sky as it supports your frame.

c) Become aware of your feet anchoring you to the earth.

d) Breathe normally.

e) Remember a time when you felt calm and relaxed. If you cannot remember such a time, imagine how amazing it would feel to unwind. Make it into a movie in your mind.

- What did you see and hear?
- Which emotions did you feel and enjoy?

f) Make any colours brighter and richer so the image in your head/mind is more appealing.

g) Enhance any pleasing sounds so they are louder.

h) Focus on the good emotions and allow the feeling of calm to intensify.

i) Notice where the feeling is strongest in your body.

j) Imagine it is a ball of brightly coloured light – choose any colour that you think of as happy or relaxing.

k) Allow the ball of light to radiate out until it has filled your entire body.

l) Repeat the exercise four or five times, adding more details to the visualisation each time.

m) Enjoy feeling calm and relaxed.

n) Practise often and enjoy doing so.

2. Calming anchor:

a) Remember a time when you felt totally calm and relaxed. If you can't think of one, remember how it feels just as you are about to drop off to sleep or as you awaken in the morning before disturbing thoughts rush into your head.

b) Recall the memory as vividly as possible or imagine as much detail as you can.

c) Focus on how great you feel and how nice it is to feel so calm.

d) Allow the pleasant feeling of calmness to intensify.

e) When you feel really happy, calm and relaxed, squeeze the knuckle at the base of the thumb of either hand using the opposite thumb and index finger.

f) Continue to squeeze for a moment or two while the feeling of calm is still intense.

g) The second you notice the feeling of intensity subsiding, stop squeezing.

h) Repeat the exercise five more times, each time adding more details to the event.

i) Enjoy the feeling.

j) Practise every day until triggering your anchor allows you to recall feelings of calmness instantly.

k) The next time you face a challenging situation and are beginning to feel anxious, trigger your calming anchor by squeezing your knuckle at the base of the thumb.

l) Concentrate for a few moments and access your inner calmness.

Don't underestimate the value of Doing Nothing, of just going along, listening to all the things you can't hear, and not bothering.

Pooh's Little Instruction Book
(Inspired by A.A. Milne)

Eye of the Storm

Sometimes when we are dealing with a particularly challenging short-term situation, it is like being in a violent storm. We can become panicked, vulnerable and anxious, which can affect our ability to make the best choices. The secret for staying calm in the midst of chaos is to find the eye of the storm.

If your life feels like it is out of control it is important to learn to relax. Using brief sessions of mindfulness and breathing exercises, and by bringing your attention inward, you can achieve a sense of calm. Even if this sense of peace and calm lasts for just a short period, each day you will benefit more from the respite than you might imagine – so give it a go.

Everything Passes

When we are enduring something unpleasant it helps to remind ourselves that everything passes. Nothing in life stays the same or lasts forever. We would all like pleasurable experiences to last as long as possible and for the unpleasant or painful experiences to be over immediately, but that is often not reality.

Experiment with the concept and remind yourself that everything passes, one present moment followed by another. Keeping this awareness close to your heart is not easy, especially in the face of adversity, but it is usually very helpful.

For some people coping with a difficult situation like the death of a loved one is so overwhelming that they need specialist counselling. If you believe that you might need help coping with a particularly difficult situation, don't be afraid to seek professional help or at the very least, talk to relatives or friends who you think might be able to help.

As you embrace a new way of living, take charge of your emotions in order to feel liberated. But don't be hard on yourself if you cannot achieve the results you want overnight, for your behaviours have been developing since the day you were born. The more you practise, the quicker and the more amazing the results will be.

The Little Boy and the Sweets

At the end of the school year the teacher brought in a jar of sweets then invited the children to line up and take some. They each took turns, smiling happily, until one boy put his hand into the jar and grabbed as many as he could possibly hold. But when he tried to pull out his hand, he was prevented from doing so by the neck of the jar.

Scowling with disappointment, he looked at his teacher, unwilling to let go of any of the sweets but still unable to remove his hand.

Smiling tolerantly, his teacher said: 'Be satisfied with half and you will be able to remove your hand.'

Notes to Self

- Asking the right questions will help me resolve problems.
- I need to focus on what is right and good in my life.
- I have the power to halt negative thought cycles.
- Everything I do in life is a choice.
- I don't need to be perfect.
- Nothing has to be perfect to make me happy.
- Everything passes.
- In the midst of chaos, I can find the eye of the storm.

Take Action

- Stop the negative dialogue in your mind by controlling your inner voice.
- Learn to recognise the signs that your stress levels are rising then manage thoughts before they get out of hand.
- Become skilled at bringing your attention back to the present.
- Write down your worries and possible solutions.
- Look for the extraordinary in the ordinary things in life.
- Write a gratitude list, take time each day to appreciate the things on it and add to it on a daily basis.
- Practise distracting yourself.
- Stop worry in its tracks and learn to control your monkey mind.
- Notice your thoughts at any given moment in order to control your responses and emotions.
- Create your calming visualisation.

- Build your calming anchor.
- Learn to tense and relax your muscles.
- Use the practical ways to help you relax.
- Seek specialist help if needed.

Chapter Five – De-clutter Your Mind, Life and Emotions

For every minute you are angry, you lose sixty seconds of happiness.

Author Unknown

Introduction

This chapter is all about having a clear-out and not filling our every moment. When we are stressed our lives, minds, hearts and sometimes our homes are full to bursting. We have already looked at negative thoughts in some detail and now I want you to focus on clearing out any negative emotions you have been carrying around with you.

☺ In my opinion, negative emotions have a very short use-by date and once passed, they belong in the bin with the mouldy bread.

We may not always be conscious of it, but our emotional state varies throughout the day in accordance with what is happening at the time and any thoughts that we may have about a particular event.

Because emotions are very complex, it is impossible to give a full description of the vast array that we experience. There are emotions – both positive and negative – that we all recognise, although how we experience them is unique to us. For instance, two people may feel sad, but how the emotion manifests itself and the intensity of it might be very different between individuals.

There are some emotions, however, that will send our stress levels soaring and it is these that we need to learn to deal with effectively.

Anger

If you are not constantly blowing your top you might think you are not an angry person. But anger does not always manifest itself in shouting, throwing objects or violence. Angry people often bottle up their feelings and as a result can be impatient, irritated, frustrated, resentful or bitter.

Anger can be a crippling emotion and it is one that a great many of us handle badly. Appropriate anger is not necessarily a bad thing, but when you are feeling stressed even the smallest thing can make you feel angry.

> *If a small thing has the power to make you angry, does that not indicate something about your size?*
>
> *Sydney J. Harris*

Unresolved anger

Unresolved anger can simmer away and then days, weeks, months, even years after an event it can still cause underlying stress. While coaching I frequently find that people are angry and bitter about events that occurred many years earlier. Often they are angry with family members, colleagues and friends, which leads to resentment that festers for many years.

Sometimes there is no way to resolve the issue; for example, if the person concerned has passed away. If this is the case and you don't think you can simply let the negative feelings go because you never got to tell them how you felt, consider writing them a letter expressing your feelings. Obviously they will not be able to read it, but for some people the act of writing down your thoughts can offer a sense of release.

If you are still in contact with the person who made you angry, you can of course choose to discuss the matter calmly with them. However, this may lead to more disagreements, so perhaps for your own sake it is best to choose to forgive them and let the matter go.

Are you an angry person?

Anger is destructive, often ruining relationships between spouses, family members and work colleagues – although the most damage is done to ourselves.

You were not born angry. Anger is a learned response, often stemming from childhood, when somehow it appeared that anger was the only way to deal with issues. Generally, you will find that people who are angry were raised in an 'angry home', where they witnessed episodes of uncontrolled anger from parents or older siblings. Or where they felt so repressed that they felt unable to express their emotions appropriately.

Sadly some people, particularly those who are stressed, are always ready to explode. This is because they permanently have a low level of anger bubbling away under the surface. Not only is this an extremely unpleasant way to live but, in my opinion, it is also a very unhealthy way to live, as it means they are living life in fight or flight mode.

People who carry anger with them all the time are often very unpleasant to be around. Some people can find them intimidating, whereas others can feel unhappy around them because they know that the angry person could kick off at any moment. This can leave them feeling as though they need to be ready to defend themselves should the need arise.

If you are suffering from anger, it may make you feel powerful and in control, but in fact you are just the opposite. Consider the following to help you assess how much residual anger you are carrying around:

- Do friends, family or colleagues think you get angry too often or too quickly?
- Has your anger caused issues in the past?
- Have you lost friends because of your outbursts?
- How have you hurt those you love? (For example, shouting at children.)
- Do you blow up over little things?
- Do you lose control?

In my opinion, if you have answered yes to one of these questions then you need to learn to deal with anger.

You may be thinking that expressing anger is not all bad in that it stops you from being pushed around and releases tension. Perhaps you feel anger is mobilising or that it makes you feel powerful. Maybe you see it as a way of achieving results or feel that it makes you appear assertive and strong. Whilst moderate anger can occasionally be appropriate, it is rarely the best solution if it takes the form of shouting, screaming or violence.

When you are angry, you are not in the best mindset to make decisions. In fact, my advice is never to make big or important decisions when you are feeling angry.

Learning to control your temper

Start by keeping an anger diary and note down the following:

- any angry thoughts you have each day
- situations that trigger angry feelings
- people who often make you feel angry

Once you are aware of what or who makes you feel angry, you can begin to deal with inappropriate feelings or reactions in a calm and controlled way, without escalating the problem in the form of uncontrolled outbursts. If you fail to deal with the things that make you angry, it will lead to additional stress. Begin by asking yourself questions like:

1. What can I do to be more tolerant of this person or situation in future?
2. Are there any aspects of this situation that are okay?
3. How can I separate how I feel about the behaviour from how I feel about the person?
4. Am I angry because they have broken one of my rules? If this is the case acknowledge that we all have our own rules that we want others to abide by – but even if your rules are fair and reasonable in your opinion, others may not feel the same way.
5. Is this worth getting angry about?
6. Will it matter in a year, six months, a month, a week, tomorrow?
7. How can I avoid the things, situations or people that make me feel irrational and angry?
8. Are my expectations unrealistic? Your knee-jerk reaction to this may be a resounding *NO*. But it is important to consider

the question carefully because if you have unrealistic expectations of people, situations and life in general, you are going to feel disappointed more often. For example, it would be ridiculous to expect your children never to leave toys lying around or for your spouse never to do anything to irritate you.

9. Would people I respect agree with this way of thinking?
10. What evidence is there to disprove what I am thinking about this situation?
11. Am I being inflexible?
12. Can I move away from my current position?

Tolerance

People who are stressed don't just get angry when the situation warrants it. They can feel inappropriate anger at insignificant everyday occurrences such as:

- traffic and other people's driving
- queuing in the supermarket
- computer software problems
- people making genuine mistakes

If you feel you really do need to release your frustration in some way, I would recommend exercise, a stress ball or even punching a pillow. But always avoid venting at others as a way of letting off steam. Better still, practise being more tolerant.

This exercise can be quite challenging, but it is well worth the effort. What you need to do is to practise tolerance. If one of the things that makes you angry is waiting in a queue at the bank, then the next time you go in, choose the longest line or the clerk you know is the slowest and the least efficient. While in line, practise this quick meditation:

1. How am I feeling?
2. What thoughts are in my head?
3. How does my body feel?
4. Focus on your breathing.
5. Take slow, controlled breaths.
6. Do this for a few moments.

7. Repeat the following affirmations:

- I can stay calm and relaxed in this situation.
- I don't have to be angry about this if I choose not to.

Acceptance

Some people believe that suppressing anger is bad for you. Indeed, bottling things up and becoming resentful is definitely not something I would recommend. But shouting and screaming won't make you feel better, either. In fact, venting anger often escalates the problem and hurts people in the process.

Instead, if you are angry about something, express your feelings calmly and then let it go. This way, you are more likely to be able to help others see your point of view. However, you may have to accept that whatever you do, you will never be able to change another person's opinion or view to match your own. Alternatively, look for compromises and win-win situations, where you both get a resolution you can be happy with.

The Lion and the Oxen

Four oxen lived happily together in a field, but every day a lion came and prowled around the field in the hope of feasting on one of them.

Each time he tried to attack them, the four oxen turned around with their tails towards each other and their heads facing the lion. No matter which way the lion approached, he was met by the horns of one or other of the oxen. Eventually, he went on his way, his hunger unsatisfied.

Then one day the four oxen began to quarrel and no longer wanted to be friends. Angrily, they went off to graze alone, each in a different corner of the field.

When the lion came by that day he was able to attack them one by one and feasted all day.

Tapping away anger

As with most things in life, you have to have a strong enough motivation for you to take action. Perhaps your anger does not bother you – indeed, you may even find it satisfying to lash out. Maybe you believe it is okay to vent at home because you can control your temper at work and simply expect your family to accept it. You may even find it releases some of the stress you are feeling.

But if you want to your personal relationships to thrive and for your loved ones to relish being around you, it is vital to learn to control your temper. As much as they may love you, no one can be really happy if they are on edge waiting for you to explode at the slightest thing.

Humans are habitual creatures and once a habit has been established, it will carry on running forever, unless or until something is done to break it. The key is knowing how to change the automatic response.

Sometimes we don't feel able to express our anger and bottle up our emotions; for example, if a friend or colleague has behaved in a way we find intolerable. This can lead to more stress. The answer is to learn to express our displeasure in an appropriate way.

Bottling things up can result in inappropriate anger over something very small and often unrelated to the issue at hand. This can involve you hurting those you love the most and not the people or situations that warranted it, thereby leading to feelings of guilt and increased stress. Lashing out at those you love should be sufficient motivation to learn to deal with any anger issues you have.

EFT (Emotional Freedom Technique) is an energy therapy that can be used for anger management. It is growing in popularity with therapists who use it alongside their regular therapies and it is 100 per cent safe to use.

The tapping routine that I am going to share with you has been adapted from various techniques and can be used to help you to overcome your automatic anger response, Practise it when feeling calm and then you will be ready to use it when you are feeling angry:

1. Close your eyes and take three deep breaths.
2. Using two fingers of either hand, tap your chin five times.
3. Tap the 'karate chop' point on the side of either hand, below your little finger, three times, using the side of your opposite hand.

4. Using two fingers of either hand, tap your collarbone five times – level with where you would fasten a tie; repeat on the other side.

5. Tap under each eye five times, again using two fingers of either hand.

6. Open your eyes.

7. Close your eyes.

8. Open your eyes and look down and to the left.

9. Next, direct your eyes down and to the right.

10. Rotate your eyes around in a circle in a clockwise direction.

11. Rotate your eyes around in an anticlockwise direction.

12. Recite the following:

   - this anger hurts me
   - anger hurts those I care about
   - I choose to release anger
   - I allow myself to let these feelings go
   - I can deal with this situation in a better way

13. Repeat the exercise until you feel calmer.

I still feel angry at times and I find certain situations or people's behaviour irritating. However, I am now far more in control of my feelings; although I do tell people I am displeased once I have stepped back to ensure that I am not being intolerant for no reason.

After all, if someone continues to behave towards me in a way that I have previously explained that I find unacceptable then they should be prepared to accept that their behaviour might result in me expressing my displeasure.

However, the type of person who continues to do something you have asked them not to is likely to feel that you are just moody or intolerant, or that you get mad for no reason because you are stressed. This is because they unlikely to accept that your reaction could have anything to do with them.

   ☺ Be mindful, though, that if you are stressed, they could just be right!

Whilst I no longer feel I have to put up with whatever comes my way, I have also learnt not to take things out on my loved ones, which has saved me a heap of guilt!

Guilt

First and foremost, guilt is an emotion. If we do something that our conscience believes is wrong or has caused harm, generally a sense of guilt will follow. Although guilt can be a crippling emotion, its purpose is not destructive; in fact, it is useful at assisting us to act in line with what we believe is right.

However, if you:

- suffer from chronic guilt
- frequently feel guilty without justification
- have difficulty letting go of guilt
- feel excessive guilt

like all negative emotions and thoughts, it can lead to feelings of stress. Wallowing in guilt can actually become more about you and how bad you feel about what you did rather than the harm you perceive you caused.

There are many reasons people feel guilty and they fall into a few basic categories:

1. Guilt about your past behaviour

In this type of situation there is no doubt that the behaviour occurred. You violated your own ethical or moral code, by cheating, lying or stealing, for example. Or by doing something you swore you would never do again, such as smoking, drinking, overeating or shouting. Put things right where you can. More importantly, resolve to act in line with your moral code of conduct going forward, as you cannot change the past no matter how much you may wish to do so.

2. Guilt over something you have not done but want to do

Although you have not actually done anything wrong, the very fact that you are contemplating something that goes against your own standards can lead to feelings of guilt. This kind of guilt can be felt as keenly as if you had actually committed the action. If your guilt relates to thoughts you have had, accept you have had these illicit thoughts as part of who you are right now. Acknowledge the fact that you have not followed through with the act. If having the thoughts continues to bother you, work on reducing them through conscious effort.

3. Guilt over something you think you did

Our memory of past events is highly flawed. It is entirely possible to have a sense of guilt over something you think you may have done. Indeed, it is even possible to feel guilt because of your thoughts. For example, if you believe your bad thoughts have caused harm to happen to someone. If you are distorting your recollection of events to make you seem more at fault than you are, question the reality of your thinking about the event.

4. Guilt about not doing enough

This is quite common when someone has died. Despite spending days, weeks, months, even years caring for someone, people will often focus on the one thing they feel they did not do well enough or sufficiently, resulting in an enormous sense of guilt. If you are in a situation where you believe you should be doing more, it is important to separate your desire to help from the guilt you fear will overwhelm you if you don't. Acting out of guilt can only drain you further and cause stress.

5. Guilt over what you have

If you are doing well, achieving and enjoying the pleasures in life, this can be accompanied by a sense of guilt and feelings that you don't deserve your good fortune. For instance, perhaps your ability to go on nice holidays and own an executive car makes you feel guilty when you hear on the news that others are struggling. It is worth remembering that your success does not diminish opportunities for others. Additionally, you can still enjoy life and help others by donating to charities for those in need.

6. Survivor's guilt

Soldiers often suffer from feelings of guilt when they have lost colleagues and it is accompanied with thoughts of what they could have done differently. However, this type of guilt is not restricted to the armed forces. If you suffer from this kind of guilt it can often be tied to grief. So if you cannot accept that your survival is a blessing that will allow you to contribute further to the world, consider seeking help from a counsellor.

Guilt is a complex and interesting emotion that is best dealt with.

Anxiety

The line between stress and anxiety can become blurred as they are similar in many ways and result in many of the same symptoms. But when someone is feeling stressed they generally know the cause, in that they feel too much pressure from one or more areas of their life. When the cause of the stress has gone the feelings of stress generally subside. With anxiety the cause is often less clear; indeed, they can become anxious about feeling anxious. Stress comes from overwhelm and frustration, whereas anxiety comes from fear and worry.

Living life with a constant or frequent feeling of anxiety means you are putting yourself under immense and unnecessary stress. In order to reduce that stress, you need to learn to substitute that feeling of fear for faith in life, yourself, God, the universe. You can choose to have faith in whatever belief best suits your model of the world.

Anxiety busting

Anxiety affects us all at different times and in different ways. When anxiety persists, it can become a significant factor in our lives. Anxiety that is not dealt with can escalate and result in panic attacks and anxiety disorders such as obsessive compulsive disorder (OCD).

Anxiety can make things appear worse than they really are and prevent you from confronting your fears. However, anxiety is normal and exists as part of the body's fight or flight response.

If your stress levels are generally high and you continually add stressors, no matter how small, it can trigger and cause feelings of anxiety. When anxiety is building, it is doing so as a direct result of the thoughts you are having. Anxiety brings with it physical responses, such as a feeling of tension in the muscles or shallow breathing. When you notice either the physical response or the anxious thoughts, you can stop anxiety in its tracks by using visualisation techniques.

The following exercise will help you to feel calmer by bringing your attention inward. Repeat the exercise in order to reduce your anxiety further. By practising this technique you will intensify its effects:

1. Emotions are energy, so the feeling of anxiety will be moving.
2. Notice where you feel the anxiety in your body and imagine it spinning.
3. Pay attention to the direction in which your anxiety is spinning.
4. Next, give it a colour; whatever colour your unconscious mind chooses is fine.
5. Visualise it still spinning but moving up your body and out through the top of your head, out of your body.
6. Change the colour to a positive, relaxing colour.
7. Visualise it spinning in the opposite direction.
8. Picture it spinning back inside you, through the top of your head.
9. Allow the spinning to slow down and stop before the colour spreads throughout your body, filling you with calmness.

Forgiveness

Nearly everyone has been hurt at some time or other by the actions or words of another. But there is no benefit to be gained in refusing to forgive or get beyond past betrayals, disappointments and hurts. No matter what you believe you have suffered, the process of forgiveness is the same: You let go of anger and hurt by being mindful and by focusing on gratitude and kindness. The fact is you *can* forgive the person without excusing the act.

Deciding to forgive means letting go of resentment and thoughts of revenge. Forgiveness may lead to feelings of understanding, empathy and even compassion for whoever it was who hurt you. This doesn't mean that you deny their responsibility or justify the wrongdoing. It is just a case of deciding not to allow it to hurt you any longer.

Forgiveness brings a kind of peace that helps reduce its impact on your here and now, allowing you to enjoy life more. Forgiveness can lead to:

• healthier relationships
• greater spiritual and psychological well-being

- less anxiety and stress
- lower blood pressure
- fewer symptoms of depression
- lower risk of alcohol and substance abuse

> ☺ Negative emotions become trapped in your body and are harmful, so let them go – you will feel great!

I believe that the ability to embrace forgiveness and focus one's energies on the future is vital to a happy life.

> *Feeling resentful and bitter towards someone is like 'drinking poison and expecting the other person to die'!*
>
> *Unknown*

Grudges

People who are negative about things blame others for what has happened in the past, which is actually ruining their now, their present moment and their future. Often, they will tell you it does not bother them any more, but the signs that they are still holding a grudge are still there. These may include a change in their tone of voice, a slight tensing of facial and other muscles, and the fact that if anyone mentions a related topic, they immediately remember the situation.

The visual signs are not always subtle. One very attractive client of mine was adamant that she was no longer angry about an event from three years ago. However, every time she spoke about it her face contorted and changed so much that it was as though she had been through several hours of visual effects in the make-up department. It actually made her look twenty years older and far less attractive.

> ☺ Had she seen what it did to her lovely face then she would have let go of the anger years before.

In other cases, people don't even try to pretend they are over whatever the incident was. In fact, it begins to define them. They take a certain amount of satisfaction, pride or even status from being the injured party, the abandoned wife, etc. They say things like: I will never get over what he did to me; I will never forgive him; I will never trust men again.

This simply prolongs the painful feelings. Often, they will struggle to ensure they are seen as the injured party or proved right, rather than accept some responsibility for the situation or simply forgive.

What I would like you to do now is recognise:

- what it is that you are still festering about
- that it is time to stop renting the person or the situation space in your head

Then learn to forgive as many people as you feel you can.

Deal with negative situations and forgive

When I did this next exercise I was not a bitter person and I did not feel that I held any grudges from my past. But to forgive was such a liberating and joyful experience that I now recommend it to all my clients and friends:

1. Make a list of all the people you need to forgive.
2. Find a quiet time and place so you can focus on forgiveness, visualising the other person or people involved.
3. For only a few moments focus on each person.
4. Ensure that you are seeing the event or person from a safe distance so that you feel no emotion.
5. If you feel any emotion, push the event further away in your mind's eye until you feel able to view the event without emotion.
6. Next, imagine your negative emotions floating away, releasing you from their grip.
7. Then ask your unconscious mind what you need to learn from this situation that could help you in the future.
8. Next, simply choose to forgive them.
9. Now think about each person or event again – go in closer this time and check there is no residual emotion.

This exercise will free up space in your mind and heart so it can be filled with positive feelings.

Negative press – negative emotions

Technology allows tragedies that happen across the globe to be relayed to us almost instantly, often in graphic detail. This can evoke a feeling of despair, a desire to change the world and feelings of inadequacy. In turn, it can bring spirits crashing down and can cause stress levels to soar.

If the things you see in the media have a negative effect on you, then stop watching the news or reading newspapers and magazines filled with depressing stories and features. If you don't want to live in a bubble and feel you need to know what is happening in the world, take just a couple of minutes each day to read or listen to the headlines and don't wallow in the detail. The Internet is good tool for this as long as you don't get drawn into spending hours on any websites where the news is being sensationalised.

The best thing is that to make the world a better place, and to avoid feeling frustrated and inadequate, we only need to channel our energy and care into doing small acts that make a difference. It is unlikely that you are going to be in a position to go rushing off to the other side of the world to assist, so make a financial donation if appropriate, or take any action you can, and then carry on with your day. This is not being callous – it is about recognising that constantly hearing about the suffering of others won't help you manage your stress levels in any way.

If reading articles about celebrity lifestyles causes you to feel your own life is lacking, give them a miss until you are feeling in a better place. Or at the very least question why it is that if their lives are so wonderful, they seek media attention for events that should be personal.

> *We cannot do great things on this earth. We can only do little things with great love.*
>
> *Mother Teresa*

Multitasking

Do you feel like the only way to get through things is to multitask? This is a common mistake because, unless one of the tasks can be done completely unconsciously, what is actually happening is that you are dividing your attention. Although you may be able to do a simple task like fasten your shoelaces whilst thinking about something else, you cannot hope to achieve the same quality of result if you are engaged in more complex tasks. If the two tasks require you to use the same part of the brain – for example, writing an email while talking on the phone about another subject – your brain simply slows down.

☺ So sorry, you might not want to read this, but no matter how skilled you are at dividing your attention, you will always achieve better results when you are 100 per cent focused.

In fact, multitasking essentially causes more problems than it solves. For example:

1. It causes stress. When people multitask stress hormones, like cortisol and adrenaline, significantly increase.
2. Tasks may actually take longer to complete, leading to additional feelings of stress and anxiety because you are not getting everything done that you should do.

   All this will result in is the need to multitask even more in order to rectify the situation. This actually has the reverse effect, in that tasks remain unfinished or are completed to a lower standard.

3. Multitasking uses up far more energy than when you are concentrating on just one task at a time, which can leave you feeling drained and stressed.
4. It reduces your enjoyment in that when you are only half focusing on a task, you are only getting half the enjoyment. Take a look at these two examples:

   a) I love to paint, but if I were thinking about whether or not I was going meet a work deadline whilst performing this task, I would not derive the same pleasure from each brushstroke.

   b) If you eat sweets while watching television, you will not enjoy them as much as you would otherwise. Often you will find that you get to the end of the bag before you have even been aware that you are eating them.

5. Multitasking reduces the speed with which you can complete a task accurately. If you don't believe me, try 'single-tasking'

on something you would normally combine with another task and time yourself.

6. As explained, when multitasking you are actually dividing your attention. Therefore, you are more likely to make mistakes or forget things.

How many times have you forgotten where you put something or what you went into a room for? The main reason multitasking is so hard is because it means you are continually switching your attention between tasks. This requires you to retain the previous tasks in your mind ready for when you switch back to them.

So if you swear by multitasking and think you can do it as well or better than single-tasking, research has bad news for you: performing two tasks at once, instead of sequentially, makes things more difficult. After years of multitasking it is not easy to focus on one task at a time, but it is worth it. Be persistent and focus fully on at least one task every day for a minimum of five minutes.

Do nothing

I never feel bored. My life is full of activities that I enjoy – and the occasional one that is not so good like cleaning the bathroom.☺ I generally have lots of pleasant things to think about, but sometimes it is lovely just to do nothing for a few moments.

Find a comfy chair – preferably in a pleasant room or one with a nice view – and just sit for ten minutes doing absolutely nothing. This is not a meditation session; it is just a session of being. Simply enjoy sitting with the thought of having nothing to do for the next few minutes. If thoughts pop into your head, just let them go without giving them any attention.

De-Clutter Your Life

This guide is packed with exercises and ideas on how to de-clutter your mind and reduce stress levels. However, if you are living in a cluttered environment then you need to deal with that, as well.

The sense of stress caused by clutter can be enormous, especially if you have to deal with other people's clutter. A clutter-free environment, however, helps you to feel in control and it also increases your sense of calmness. In addition, clutter often makes tasks more difficult, thereby increasing stress levels.

Make a commitment to de-clutter – you might just be surprised by the positive results, the satisfaction and the sense of calm that come from the act of de-cluttering itself.

Once you have decided to let things go and get rid of them, it is crucial to get them out of the house as soon as possible so they do not become piles of clutter.

Tips for de-cluttering

1. Scan any photographs and sheets of paper that can be stored as digital images. If you don't feel you can part with the originals, store them in the loft, shed or garage so you can at least clear your living space until you feel able to let them go – providing your loft is not bursting at the seams. ☺

2. Opt for digital copies of utility bills, insurance documents, etc.

3. Storing and holding on to books can bring pleasure, but if they are cluttering your home invest in an e-reader. Downloading and storing books on an electronic device has the added advantage of being able to obtain books instantly and they are generally less expensive, too.

4. Similarly, storing music on an electronic device could potentially save a great deal of space in the home.

5. Choose a beautiful box in which to keep sentimental items.

6. If someone gives you an unwanted gift, consider giving it to a charity shop to help raise money for a good cause.

7. If you are worried about needing something the day after you let it go, store it for six months in the loft or shed. If you still haven't used it after this period then give it away.

8. Operate the 'touch it once' principle in that when you have finished with an item, put it away in the correct place. This will save you loads of energy because it means you will never have to tidy again as everything will already be put away.

9. If your children or spouse are untidy, lead by example. If you don't put things away immediately, how can you expect them to do so?

Notes to Self

• I have choices; I am not trapped.

- All that is real is the present moment.
- I can control my temper.
- Forgiveness is a liberating experience.
- I choose to make amends and let go of guilt.

Take Action

- Become aware of your negative inner dialogue and learn to dismiss it.
- Use the anxiety buster.
- Practise forgiveness.
- Work out what your anger triggers are.
- Practise tolerance.
- Tap away anger.
- De-clutter your life.
- Don't try to change the world.
- Avoid multitasking.
- Schedule some time to do nothing.
- Restrict worrying to a short, planned time and place.

Chapter Six – Overcome Sleep Difficulties

You're the happiest while you're making the greatest contribution.

Robert F. Kennedy

Introduction

My aim is not to help you become an expert on the science of sleep. However, it is important that you understand its importance and how to ensure you get sufficient quality sleep every night. Even without any knowledge about sleep, it is fairly obvious that it is beneficial. This is simply because a lack of sleep makes us feel dreadful, while restful sleep can make us feel ready to take on the world.

Sleep and Stress

Difficulty sleeping and stress are like two sides of the same coin. When you are stressed, it is incredibly difficult to sleep, no matter how tired you are. To state the obvious, lack of sleep makes you feel tired, which in turn makes it more difficult to cope with everyday life, leading to increased feelings of stress. In other words, it is a vicious cycle.

How many hours of sleep have you lost worrying about the future and agonising over the past? It might surprise you to learn that many of the things we worry over that we think might occur never actually happen. As it is too late to change the past, these hours of worry are simply keeping you awake and spoiling your enjoyment of life. Thankfully, dealing with your stress so your inner monster will sleep soundly can benefit you greatly.

Definition and Causes of Insomnia

Insomnia is generally defined as an inability to sleep. It is characterised by a persistent difficulty in falling asleep and staying asleep, waking too early or where sleep is unrestful. Often, the sufferer will experience difficulties while awake. It is frequently thought of as a symptom of medical and psychiatric disorders. Insomnia is not the same as sleep deprivation, which is where there is a limited opportunity for sleep, such as a nursing a baby or a sick relative.

Insomnia is classed in two categories: acute or short-term insomnia – lasting one to four weeks – and chronic or long-term insomnia, which lasts for longer periods.

Primary insomnia may also be referred to as insomnia syndrome. It is a disorder in its own right and often has no obvious cause, but may arise from behavioural factors, such as negative conditioning or physiological issues, including hyper-arousal (fight or flight response).

Secondary insomnia arises from other conditions, such as:

1. Psychological: stress, anxiety, depression and grief.
2. Environmental factors: an uncomfortable bed, noise, or being too hot or cold.
3. Shift work: varying shift patterns and corresponding changes in sleep/wake schedules.
4. Lifestyle: eating too late at night, alcohol consumption, nicotine, drugs.
5. Substance use, including prescribed medicines: if you believe you may be suffering from the side effects of any medication, you should consult your GP or medical provider.
6. Jet lag: a temporary condition that can cause disturbed sleep patterns and fatigue following air travel across a number of time zones.
7. Medical: for example, chronic pain caused by various conditions such as fibromyalgia, osteoarthritis, severe headaches and rheumatoid arthritis.
8. Neurological disorders: including Parkinson's disease, Tourette's syndrome and epilepsy.
9. Sleep disorders: including sleep apnoea syndrome and restless legs syndrome.

paralysed to prevent you from acting out the actions in your dreams. REM sleep is important for processing emotions, retaining memories and relieving stress.

Non-REM sleep

NREM sleep is made up of varying levels, from light sleep through to very deep sleep. There are three stages:

1. Drowsiness – this is the beginning of the sleep cycle, lasting for around five to ten minutes. Because it is the transition period between wakefulness and sleep, if you are woken during this stage you might believe that you weren't asleep.

2. Light sleep – during this stage the body temperature decreases, the heart rate slows and the brain begins to produce bursts of rapid, rhythmic brain wave activity. It is more difficult to wake someone from this stage, which lasts for approximately twenty minutes.

3. Deep sleep – this stage lasts for around thirty minutes, during which people become less responsive to noises and activity in the environment, even failing to generate a response altogether.

Too Stressed to Sleep?

It is vital that you get sufficient sleep covering all stages on a regular basis if you are going to feel ready to take on the day ahead. While there is medication available to help you sleep, in my view it is far better to use your own internal resources to improve your ability to sleep soundly.

This guide is packed with information to help you reduce stress and sleep better, which in turn means you will cope with challenges better, reducing the stress you feel even further.

It is very hard to fall into a deep, peaceful sleep if you are feeling frustrated about all the things that are wrong in your life or are anxious about the future.

The steps overleaf provide a formula you can use every night for getting to sleep, sleeping better and waking up in the best possible way to start your day.

Appreciate your day and relax

1. Deal with the day's challenges

A couple of hours before bed, take no more than five minutes to jot down any concerns or worries you have had that day. Resolve to work on a solution to the problem the next day and then forget about it. This way you will allow your unconscious mind to formulate a plan whilst you sleep. If you don't believe this can happen, perhaps you will at least accept the fact that you will be better able to come up with a solution after a good night's sleep.

2. Review your gratitude list

An hour before bed, spend fifteen minutes reviewing your gratitude list. Enjoy the process and really focus on the pleasure you get from each item you have listed.

3. Relax

Thirty minutes before bed carry out one of the relaxation exercises in this guide. Alternatively, if you find it too difficult to relax alone, listen to a relaxation CD that is made up of soothing sounds or music. This can be equally effective, especially when it is tailored to your condition – stress.

Set a Sleep Switch

The sleep switch is designed to provide a powerful anchor for sleep. It provides the brain with a cue like a poem, rhyme or prayer that it associates with going to sleep. Anchors are stimuli that bring thoughts or emotions to the forefront of your mind along with corresponding actions.

In addition to affecting your mood, they might produce an automatic involuntary reaction or memory. For example, if your grandma's house always smelt like roses and it was a place where you felt safe, then the smell of roses may invoke instant feelings of security. Likewise, the sound of the phone ringing will cause you to answer it without even thinking about it. But if it always heralds bad news, you will soon come to dread the sound of the phone ringing. I have become so used to exercising to certain songs that as soon as I hear them, I feel energised.

You may very well have built up unconscious anchors around bedtime and sleep that are negative, but these can be changed by replacing them with positive ones. These can develop from following a good bedtime routine and setting your own sleep anchor:

1. Choose a poem, rhyme or prayer that you like that you can recite by heart. For this exercise it should be one that is neutral with no memories attached or one that stimulates pleasant and peaceful thoughts. If you prefer, you can choose to count backwards from 300 instead.

2. Lie in a comfortable position, breathe normally and recite whatever it is that you have chosen in your head.

3. Continue to recite it slowly, focusing on the words until you fall asleep – don't rush through it.

4. If other thoughts or concerns come into your head, let them go and start at the beginning, without giving them any attention.

5. It is natural to get distracted and lose your place, so when this happens relax and simply start again at the *beginning*.

6. Focus on the words and nothing else.

7. Repetition is key and you will need to be dedicated at doing this exercise every night, and whenever you wake up during the night, until you fall sleep.

8. To start with it may take you awhile before you fall asleep.

9. Just keep persevering and the more you do so, the quicker your brain will associate the verse with sleep and the faster the results will be.

As your switch becomes more effective, you will find that you begin to fall asleep before the end of the verse.

☺ My sleep switch is incredibly effective and I am asleep before I have recited it even once. However, I rarely need to use it now as the rest of my bedtime routine works wonderfully.

Establish a Bedtime Routine

It is vital to establish a good bedtime routine:

1. Make sure your bedroom is quiet, dark and at a comfortable temperature.

2. Stick to a regular schedule by going to bed and getting up at the same time every day, including weekends, even if you are tired. This will help you to get back into a regular sleep rhythm. Once you start moving around, preferably outside in the fresh air, you will feel more alert.

3. Avoid stimulating activity, big arguments, heated discussions or stressful situations before bedtime.

4. Consider turning off all electronic appliances at least fifteen minutes before going to bed, as it is never a good idea to watch TV or play on computer games just before you are trying to wind down to sleep.

5. Restrict your alcohol and caffeine intake ideally at least six hours before bed; although alcohol can make you feel sleepy, it interferes with the quality of your sleep.

6. As nicotine is a stimulant, consider quitting smoking or avoid it at night.

7. Train your body to associate bed with sleep and nothing else – especially not frustration, anxiety and stress. Use the bedroom only for sleeping and intercourse, so that your brain and body receive a strong signal that it is time to sleep when you get into bed. Don't work, read, watch TV or use your computer in the bedroom – the aim is to associate the bedroom with sleep alone.

   However, it is worth pointing out that reading can distract the mind from other matters and can be a relaxing experience that allows you to drift off to sleep easily. Experiment with what works best for you.

8. Use conscious breathing in order to relax deeply and aid sleep:

   • When you get into bed, close your eyes and take deep, slow breaths, making each one deeper than the last.

   • Ensure each exhalation lasts a little longer than each inhalation.

   • Breathe deeply by involving not only the chest, but also the lower back, rib cage and belly.

   • This can be combined with reciting the sleep switch explained earlier.

9. Avoid naps as napping during the day can make it more difficult to sleep at night. If you feel like you have to take a nap, limit it to thirty minutes before 3.00 p.m. and where possible, do a meditation instead.

Battle of the Wind and the Sun

The wind and the sun were disputing which was the stronger, when suddenly they saw a traveller walking down the road.

The sun said: 'I see a way to settle our dispute. Whichever of us can cause that traveller to take off his cloak shall forever be regarded as the stronger.'

'Good,' said the wind. 'I will begin.'

The sun retreated behind a cloud while the wind began to blow as hard as it could, directing all its force onto the traveller. But the harder it blew, the more tightly the traveller wrapped his cloak round him, until at last the wind gave up in despair.

Then the sun came out and shone with all its brilliance, warming the traveller and the earth around him. Within minutes, the smiling traveller decided it was too hot to walk with his cloak on.

Notes to Self

- Insomnia can be overcome.
- The sleep switch is my key to restful sleep.
- Many of the things I worry about never occur.

Take Action

- Become aware of any unconscious anchors you have set around bedtime and sleep, then break the pattern to change any that negatively affect your ability to sleep well or that add to your feelings of stress.
- Aim for six to nine hours of sleep a night.
- Take time to appreciate your day and relax.
- Develop a stress-reducing bedtime routine.
- At the end of every day review your gratitude list.
- Set a sleep switch.

- Go to bed and get up at the same time every day.

Chapter Seven – Financial Worries

The real measure of your wealth is how much you'd be worth if you lost all your money.

Author Unknown

IMPORTANT NOTE

The information contained in this guide is general budgeting advice. It should not be used as a substitute for professional financial advice. If you are concerned about debt, you should contact a free, independent advice service such as the National Debt Helpline or the Citizens Advice Bureau in the UK for confidential advice on how to deal with debt problems. If you are not resident in the UK, make enquiries as to the services available in your country of residence.

Introduction

nsufficient money coming in each month can certainly be one of the most stressful things in life to deal with. Spending more than you earn each month isn't sustainable in the long term, driving people further and further into debt, causing even more stress.

Whilst it is certainly true that money cannot buy happiness, there is no doubt that a lack of it can cause a great deal of unhappiness. Feeling worried or anxious when facing debt and financial problems is a normal response. But as you have been discovering throughout this guide, there are many things you can do to help yourself through difficult times. Depending on your circumstances, addressing your financial issues may take months or even years to sort out, so it is important that you use stress-relieving techniques at the same time as dealing with the financial issues.

Living in a Consumer Society

These days we live in a consumer-based society and that in itself is a major cause of stress to many people. We constantly strive for the latest fashions, new versions of smart phones or bigger 3D, surround-sound televisions, etc. Often, the minute we have acquired them there is a new version available and the cycle starts again.

There is even a new form of snobbery developing as people try to improve what they think of as their perceived status by buying gadgets and designer labels they hope will impress others. They are generally quite easy to spot, as their designer label will be proudly displayed. Or they will immediately tell you the brand of their latest jacket, shoes or gadget – even if you show no interest whatsoever.

We have developed a 'must-have now' culture. From expensive holidays to designer goods, we are encouraged to buy on credit rather than wait and save for what we want. Many of us have forgotten or never experienced the additional pleasure that comes from buying something that we have saved for.

There is absolutely nothing wrong with wanting nice things or having aspirations, as long as the desire for them is not causing stress or leading you into debt.

I rarely meet anyone who believes that they have enough money to live the life they wish to lead. But often, when they really think about what makes them happy, it is the things that cost little or no money that are genuinely important to them.

Richness is relative

Everything is relative, so what people perceive as poverty or money worries can vary drastically from person to person. What is important is that it is not our situation that causes the feeling of stress, but our perception of it.

I have known people to become incredibly stressed at the thought of having to sell one of their cars, or letting the cleaner or gardener go. Whereas someone else, who doesn't have enough money for next month's rent and faces possible eviction, has taken it in their stride.

Our feelings and thoughts around money are all subject to our beliefs, values and past experiences. These very simple examples illustrate the point well:

1. If someone makes the following statement: 'I spent a fortune on this handbag,' they could mean anything from £10 to £1,000 plus, depending on their circumstances.

2. If they say: 'We have absolutely no money for non-essentials,' this could mean that they only have £1,000 a week to spend on luxury items, that once the rent, utility bills and food are paid for they have less than £5 a month left over or anything in between.

I was raised in what I believe was poverty. When there was no food we ate bread dipped in Oxo gravy. When it was cold and there was ice on the inside of the windows, because we could not afford to put the heating on, we wrapped newspaper around us to keep warm. Often we would use salt to clean our teeth because there was no toothpaste. I rarely had new clothes and I remember at sixteen having to borrow shoes from a friend so I could go to school to take my final exams.

Our childhood experiences left my sisters and me with a strong desire to ensure our children never experienced the extreme poverty that we did. However, it is not the poverty we reminisce about – it is the good times we shared. In later life, we realise just how amazing our mother was at managing money and, perhaps more importantly, we have a deep respect for the woman who in later life still had nothing by today's standards but was contented.

Perhaps it was my childhood experiences that led to my spending over twenty years working in the world of credit and finance, or maybe it was simply coincidence that led me in that direction. Whatever it was, from the very first day I was fascinated by what a difference careful financial planning could make and as a result I became passionate about managing my budget.

☺ When I was growing up we lived in a council flat in a very poor neighbourhood. Our next-door neighbour had red quilted wallpaper, which she decided to change. When it was taken down, it came off in full strips, so my sisters and I put it up in our lounge. We still laugh about having second-hand wallpaper now.

Managing Budgets

If even thinking about taking a close look at your finances brings you out in a cold sweat and you have not looked at them for a long time, then making a budget can be a daunting prospect. However, it can also be a satisfying process. Once you have drawn it up, although you may not be happy with your financial situation, you may even feel relieved that you are taking control of your finances.

Mr Micawber's often quoted recipe for happiness:

Annual income twenty pounds, annual expenditure nineteen [pounds] nineteen [shillings] and six [pence], result happiness. Annual income twenty pounds, annual expenditure twenty pounds ought and six, result misery.

Charles Dickens, David Copperfield

Compiling your budget

A budget is quite simple. It is merely a plan that takes into account your monthly income and expenditure. By completing a budget fully you will have a clear view of where your money goes.

If you stick to your budget, it will help ensure you are not spending more each month than you have coming in, thereby helping you to live within your means. Another unexpected benefit that often results from effective budgeting is that you may find you are wasting money on non-essential items that are not bringing any real value into your life.

For example, if you discover that you are spending £5 a day buying lunch on your way to work, that equates to over £1,000 per year. Now if what you are buying for lunch is the most amazing sandwich or salad that really makes your day, then you may choose to make no change. However, if it is a mediocre meal that you would not miss then you might choose to make your own lunch, which even after buying the ingredients could mean a possible saving of £800 pa.

☺ Whilst considering the fact that it must be one hell of a sandwich to outweigh the stress caused by overspending, have a think about how the money could be put to better use.

If you have a financial goal, such as getting out of debt, saving up for a deposit on your first home, putting money aside to enable you to start a family or putting something away for your retirement, a sensible budget will help you work towards this.

Important points about budgeting

1. Revisit your budget on a regular basis and also whenever there is a significant change in your employment or living situation, to ensure your budget still works.
2. Set aside at least an hour before you begin trying to draw up your budget. Rushing is likely to lead to mistakes.
3. It is important to ensure your budget reflects all of your everyday expenses, needs and income as closely as possible. This will mean you are balancing your earnings and spending effectively. Missing out one significant item or a few small ones such as having your hair or nails done or going for a pint or a game of pool with your mates will provide you with an inaccurate budget. This will result in discrepancies between your plan and your actual financial situation.

Drafting an effective budget plan

Whether you use a spreadsheet, a specially designed computer program or just a notebook to create your budget, the following tips will help you create an accurate account of your income and expenditure:

1. Gather together all the paperwork you will need before getting started:

   - bank statements for the previous twelve months – this will ensure you have covered irregular significant expenditure such as insurance, Christmas or holidays
   - credit and store card bills for the previous twelve months
   - copies of household bills

- your most recent payslip – if your income varies from month to month you may need several months' worth
- details of any savings, shares and pension contributions
- information on any other income you may have.

2. Next, calculate your income, taking into account the following:

- your regular earnings from employment, after tax and National Insurance have been deducted; take care if you are including overtime
- income received from savings, investments, self-employment or rental of any properties you own
- include any yearly or sporadic earnings such as dividends from shares and annual salary bonuses
- Separate regular income and sporadic income into two columns and then add the two totals together at the end, to give you a grand total of your income.

3. Now, you need to work out how much you are spending:

- Look through your bank statements, household bills, and credit and store card bills, placing each item of expenditure into a category such as food, mortgage, rent, leisure, clothing, etc.; the more accurate your figures, the more useful your budget will be.
- Take into account all occasional spending, such as Christmas, insurance policies, holidays, birthdays, car tax and MOT, etc., and add costs like these to your list of expenses.
- Separate regular outgoings and sporadic expenditure into two columns.
- Add the two totals together at the end, to give you a grand total of your expenditure.
- Divide the total of your sporadic expenditure by twelve, to give you the amount you will need to set aside each month for irregular expenses.

Once you have these figures, you need to compare what is coming in and going out on both a monthly and an annual basis. Then you can deduct your annual and monthly expenditure from your annual and monthly income figures. The balance is yearly and monthly surpluses – or shortfalls – in your finances. A shortfall will be indicated by a negative number.

Remember that if you have included sporadic income that is not guaranteed, such as an annual bonus, and have spent money based on this total income, you may have a shortfall at the end of the year if the income does not materialise. If possible, it is best to live within the constraints of your monthly income and reserve extra payments for treats or savings.

Even if you find you have more money coming in than going out, whilst that is great, it still makes sense to have a budget to ensure you keep spending sensibly. It could also help you find opportunities to save for the future or pay off debts more quickly.

If you discover that your spending exceeds your income at present, a budget is crucial if you are to avoid spiralling into debt. It won't help if you don't address the situation and a budget will enable you to do this. If you find yourself in this situation, it is time to work out what you can cut from your monthly spending and thereby reduce the stress in your life.

It is not my place to tell you what you can or cannot afford, or what your priorities should be. Only you can decide if your round of golf, your child's dance lessons, your monthly visit to the nail bar, a pint down the pub or the twenty cigarettes are vital to your happiness. It is no one's place to judge your choices, as we all have things we feel we cannot do without. But if you need to make spending cuts, be realistic about how essential the items are.

Reducing expenditure without feeling deprived

Even if your income exceeds your expenditure, why spend more on something than you have to? This can be particularly important when making a large purchase, as even 10 per cent difference in price can be a significant amount. However, shopping around can be time-consuming and if one of your stressors is a lack of time, try shopping online to save time.

If you need to reduce your expenditure and free up some cash, cutting the cost of essential household goods and services should be top of your list of priorities. The following may give you some ideas from where to start when cutting down on bills:

1. Energy costs – becoming more energy efficient and reducing expenditure could save hundreds of pounds a year. Check whether a different supplier could offer you cheaper energy or a better tariff.

2. Don't leave appliances on standby; turn off your television, etc., when you are not using them.

3. Turn off your mobile phone charger at the wall when you are not actually charging your phone.

4. Switch off lights when you leave the room and don't have more on than you need.

5. Don't heat more water than you require when boiling a kettle.

6. Use lids on saucepans as the contents heat quicker.

7. If you have a dishwasher or washing machine, use the half load or economy cycle if it isn't full.

8. Turn down the thermostat on your hot water to 60°C.

9. Fix leaky taps and ensure they are properly turned off; a dripping tap can waste enough water in a week to fill a whole bath.

10. If you can, keep active to stay warm; even doing some housework will raise your metabolism and make you feel warmer.

11. Don't heat rooms continuously throughout the day if they are not being used.

12. Tuck curtains behind your radiators when they are on, so you heat the room and not the window.

13. Reducing your room temperature by as little as 1°C could cut your heating bills by up to 10 per cent.

14. Tumble dryers are very expensive to run and produce a lot of heat. If you are able to dry your clothes outside or on indoor racks, do so.

15. Wear an extra item of clothing instead of turning on the heating; it might be all that you need to stop you from feeling chilly.

16. Turn the heating off or down if you go out. While it is nice to come back to a warm home, it only takes twenty minutes to

warm up. Alternatively, if you have an efficient boiler, it may be more economical to leave the heating on at a constant low heat. Take some independent advice before deciding what is the most economical and efficient for your home.

17. Remember that you need to retain some warmth in all the rooms to prevent damp and mildew.

18. Don't use an electric fan to keep you cool unless you have to as they are very expensive to run and turn it off if you are not in the room.

19. Insurance – don't just accept the renewal quotes you receive for insurance products. By sticking with the same insurer year after year, you will miss out on the best deals.

20. Food shopping – supermarkets are a convenient way to get all your shopping from one place. Shop around for the best deals, consider own-brand labels and only buy three-for-two deals if they are things you actually want and will use. It is not good value if products sit on the shelf in the fridge and are then thrown away when they go out of date.

21. Instead of just pulling into the same petrol station each week, check the pump prices and fill up where you can get the best deal. Remember: driving 30 miles out of your way to fill up might cost more than you are saving.

22. If you have credit and store card debts, consider transferring to a zero per cent balance transfer card or a life of balance transfer card (where you transfer the balance and get a super-low rate of interest for the life of the balance). Cards like these could cut your interest costs dramatically, allowing you to pay off your debt more quickly.

23. If you are thinking of applying for a loan to pay off existing debts, ensure you have a plan to clear what you owe on the new loan before spending more. Bringing all your borrowing together in one place and then continuing to use credit/store cards will make the situation worse.

How far you have to cut back will depend on your personal situation. Cutting back isn't easy, but failing to do so will result in debts that spiral out of control. Every month that you reduce your debts will mean you are moving towards being less stressed.

Getting your partner to cooperate

If you have a partner or spouse you will need their cooperation to reduce expenditure and manage your budget. It could be that they are as stressed out as you are by your collective financial position. But if they are not fully aware, explain the circumstances and enlist their help in gathering the information. Alternatively, when you have all the facts together, sit them down and explain the full extent of the situation. Then obtain their agreement to economise.

If you are unable to gain the support of your significant other with regard to financial restraint, it may be necessary for you to take control of the finances and expenditure until things improve. In extreme cases, lack of support with regard to financial matters may be a result of much deeper issues in the relationship.

Increasing Your Income

If you still can't make ends meet, you could consider new ways to increase your income by:

1. Making sure any savings or investments you have are performing as well as possible.

2. Considering ways you could use your skills to generate extra income by working in your spare time either in a second job or through freelance work.

3. Selling unwanted items via the Internet or at car boot sales, etc.

4. Using cash back credit cards (where you get cash back on your spending) instead of your debit card for everyday spending could help you generate hundreds of pounds extra each year. A cash back credit card is one where you receive money for every purchase you make on the card.

   For example, a card that gives 1 per cent cash back means you will earn £1 on a purchase of £100. By providing this incentive the credit card providers hope to encourage you to use your card more. Which is fine as long as you are able to clear the balance each month and providing you do not incur interest charges. Beware, however, of cash back cards that incur an annual fee.

5. Depending on your situation you may be entitled to some form of benefits such as Family Tax Credit or Working Tax

Credit (in the UK). If you think this is the case, seek advice and make the appropriate claims. Every day we hear of people making fraudulent claims and people living off the State whilst making no effort to support themselves. But remember, if you have a genuine claim there is no shame in claiming available benefits. After all, these things are there to help those in need.

Financial Goal-Setting

Whatever your financial goals, once you have compiled your budget, it is time to draw up a plan that will help you achieve them. Be as realistic as possible. There are certain costs that will be impossible or very difficult to cut, while others will be easier to tweak.

Once you have assessed your current financial situation and drawn up your budget, it is not the time to sit on your laurels – the most important task is sticking to the spending plan you have made. Reviewing your spending on a monthly basis will highlight any issues so you can cut back immediately if necessary.

Checking your bank statements on a weekly or monthly basis is crucial if you are keen for your budget to stay balanced. Make sure you check that the transactions have been processed correctly. This also means you can spot fraudulent activity on your accounts sooner rather than later, should this occur.

Cash Spending

If you tend to make most of your purchases with cash, you may have difficulty keeping track of where the money goes. The only accurate way to track expenditure it is to write down what you spend daily in a notebook so you know where all your money is going.

Be realistic and keep all receipts so you don't miss one or two. Ensure your partner does the same if you are to gain an element of accuracy. Although the idea of doing this might appear tiresome, try making a note of all your spending for at least a few weeks – you might just be surprised where your money is going.

What is a Debt Problem?

Being in debt means that you owe somebody or an organisation money. Owing money is not in itself a problem. Many people owe money in different forms – such as on a mortgage, credit cards, store cards and loans – and are able to manage their finances without any worry. However, if you have insufficient money to pay for essentials like food, rent and bills, or to make at least the minimum repayments on all your debts, then you have debt problem.

Money won't create success, the freedom to make it will.

Nelson Mandela

If you realise that you have a debt problem, there are things you can do about it and the quicker you get started, the better. Facing up to a difficult situation may not be easy, but ignoring it will not help your stress levels or make it go away – so burying your head in the sand is not an option. In fact, if you ignore it, the problem will only get worse, leading to more stress.

Once you have a plan of action, you are likely to feel better. It is outside the remit of this book to advise you on debt issues; however, as already mentioned, there is free, independent advice available from the National Debt Line and from the Citizens Advice Bureau (in the UK), which can show you how to:

- work out your personal budget
- decide which debts to deal with first (priority debts)
- work out offers of payment
- deal with court procedures

Debt management

Debts can be split into two distinct groups – priority and non-priority:

1. Priority Debts

Debts that might result in the loss of a home or legal procedures are called priority debts. Because of the implications, they are likely to be the cause of most stress. Sometimes, people can negotiate payment amounts with creditors for priority debts. It is important to focus on repayment of these debts first, owing to their legal impact. Priority debts include:

- rent or mortgage
- secured loans

- council tax
- electricity and gas suppliers
- child support or maintenance
- magistrates' court fines
- business rent or rates
- hire purchase or conditional sale rented and hired goods
- income tax/VAT
- TV licence

2. Non-Priority Debts

Non-priority debts are those that do not affect your home or present an immediate threat in the form of fines or legal action. However, they can often feel very important if they are for large amounts of money or if there is a personal obligation to pay back debts promptly. Non-priority debts include:

- defaults on loans that are not secured against a home
- benefit and tax credit overpayments
- student loans
- money borrowed from family and friends
- credit or store card debts
- overdrafts
- water charge arrears – water companies may no longer disconnect supplies to enforce payment, but payment of water bills should still be high up on the list of priorities
- county court orders – where someone has been ordered to pay a debt via a county court order; however, courts take into account a person's ability to pay

If you are aware that you are facing financial difficulties and you might have problems meeting your current commitments, you should contact the people or organisations involved as soon as possible to advise them of your circumstances.

Often, if you explain you are in difficulty, they may agree to let you pay less than the required monthly repayments on non-priority debts and sometimes even on priority debts. The important thing is to take one step at a time and to do so straight away, before things spiral out of control.

In order to work out how much you are able to pay back to the people to whom you owe money (your creditors), there are a number of things that you need to do. These include identifying:

- what debts you owe
- your priority debts – those that you must repay first, to avoid legal action
- your other debts

You then need to work out your budget and calculate how much money you have left over, as explained earlier. Be realistic about how much you can afford to pay back. You should not agree to arrange repayments that are going to be difficult for you to keep. If you continue to be anxious about whether or not you can pay back the agreed amount, you will merely have replaced one worry with another. If you are not able to reduce your debts, consider contacting one of the organisations mentioned earlier for help and advice.

Debt management companies

This type of company usually arranges a debt management plan, avoiding the need to speak directly to your creditors. It also means that you are only required to make one payment to the debt management company. In turn, the company will distribute payments on your behalf to your creditors, based on the amount you owe them and your disposable income.

Most debt management companies will charge you for their services. However, some provide this service at no cost to the person in debt. *ALWAYS CHECK BEFORE YOU ENGAGE THEIR SERVICES.* Ensure that you fully understand the charges and are sure you want to use them before you agree to let them act on your behalf.

Consolidation loans

The rationale behind a consolidation loan is that all of your outstanding debts are cleared by one larger loan with a fixed, lower, more manageable interest rate and therefore lower monthly repayments.

If you are thinking of taking out a consolidation loan, shop around for the best deal and make sure you can afford the repayments. They can often be secured against your home if you have sufficient equity. Remember: if a loan is secured, you may lose your home if you fail to make the repayments.

Interest-free and balance transfer credit cards

There are a number of deals available in the UK that offer interest-free balance transfers. If you have debts on credit cards and are paying a high interest rate, this may be a viable option for you. But before you take one out, always:

- shop around for the best deal
- read all the terms and conditions
- seek independent advice if you are unclear about any aspect of the deal

Moving all of your credit card debts to one where it is interest-free for twenty months could give you the opportunity to reduce your debts rather than simply paying the interest charges. But it is essential you know what you are agreeing to and that you do not take this as an opportunity to continue to overspend.

Seek help immediately

The stress that is caused by financial pressures should never be underestimated. If you start feeling like you really cannot cope or that life is isn't worth living, these are dangerous signals. Seek help immediately. Either see your GP or call a support line such as the Samaritans (in the UK) for confidential support.

Take it week by week

Having looked at ways to reduce your expenditure and address any debt problems, it is unlikely that you will have an immediate turnaround in your financial situation and be debt-free overnight. Therefore, it will be necessary to manage any stress relating to your financial situation whilst you are working on rectifying the problem.

The exercises throughout this guide will help you deal with any stress relating to financial matters, in the same way as any other form of stress. However, the most important thing you can do to reduce anxiety associated with money is to remain focused on your goal and the fact that your situation will be improving each week. Finding ways to spend time with family and friends that are cheap or free – like picnicking in the park or on the beach, or watching a movie while having a home-cooked pizza – can be great fun and will distract you from stress.

Sometimes it may be necessary to make difficult decisions like selling your home. There is no doubt that this can be a difficult decision to make and indeed perhaps not something you would desire to do in an ideal world. Perhaps even the thought of it makes you feel more stressed. But if living in your current home is causing stress anyway, although it may not feel like it at the time, you may actually be happier once you move. I have known several cases where people have done just that and far from ruining their lives, things greatly improved:

> One couple were faced with a situation where their house was likely to be repossessed. The interest rates at the time had risen to the degree that they were unable to manage their budget. They chose to move not only to a smaller house, but also to a slightly cheaper area. As a result, their repayments reduced greatly and because this freed them from stress, they were able to focus on other areas of life, like their careers.
>
> The wife managed to achieve two promotions within a couple of years. As a result of her increased income, combined with the husband's steady income, the lower payments meant that they were able to afford holidays, nights out, a better car and a few luxuries. After speaking to them, it was clear that the difficult step they took improved both their lives and their marriage.

The Sisters

> There were two very beautiful sisters, Mira and Carina, who grew up in a poor but happy home. Eventually, they both got married. The first sister, Mira, married the town's richest merchant in the land and suddenly had great wealth. Although she and her husband had fine clothes and the best food, they trusted no one, keeping their doors and windows locked tight each night, for fear they would be murdered and their gold stolen.
>
> The second sister, Carina, married a nearby farmer and although they were very poor, their home was blessed with love and happiness. They welcomed friends into their home to share their meagre repast, they never bothered to lock their doors or windows and they slept soundly every night.
>
> One day Mira, who loved her sister dearly, visited Carina and gave her a large chest of cash, because she could no longer bear to see her sister struggle.

Carina and her husband were overjoyed and spent the day planning what they would buy and considering how their lives would change by moving to a bigger farm in another district. As they chatted happily, they realised that it would mean they would have to move away from their friends and neighbours, and they began to feel sad. That night, they found themselves locking all the doors and windows, but still they could not sleep as they kept watch on the chest of gold for fear it would be stolen.

Early the next morning, they took the chest of gold back to Mira, saying: 'Thank you, dear sister. We are very poor, but our lives are rich and your gold took our peace away.'

Notes to Self

- If I make a budget and stick to it, I can improve my financial position.
- Material possessions are not vital to my happiness.

Take Action

- Gather all your financial information together, compile a budget and review it on a regular basis.
- Learn to manage your budget.
- Deal with any priority debts first.
- Seek specialist financial advice if necessary.
- Increase your income and reduce your outgoings where possible.
- Seek help immediately if you are feeling overwhelmed by your debt problems.

Chapter Eight – Diet and Exercise

Take care of your body. It's the only place you have to live.

Jim Rohn

PLEASE NOTE:

The information provided is not intended to be a substitute for medical advice. If you have any concerns about your weight or diet, get in touch with your GP, medical practitioner or a dietician.

Introduction

Given that your body and mind are like a machine, it makes sense that you need to take care of them both in order to ensure that they perform well in all areas. However, it is certainly easier said than done. I personally find that one of the most difficult parts of eating healthily is gaining a clear understanding of what foods are good or bad for health. This is quite simply because the information appears to change constantly. Therefore, I choose a diet mainly consisting of natural foods that are low in fat, salt and sugar that I enjoy eating, as I know that I feel at my best when eating in this way.

☺ But I do not stick rigidly to any particular regime. I definitely have a weakness for ice cream and chocolate.

Monitor your diet for a few weeks to ascertain if certain foods are having a negative effect on how you feel. For example, if certain foods make you feel sluggish after eating, you may choose to omit that particular food from your diet.

Unhealthy Eating Habits

Stress is often a trigger for unhealthy eating habits or binge eating. Emotions are the body's way of telling us that something is wrong and we need to take action. Although I understand the temptation to comfort eat when you are feeling stressed, eating only makes us feel better on an emotional level for a few minutes and often makes us feel worse.

> *A crust eaten in peace is better than a banquet partaken in anxiety.*
>
> *Aesop, Fables*

Stress-Induced Overeating

There are many reasons that people overeat, most of which are not related to hunger. Stress can induce comfort eating, which means simply reaching for food in an effort to suppress negative emotions. Sadly, not only are you unlikely to enjoy food eaten whilst in a state of anxiety, but the negative emotions are also a signal that something is wrong and no amount of food will address the problem. The techniques in this book will help you deal with any negative emotions in an appropriate manner.

☺ So keep reading – there is lots of help coming up.

Stress-Induced Under-Eating

Stress-induced under-eating or eating less in response to stress is not as common as emotional overeating, but it does have negative implications on health and well-being. Under-eating for prolonged periods causes health problems:

- Sex hormone production can be interrupted, sexual drive reduced and menstruation affected.
- The heart can be damaged or weakened, as is a muscle that can be eroded by extreme under-eating.
- Blood pressure can drop to dangerous levels and the pulse rate can slow, resulting in sluggish circulation that can lead to ulcers on the legs and feeling cold.
- The digestive tract can become sluggish, whereby food moves slowly through it and feels uncomfortable.
- Skin can become dry, leading to signs of premature ageing.

- Hair and nails can become brittle.
- Sleep difficulties can arise, where one wakes early and experiences a feeling of restlessness.
- Lack of energy; being underweight can leave you feeling drained and tired.
- Nutritional deficiencies; you may be suffering from a lack of the vital nutrients your body needs to grow and work properly. Calcium, for example, is crucial for strong and healthy bones.
- Weakened immune system; your immune system is not 100 per cent when you are underweight, so you are more likely to catch a cold or the flu and other infections.
- Damage to future fertility; if your periods stop because you are underweight, you risk having problems getting pregnant later in life.

Eating sensibly is not the same as dieting. When developing a sensible eating plan, you need to make life choices that are not so restrictive that you feel deprived.

For example, if you decide you will never eat chocolate again, you might become obsessed with desire for what you cannot have, thereby making yourself unhappy. Instead, make choices that you will be able to sustain and enjoy throughout your life.

Irritable Bowel Syndrome – IBS

Nerves in the digestive system send signals to the brain if you are hungry, full or need to go to the toilet. It is possible that people with IBS may be oversensitive to the signals received by the digestive system. As a result, what would be felt as mild discomfort from indigestion can feel very severe in IBS sufferers.

Although the exact cause of IBS is unknown, most experts agree that it is connected to increased sensitivity in the gut, which can be caused by:

- food poisoning
- oversensitivity of the nerve endings, thereby increasing the amount of pain felt
- psychological factors, such as stress

- changes in the body's ability to move food through the digestive system

When the body is functioning normally, the muscles of the intestines squeeze and relax in a rhythmic way in order to move food through the digestive system. It is thought that this process is altered by IBS, resulting in food moving either too quickly (causing diarrhoea) or too slowly (causing constipation), leading to discomfort within the abdomen. Diarrhoea occurs because the body does not have sufficient time to absorb water from food. Constipation is a result of insufficient water in the stools, making them hard and difficult to pass.

Stress aggravates IBS

IBS is definitely not all in the mind and symptoms are very real. It is thought that an increase in the level of a chemical called 5-hydroxytryptamine (5-HT) during stressful periods may affect the normal functioning of the gut. Evidence suggests that stress can cause a flare-up of IBS symptoms. Even people without IBS can experience sudden changes in bowel habits if they are facing a particularly stressful situation.

Many people with IBS have experienced stress as a result of a traumatic event during childhood, such as abuse, neglect, a serious illness or bereavement. It is possible that stress caused by this type of event at an early age may make people more sensitive to stress in addition to the symptoms of pain and discomfort, which can result in IBS.

Try keeping a journal in order to identify a correlation between your stress levels, diet and IBS symptoms.

A Healthy, Balanced Diet

A healthy, balanced diet means eating healthy, nutritious food that has no side effects. Current UK Government guidelines state that a healthy, balanced diet means eating from all the food groups in sensible proportions, based on the following daily servings:

- fats, oils, sweets – eaten sparingly
- milk, yogurt, cheese – three servings
- meat, poultry, fish, dry beans, nuts – two servings
- fruit – two servings

- vegetables – three servings
- fortified cereal, bread, pasta – six servings
- fluid – eight glasses/2 litres of water a day

A balance of the correct vitamins and minerals can help reduce stress. Fresh fruit and vegetables provide a vast array of vitamins and minerals that are great for reducing stress. Vegetables also have a high fibre content, which is helpful in treating another long-term effect of stress – constipation. Certain foods and drinks can aggravate stress. This means they should be consumed in moderation. Foods and drinks that may be linked to stress include:

- tea, coffee, cocoa, energy drinks
- alcohol
- fast food, takeaways and junk food
- butter, cheese
- red meat and shellfish
- sugar
- carbonated drinks
- almonds and macadamias
- coconut oil

To ensure your diet is not aggravating your feelings of stress and to eat food that promotes good health, plan your meals in advance.

Real Food Versus Processed

One aspect of my diet that is becoming increasingly important to me is eating real food as opposed to processed food. The term processed food can be confusing, so to clarify, most foods that we eat are processed in some way. Fruit is picked from a tree, minced meat has been put through a machine and butter is cream that has been separated from the milk and churned. But there is a difference between mechanical processing and chemical processing.

If a product is combined with another real food and then frozen, canned or placed in a jar then in my opinion it is still real food. Whilst fresh may be best, it is not always available or practical. On the other hand, foods that have been chemically processed and made solely from refined ingredients and artificial substances are generally 'processed'.

Negative aspects of processed foods

1. If you consume lots of processed foods it is a mistake to assume that because you are not adding large amounts of sugar or salt to your food, you are not in fact eating these things. This is because many processed foods contain large amounts of sugar and salt.

2. Processed foods can lead to overconsumption. Our appetite gravitates towards foods that are sweet, salty and fatty. This is because we know on an instinctive level that such foods contain energy and nutrients needed for survival. Understandably, food manufacturers want people to buy their products, therefore they make them as desirable as possible, which can lead to overconsumption.

3. Processed foods often contain a long list of artificial ingredients or chemicals that are added for various purposes, such as:

   • preservatives: chemicals that prevent food from rotting
   • colourants: chemicals that are used to give food a specific colour
   • flavour: chemicals that give food a particular flavour
   • texturants: chemicals that give a particular texture

   Because manufacturers are not required to disclose exactly what the food contains, the wording 'artificial flavour' on labels could actually be a combination of ten different chemicals that have been added to produce a specific flavour.

4. Processed foods are often high in refined carbohydrates. Some sources think that the majority of our energy intake should be from carbohydrates, while others advise us to avoid them like the plague. But the one thing that is generally agreed on is that carbohydrates from whole foods are much better than refined 'simple' carbohydrates.

   One of the main problems is that refined carbohydrates are quickly broken down in the digestive tract, leading to rapid spikes in blood sugar and insulin levels. This in turn can lead to carbohydrate cravings.

5. When compared to whole unprocessed foods, processed ones are extremely low in essential nutrients. If your diet is made up of mainly processed foods you may be missing out on the vitamins, minerals, antioxidants and trace nutrients found in natural foods.

6. Processed foods tend to be lower in fibre, which is required for a healthy gut. It takes less time and energy to digest processed foods. They are often very easy to chew and swallow. Sometimes, it is almost as if they melt in the mouth. This is because much of the fibre has been removed and the ingredients refined.

   One consequence of this is that it takes less energy to eat and digest processed foods. Therefore, we can eat more of them in a shorter amount of time, thereby burning less energy (calories) digesting them than we would if they were unprocessed whole foods.

7. Processed foods are often high in trans-fats or processed vegetable oil.

The following simple, practical information can help to improve your diet if you feel it is necessary:

Starchy Foods

Starchy foods such as bread, cereals, rice, pasta and potatoes play a significant part in a healthy diet. Wholegrain varieties of starchy foods are the optimum choice as they are a good source of energy and form the main basis of a wide range of nutrients in our diet. In addition to starch, these foods also contain fibre, calcium, iron and B vitamins.

Fibre

Like them or not, foods that are rich in fibre are really good for you. So if you can include things like wholegrain bread, brown rice, pasta, oats, beans, peas, fruit and vegetables, you are making a healthy choice. There are two types of fibre – insoluble and soluble:

1. Insoluble fibre

Because fibre such as wholegrain bread, wholegrain breakfast cereals, brown rice, fruit and vegetables cannot be digested, they pass through the gut, helping other food and waste products move through more easily.

2. Soluble fibre

Oats and pulses such as beans and lentils are good sources of soluble fibre that can be partially digested, even helping to reduce the amount of cholesterol in the blood.

Fruit and Vegetables

Most people know they should be eating more fruit and vegetables, but most still don't eat enough. Once they expand their choices they find there is a great variety available.

☺ Snacking on fruit and vegetables is far healthier than reaching for the biscuit tin.

Fish and Shellfish

Fish and shellfish are good sources of a variety of vitamins and minerals. Oily fish is particularly rich in omega-3 fatty acids, which help prevent heart disease – mackerel, sardines, trout, herring and salmon containing the richest source.

There are maximum levels recommended for both oily fish and crab, as well as some types of white fish, so please check with your dietician or healthcare provider for the recommended daily amounts. T this is particularly important if you take supplements containing vitamin A.

Eggs

Eggs are a good source of protein, they are easy to prepare and they contain both vitamins and minerals. However, eggs also contain cholesterol and high levels in the blood increase the risk of developing heart disease. People who are concerned about their cholesterol levels and who have a balanced diet should consult their medical practitioner or dietician.

Pulses and Lentils

An edible seed that grows in a pod, pulses include things like chickpeas and kidney or lima beans. Pulses and lentils are a healthy choice for both vegetarians and meat-eaters, as they are a great source of protein.

Seeds

Sources of protein and fibre, in addition to vitamins and minerals, seeds can be added to various dishes to provide extra texture and flavour or to coat breads. They can make a healthy snack and can be added to salads, casseroles and breakfast cereals.

Nuts

High in fibre, rich in a wide range of vitamins and minerals, and a good source of protein – important for vegetarians – this food group also contains other unsaturated fats called 'essential fatty acids', which the body needs to sustain health.

Meat

An excellent source of protein, vitamins and minerals – such as iron, selenium, zinc and B vitamins – it is also one of the main sources of vitamin B12.

Fats

Fat helps the body to absorb certain vitamins, it is a good source of energy and it provides essential fatty acids that the body itself cannot produce. There are two main types of fat found in food, plus trans-fats:

1. Saturated fat

Sustained over a period of time, a diet that is high in saturated fat can raise the level of cholesterol in the blood, thereby increasing the chance of developing heart disease. Foods high in saturated fat include:

- fatty cuts of meat and processed meat products such as sausages and pies
- butter and lard
- cream, soured cream, crème fraîche and ice cream
- cheese; particularly hard cheese
- pastries
- cakes and biscuits
- some savoury snacks

- some sweet snacks and chocolate
- coconut oil, coconut cream and palm oil

2. Unsaturated fat

Unsaturated fat provides the essential fatty acids that can help lower blood cholesterol. Foods that are rich in unsaturated fat include:

- oily fish
- avocados
- nuts and seeds
- sunflower, rapeseed, olive and vegetable oils, and spreads.

3. Trans-fats

Trans-fats are found naturally at low levels in some foods, such as those from animals, including meat and dairy products. They can also be found in foods containing hydrogenated vegetable oil.

Trans-fats raise overall and LDL (bad) cholesterol levels in the blood, increasing the risk of coronary heart disease. Items that contain 'hydrogenated oil' or 'partially hydrogenated oil' often include trans-fats and can be used to extend the shelf life of processed foods, typically biscuits, cakes, etc.

Fluids

Our bodies need fluids in order to function properly and to ensure that we don't become dehydrated. But it is important to know what to drink and when if we are to make healthy choices for growth and maintenance.

Water and soft drinks

Water is the best choice for quenching thirst between meals and for rehydrating the body quickly. In climates such as the UK, it is currently recommended that we drink approximately 1.2 litres (six to eight glasses) of fluid a day to stop us from becoming dehydrated. In hotter climates and when exercising the body needs more than this.

Without sufficient fluid, the body can only survive for a matter of days. Water makes up 70 per cent of an adult's total body weight and is lost through urinating and sweating. One of the first signs of dehydration is thirst, but the good news is that water can be replenished through our diet. The bad news is that people often confuse this with hunger and eat more than they need instead of giving their body the fluid it needs.

Caffeinated drinks

Drinks that are high in caffeine such as tea, coffee and energy drinks might refresh you if you are feeling tired, but they should definitely be avoided when you are stressed as they contain neuro-stimulators, which are believed to heighten stress. Cutting down on tea and coffee could also help to improve iron levels in the body.

Milk

Milk plays an important part in our diet whatever age we may be as it contains vitamins and nutrients such as calcium and protein. These are beneficial for both your skin and for healthy teeth, bones and muscles. The added benefit is that it doesn't cause tooth decay. For a healthy choice, choose skimmed milk.

Fruit juice and smoothies

We all know that we should be consuming five fruit and vegetable portions daily, and a glass (150 ml) of unsweetened fruit juice counts towards this. While it contains lots of vitamins that are good for our health, especially vitamin C, we need to be aware that when fruit is juiced or blended, sugar is released.

Fizzy drinks and sports drinks

There are few nutrients and lots of calories from hidden sugars in fizzy drinks, squashes and 'juice drinks'. While low-calorie varieties are an alternative, they harbour many chemicals and so shouldn't be consumed too often. A high level of carbon dioxide in fizzy drinks can aggravate stress, so think twice before adding them to your diet.

Alcohol

In addition to causing weight gain, which can be associated with alcohol intake as it is high in calories, it is also a diuretic, which means more water than usual is lost through the body. If you have overindulged, avoid alcohol consumption for at least forty-eight hours to give your body a chance to recover. Please check with your GP, dietician or health provider for the recommended daily amounts.

Vitamins

Vitamin supplements are widely available in many stores these days, although it is far better to acquire them naturally through our diet. Essential nutrients, the body needs vitamins in small amounts in order to function properly. There are two types of vitamins – fat-soluble and water-soluble:

1. Fat-soluble vitamins

Found mainly in fatty foods such as animal fats (including butter and lard), vegetable oils, dairy products, liver and oily fish, the body needs these vitamins daily in order to function. Don't worry about consuming too many, because if they aren't required immediately, they will be stored in your liver and fatty tissues for future use. This means that stores can build up and become replenished so that they are there when you need them.

2. Water-soluble vitamins

It is important to consume this type of vitamin frequently as they cannot be stored in the body. Found in fruit, vegetables and grains, surplus stores are got rid of through urination.

Easily destroyed by heat or by being exposed to the air, they can also be lost through the cooking process, which is where they are different to fat-soluble vitamins. This is particularly so when they are boiled, which is why steaming or grilling is preferable, in order to retain as many as possible.

Minerals

Found in varying amounts in a variety of foods such as meat, cereals, bread, fish, milk, dairy products, vegetables, fruit and nuts, small amounts of these essential nutrients are required by the body in order to work properly. There are three main reasons minerals are so important:

1. Building strong bones and teeth.
2. Controlling bodily fluids both inside and outside cells.
3. Turning the food we eat into energy.

Salt

Every day twenty-six million adults in the UK consume too much salt, often without realising, as about 75 per cent is already in the processed foods that we buy.[1] To re-educate your palette, try eating at least three mouthfuls of food before adding additional salt, gradually reducing the amount.

Sugar

When stressed the consumption of sugar should be avoided, because stress causes an increase in blood glucose levels. If you have high blood glucose, it can lead to a higher risk of developing diabetes.

The Marrow Contest

Of three contestants entering a marrow contest, the first man was lazy, giving his marrows very little water. The second man's tactics were to give his marrows twice the recommended amount of water and to increase it every week, in the expectation that his marrow would grow faster and faster each week. The woman decided that she would give her marrow exactly the amount of water it required.

The first man was disappointed that his marrow was so small six weeks before the competition, but he was still convinced that his strategy was right. The second man's marrow had reached a magnificent size and would have won the competition had it been that week. The woman knew that her marrow was growing healthily and was satisfied with the result of her efforts.

The day of the competition dawned and the first man, who had deprived his marrow, was dismayed that his marrow was still so small. When the second man went to cut his marrow, whereas six weeks ago it looked like a winner, now it had burst open and was beginning to rot.

Neither of the men took their marrows to the show. The woman, who had taken a steadier, more nurturing approach, produced a magnificent marrow and won first prize!

_1. http://www.nhslothian.scot.nhs.uk/MediaCentre/Campaigns/SmallStepsBig Difference/Eating/Pages/Breakfast.aspx [accessed 25.11.14]

Exercise to Reduce Stress

People spend a great deal of time looking for ways to reduce stress, yet they overlook one of the key factors in managing stress – being active. I am not referring to the frenzied running around all day that many people do in order to cope with everything on their to-do list. I am talking about physical activity, where you break a sweat.

While we may feel like we are always on the go, technology has made our lives easier and as a result, people are less active than previous generations. For example:

- We drive to our destination or take public transport; indeed, some people rarely walk anywhere.
- Household chores are much easier thanks to washing machines, dishwashers and other labour-saving devices.
- Fewer people are employed in jobs that require physical effort.
- Many of us spend hours watching TV or sitting in front of a computer screen or games console.

Just in case you are grimacing at the thought of exercising or are dismissing it as madness to contemplate fitting it into your already hectic day, let us take a quick look at the benefits of exercise:

- In addition to reducing stress, it can reduce the risk of major illnesses – including diabetes, stroke, heart disease and cancer – by up to as much as 50 per cent.
- By maintaining a strong, healthy body that is the correct weight for your height, age and sex, you won't be putting additional strain on your joints, bones, muscles and tendons.
- Research also shows that physical activity can boost self-esteem, mood, sleep quality and energy. It can even reduce the risk of depression, dementia and Alzheimer's disease.[2]

Exercise Sensibly

Exercise should always be carried out sensibly. If you are more active and it is helping you to relax, the chances are that you are on the right track. In the past I have been guilty of over-exercising, which in itself

---

_2. http://www.nhs.uk/Livewell/fitness/Pages/Whybeactive.aspx [accessed 25.11.14]

is putting the body under stress. So when I began exercising again after undergoing major surgery, I listened to my body and measured the effects of exercise. As a result I was able to work out what would give me more energy and what would exhaust me.

NOTE:

It is vital to stretch both before and after exercising.

So how much exercise do you need to do?

Current government guidelines recommend that adults between the ages of 19 and 65 should do one of the following each week:[3]

1. At least 150 minutes (two and a half hours) per week of moderate-intensity aerobic activity such as walking fast or cycling. Unfortunately daily tasks such as shopping, housework or cooking don't count towards your 150 minutes. This is because the effort needed to do them isn't hard enough to get your heart rate up.

2. A minimum of 75 minutes (an hour and a quarter) of vigorous aerobic exercise such as running or a game of singles tennis.

3. A mix of moderate and vigorous aerobic activity every week. For example, two 30-minute runs plus 30 minutes of fast walking.

4. Two sessions of muscle-building activity, working on all of the large muscle groups in the body. For each activity, try to do eight to twelve repetitions in each set, with two or three sets for each repetition. For maximum benefit, reach the point where you struggle to complete another repetition.

Aerobic Exercise

An aerobic workout should raise your heart rate and make you breathe harder, including activities such as:

- walking
- cycling
- swimming in warm water

---

[3]. http://www.nhs.uk/Livewell/fitness/Pages/Whybeactive.aspx [accessed 25.11.14]

Strengthening Exercise

Exercises such as weightlifting need to be planned as part of a personalised exercise programme. It is vital that you are shown how to do them correctly; otherwise, they can cause muscle stiffness and soreness. Examples of muscle-strengthening activities include:

- working with resistance bands
- lifting weights
- using your body weight for resistance, such as push-ups and sit-ups

Studies show that strengthening exercises may improve:

- muscle strength
- physical disabilities
- depression
- quality of life

From personal experience I know that an exercise programme that includes a variety of activities – combining aerobic exercises, muscle-strengthening exercises and yoga – improves my mood greatly. It also helps me to concentrate better, gives me more energy and helps me sleep better.

Yoga

Yoga is comprised of a series of movements called postures. It is used to boost mental and physical wellness. In addition it focuses on strength, balance, breathing and flexibility. It is generally regarded as a safe and effective form of exercise. Evidence also suggests that regular yoga is beneficial for relieving aches and pains, including lower back pain.[4]

Walking

- ☺ One of my favourite activities is walking in the countryside, along the coast or round a city – in fact, anywhere.

_4. http://www.nhs.uk/Livewell/fitness/Pages/yoga.aspx [accessed 25.11.14]

Walking is a great way to reduce stress by releasing tension in your muscles and it can help you manage stress by:

- enabling you to observe and enjoy the environment, sky, birds, flowers, seashore, gardens, weather, etc.
- giving you a break from the situation or people contributing to your stress
- allowing you to be in the moment
- enabling you to focus on the movement of your body, so you can reconnect with yourself
- burning off additional calories consumed by being stressed
- enabling you to work through problems, possibly even coming up with solutions
- giving you an opportunity to chat and laugh with your walking buddy, if you have one
- lowering your blood pressure and the health risk to your heart, which can be increased by stress

Research shows that walking an average of 10,000 steps a day will significantly improve your health, burn excess calories, build stamina and give you a healthier heart. It can be done at almost any time, anywhere, in any weather and it is easy to fit into a daily routine.

It is estimated that the average person takes between 3,000 and 4,000 steps a day; however, some people take as few as 800 steps per day – far removed from the ideal 10,000 steps ...

The best ways to relieve stress if you are walking alone are to:

1. Focus on enjoying the surrounding countryside.
2. Think about all the things in your life that you are grateful for.
3. Listen to music.
4. Repeat affirmations related to stress management:

    - I am calm and relaxed.
    - I am grateful for the good things in my life.
    - It feels good to be outside in the fresh air.
    - I am safe.
    - I am in control.

NOTE:

Please ensure that you take sensible safety precautions and wear the correct clothing, particularly if you are walking alone.

☺ I love to begin my day with a long walk before starting work, as my job involves a lot of sitting around at a computer screen. I also find walking greatly aids concentration.

Always walk with your head held up and your shoulders back. This is important because it allows you to take in the outside world, rather than looking inward and focusing on how stressed you are feeling.

If my schedule prevents me from exercising for a few days I can really tell the difference – not only in my physical condition, but also emotionally. Exercise is part of my life and I intend it to remain that way forever, so it is important that I do not allow it to become an obligation or a chore.

For some, exercise is never going to be enjoyable. But there are ways of exercising that don't feel like exercise like joining a dance class, playing with children and gardening. Find something that works best for you and that gives you pleasure as well as exercise.

Notes to Self

- My mind and body are one machine. If I want it to last a lifetime, I need to take good care of it.
- Exercise reduces stress.

Take Action

- Ensure you have a sensible, well-balanced diet covering all of the food groups.
- Avoid food linked to stress.
- Get active.
- If necessary, take professional advice on a suitable exercise programme.
- Focus on positive thoughts while walking and exercising.
- Drink lots of water and keep well hydrated.
- Stay within the recommended healthy weight band for your height.

- Overcome emotional eating by dealing with the emotional need.
- Talk to your GP or other qualified professional if you believe you need help with your diet.

Chapter Nine – Self-Esteem

Everybody is a genius. But if you judge a fish by its ability to climb a tree, it will spend its whole life believing that it is stupid.

Albert Einstein

Introduction

Self-esteem begins to form in early childhood and by the time we reach our teens it has a big impact on how we live our lives, what we feel able to achieve and what we do with our lives.

But success does not necessarily equate to high levels of self-esteem. Low self-esteem affects a great many people regardless of their success or outer veneer.

Do You Really Understand What Self-Esteem Actually Is?

The word 'esteem' is derived from a Latin word meaning 'to estimate'. So self-esteem is how you estimate, or regard, yourself.

How would you rate your self-esteem right now? If you were to consider your own self-esteem levels at this moment in your life, how would you rate it on a scale of one to ten – one being very low, affecting every aspect of your life, and 10 being very high, enhancing every aspect of your life?

If your self-esteem is lower than you would like it to be, work on the exercises in this chapter and you will be able to move outside your comfort zone to achieve more than you previously thought possible. By celebrating your successes, your self-esteem will improve and in turn your stress levels will reduce.

If you have a good level of self-esteem, you will feel without any doubt that you:

- are likeable
- are deserving of love and happiness
- are a good human being

When you have low self-esteem it is tempting to hide your real self away, as you become fearful that people will not like the real you. Ask yourself these questions:

- Who are you pretending to be?
- What are you afraid people will find out about you?
- Who are you when no one is looking?

The answer to these questions might be difficult to face, but self-awareness is essential for growth. No matter how hard you try, you cannot hide yourself away successfully and be happy. The good news is that you are not saddled with low self-esteem for life. A big part of improving your self-esteem is recognising how your beliefs, values and thoughts affect how you feel about yourself, in turn affecting every aspect of your life.

Your Most Important Relationship

Another great question I ask myself on a regular basis is: How is my relationship with myself? This is because I recognise that if I don't have a good relationship with myself, other important relationships in my life will ultimately suffer. If you know your relationship with yourself is poor, it is time to take action.

One of the telltale signs of a poor relationship with oneself is lack of self-care. People who do not respect themselves often abuse their bodies and minds with alcohol, drugs, nicotine, overeating, under-eating, lack of exercise, excessive exercise or a general lack of self-care.

All sorts of things can reduce your self-esteem such as:

- experiences at school, work and home
- illness
- disability

- injury
- culture
- religion
- role and status in society
- how others react to you
- relationships with those close to you
- your own thoughts and perceptions

Over time, events in life and the messages you receive from people – particularly your closest relationships – will affect how you feel about yourself. If you have good relationships and generally experience positive events and receive positive feedback, you are more likely to see yourself in a positive way and have higher self-esteem. Conversely, if you have predominately negative experiences and receive negative feedback or criticism, your self-esteem levels can be adversely affected. The same can apply if you are teased or devalued by others.

Thankfully, your own thoughts have the biggest impact on self-esteem and because these are within your control, it means you are able to improve your self-esteem. It takes work and practice, but the benefits are well worth the effort.

Instead of focusing on your perceived weaknesses or flaws, you can learn to reframe negative thoughts and focus instead on your positive qualities. It is easier to get into the habit of neglecting yourself and generally ignoring your own needs than it is to nurture yourself. This means investing time, which many of us feel we simply don't have to spare. But it is important to remember to nourish and nurture yourself, no matter what the situation.

Airlines instruct us to put our own oxygen mask on before assisting those around us. It is a concept I used to struggle with, until I accepted the fact that if I ensured I could breathe properly first, I would be in a far better position to care for others. It is much the same with life in general.

Putting yourself first may require a change in what you pay attention to. For example, if most of your attention on a moment-to-moment basis is outside yourself, accommodating others or trying to fit in, you will need to change your focus. By balancing your attention so that in addition to the outside world, you also pay attention to what your body needs, you will have the ability to make healthy decisions. The added bonus will be that you are more productive after a break.

Challenge yourself to take thirty minutes every day for yourself, doing something you enjoy or pampering yourself. If you need to fit this into your working day, try going to the local cafe or coffee shop to chill with your favourite brew while you watch the world go by or read a book:

☺ Prayer:

> Lord, help me to value myself and stand up for my rights. If you don't mind, of course, and only if it's convenient and you have assisted everyone else first.

Benefits of Healthy Self-Esteem

When you have good self-esteem it feels great! It really does! You know can handle what life brings your way and you have confidence in yourself. You feel that you deserve happiness and all the good things you desire. You value yourself, you feel secure and worthwhile, and you generally have positive relationships with others.

People with healthy levels of self-esteem are:

- confident in their ability to make decisions
- assertive in expressing their needs and opinions
- realistic in their expectations
- able to develop and maintain secure, honest relationships
- less likely to stay in unhealthy relationships
- better able to cope with stressful situations and challenges
- less prone to mental health conditions such as depression and anxiety
- less prone to addictions and eating disorders
- less likely to be overcritical of themselves and others
- aware they are not perfect and that they don't have to be

> ☺ I'm okay! Great self-esteem does not mean being arrogant or showing off – these are actually traits of people with low self-esteem.

What Does High Self-Esteem Look Like?

If you cannot remember ever having healthy levels of self-esteem you may not even be able to picture what it would be like to feel good about yourself. If you had true confidence and self-esteem, how would you be? Think about it for a moment and visualise a new, more confident you. Imagine:

- how you would stand or sit
- what your voice would sound like
- what kind of thoughts you would have
- what you would say about yourself
- how you would feel inside

Play around with the image for a few minutes until it feels great. That is just a glimpse of how you could feel all the time ...

How Can You Improve Your Self-Esteem?

Improving your self-esteem is something that can take time. However, the following steps will get you off to a flying start:

Three steps to better self-esteem

1. Step one

Make a list of:

a) Achievements you are proud of – no matter how small.

b) Difficult things that you have previously handled that perhaps initially you did not think you would be able to.

c) Positive qualities you know you possess such as patience, a good sense of humour, tenacity.

2. Step two

This next one is about handling your biggest fear. Although it can be challenging, it is worth the effort as it can free you from a great deal of anxiety:

a) Acknowledge the one thing you feel you couldn't cope with.

b) Now imagine yourself handling that situation.

c) What steps would you take to get through it initially?

d) How would you change or rebuild your life?

e) Recognise that whatever it is you fear, you would handle it – we always do!

If you have done step three successfully, you should only need to do it once. There is no need to keep returning to thoughts of the worst happening once you have acknowledged that you can handle it if it does occur.

3. Step three

Sometimes we don't like to admit that we like ourselves as though it is in some way being big-headed, which is why I think this next step is so worthwhile:

a) Close your eye and visualise someone who loves, respects, admires or likes you.

b) Clearly see them standing in front of you.

c) Next, imagine yourself floating over and inside of their body, so you can see yourself through their eyes.

d) What do they see?

e) What positive qualities do they believe you have?

f) What do they like, love or respect about you?

g) Next, imagine yourself leaving their body but retaining the good feelings.

As your self-esteem improves you can start to make big changes in your life that will greatly increase your level of life satisfaction and happiness. It is important that you focus on the things that you *can* change now.

This might mean starting slowly with small steps, but gradually you will be ready to achieve things far greater than you ever imagined.

Accentuate the Positive

As long as we are still living, there is always an opportunity for growth and change, providing we want to and are prepared to take action to do so. It is okay to make mistakes – it is part of being human. The key to learning is getting things wrong before we get them right.

A man must be big enough to admit his mistakes, smart enough to profit from them, and strong enough to correct them.

John C. Maxwell

Sometimes we feel we are no good because of our past mistakes or perceived failures, which lowers self-esteem and raises stress levels. However, we can improve our self-esteem if we rethink the things we believe we have done wrong or badly in the past:

1. Consider a situation in the past that you think you handled badly or where you believe you made a mistake.
2. What were the things you did right?
3. If you believe you did nothing right or that the mistakes outweigh the errors you made, then forgive yourself.
4. Consider what you have learnt from the experience.
5. How have you grown since the event?
6. What would you do differently in a similar situation?
7. Next, write down:

   - characteristics in your personality that you like
   - what you like about your appearance
   - a list of your talents and skills

8. Commit to writing down at least one more new thing you like about yourself every day or one thing that you did each day that you can feel good about.

If you found that challenging, don't worry – it will get easier with practice.

☺ I am in competition with no one. My only aim is to be a slightly better person than I was yesterday.

Trust Yourself

It is tempting to:

- believe in other people rather than yourself
- follow the crowd
- do what others think you should

But what if you could trust yourself? What would you do if you had a difficult decision to make and suddenly got a gut feeling what the right answer was? Would you talk yourself out of it or would you stick with your instincts?

Intuition may seem to come from some mysterious inner source, but it is actually unconscious reasoning based on information stored in the brain. Throughout life we accumulate knowledge. The brain recognises and organises patterns into blocks of information, which are stored in our long-term memory. It is this information that is used to deliver our instinctive solutions to problems.

> ☺ So listen to your gut feelings instead of dismissing them. Your intuition may not always steer you in the right direction, but it can be a useful tool in the decision-making process.

Occam's razor is a principle that states: All things being equal, the simplest solution tends to be the right one. While this may be true, learning to trust our instincts takes time. Start with small decisions, without big consequences. Some people stop trusting their instincts the first time their instinct appears to have been wrong. But it takes time to tune in to our intuition, so try again and persevere.

You Are a Diamond – Are You Ready to Shine?

I love this analogy and I think it needs little explanation. We are all born as diamonds but, over time, life's negative experiences cover us in more and more horse manure. Eventually, we become completely covered and then, because we feel embarrassed and ashamed by all the manure, we paint over it with nail varnish. But no matter how many coats we apply, it does not hide the manure. If only someone told us how easy it is to wash it off in the shower.

> ☺ Every time you take a shower, enjoy the feeling of washing away any new poop.

The Stag at the River

> One hot day a stag wandering through the trees came to a river and took a drink to quench his thirst. On seeing his reflection in the water, he felt pride at the beauty of his antlers.

'They are magnificent and exquisite. I am so proud of them!' he exclaimed.

Then, noticing his legs, he became dismayed.

'My legs are too short and thin. If they could be as wonderful as my horns, I would be truly perfect.'

But while pondering on all these things, a bear appeared. Frightened, the stag ran away, its study legs carrying him quickly away from danger.

Soon, his antlers became caught in the branches of a large tree and he became easy prey.

'I can't believe that my antlers of which I was so proud are my downfall, while my legs of which I was so ashamed served me so well. Things are not what they seem to be.'

Notes to Self

- Nothing and nobody is perfect and I don't need to be either.
- I am unique in every way.
- I can increase my self-esteem.
- My most important relationship is with myself.
- I am good enough and deserving of happiness and all the good things I desire.

Take Action

- Use the Limiting Belief Buster and increase your self-esteem with my three-step process.
- Take thirty minutes every day for yourself.
- Use the self-esteem building steps.
- Focus on things you can change now.
- Accentuate the positives.
- Trust your intuition.

Chapter Ten – Relationships

Don't smother each other. No one can grow in the shade.

Leo Buscaglia

Introduction

I n the previous chapter we talked about self-esteem and your relationship with yourself. In this chapter we will be focusing on your relationships with other people, as relationships and interactions with others are often a source of immense stress. Then in the next chapter we will look at developing a healthy, romantic relationship.

☺ So stay with me, this is important stuff.

It is my belief that low self-esteem often results in poor relationships and negative interactions, which in turn leads to stress. Our self-esteem has a direct impact on the quality of our relationships. People who lack self-esteem turn to the world for approval, hoping to gain the respect of others and thereby achieve self-respect, or they look to fill an emotional void. But they rarely find what they seek. This is because no amount of respect and adoration from others will ever fill the void. They may as well be trying to fill a sieve with water.

By depending on others for validation, it makes us vulnerable and prone to overanalysing every fleeting glance and passing comment. Additionally, poor relationships can lead to low self-esteem if one party is overly critical of the other. Over time, this can undermine the other person's confidence and self-esteem.

Communication

Honest, open communication is vital for healthy relationships. Disharmony in relationships is brought about as a result of an inability to communicate effectively, causing a great deal of stress for many people. Both parties must feel able to express their views, fears and desires in order to foster strong bonds.

Most people can communicate well with certain people, but very few have the ability to communicate well with almost anyone. This is because there is a general lack of understanding of how we actually communicate. Most people focus only on the words being used; however, it is widely reported that communication is made up of three elements:

- words – 7 per cent
- tonality – 38 per cent
- body language – 55 per cent

Yes, you have read it correctly. Most verbal communication is not the words you use. That is not to say the words are not important – it is quite simply that the same phrase can have very different meanings depending on how it is said, the expression on your face and your body language as you say it. Consider the following example:

- 'You really are insane' – said with a giggle while affectionately hugging your spouse after they have told you a funny story.
- 'You really are insane!' – said very slowly in a harsh voice, with your eyes narrowed as you barge past your spouse.

I think that demonstrates the difference very well. That is also why there is no point in thinking: *I only said* ... because it is not *what* you said, it is also *how* you said it. It always makes me smile when clients relay stories to me of communications they have had and they tell me what they said in a pleasant voice, when I know that in reality it is highly likely it was said in a very different way.

If you are annoyed or stressed, it is almost impossible to hide it, which is why it makes sense to raise issues when you are feeling calm and relaxed. Never wait until things have grown out of proportion. It is very easy to stew on something small until it becomes a much bigger issue than it really is.

Instead of criticising the other person, tell them how you feel and what is on your mind. Use 'I' statements that do not criticise. For example, say: 'I felt hurt when you ...' rather than saying 'You hurt my feelings when you ...'

Most problems arise when each person is focused on their own agenda. Each individual feels sure their feelings and needs have been clearly explained, but what they have not taken into account is how the other person is feeling. They haven't ensured they have reached an agreement or understanding, resulting in a breakdown of communication.

Understand Others Before Trying to be Understood

The next time someone says something you disagree with, instead of instantly defending your own position, see if you can understand their point of view. Really hear what they have to say rather than just allowing it to wash over you or instantly dismissing it as nonsense.

The inability to listen to and understand the opinions of others limits the opportunity to learn anything new. Not to mention the stress it causes for the other person, who will feel their views are irrelevant. If you don't agree with what they are saying or don't understand what they mean, ask questions, without a hidden agenda of catching them out or proving them wrong.

It is important to remember not to transfer your anger about the other person's behaviour or the issue into dislike of the other person. Instead, ask yourself these questions:

- How could they be right?
- What is more important: my rule or my relationship with this person?
- Is there a win-win solution or middle ground where we can agree?

Once you have listened and really understood what the other person is saying, put your point across calmly. I cannot guarantee they will always listen, but you have a much better chance of them doing so if they feel heard and you remain calm.

Be Less Self-Absorbed

When you are feeling stressed it is easy to become so focused on your own problems that you monopolise conversations, talking about yourself and the current cause of your stress. If you spend the majority of your time with a friend talking about yourself, your life or problems, you will not be helping your situation or your relationship.

Although people may be sympathetic or even helpful, no one wants to feel you are only interested in talking about yourself or that you only want to spend time with them because they make you feel better. Unburdening yourself can offer an essential release but as mentioned earlier, frequently focusing on your problems will not benefit you and will increase your stress levels.

A divorced client of mine constantly talked about what had happened. She found the sympathy comforting and wanted people to agree she was not at fault in any way. Generally, even the most understanding and sympathetic people can only listen to others' negativity for so long before they become fed up with hearing it. Unless of course they are a very negative person and enjoy moaning with you – but they are not great people to be around when you are trying to reduce your stress levels.

I watched a chat show recently and one of the panellists put it very well. She said that whilst you may want to be sympathetic, if you spend months or years listening to a friend moan about their partner when they are not prepared to take action and do something about it, it is like being trapped in the film *Ground Hog Day*. For those of you who haven't seen it, the main character constantly has to relive the same day until he begins to re-examine his life and priorities.

Energy Vampires

We generally enjoy spending time with people who are similar to us and who like the same things. This works well unless the people you are spending time with are like the old stressed-out you, in which case it can have a negative effect on your stress levels.

If you are feeling great, looking forward to a nice lunch with a friend, but within ten minutes you are feeling exhausted and depressed, having listened to their negativity splurge, then it is time for a reality check. Are you spending time with energy vampires or are you one yourself?

☺ If it is you who is the energy vampire – *stop it immediately!*

However, if you find that you are spending too much time around happiness suckers, try to limit your interactions with them. When you are with them, take the lead – talk about positive things. If they become negative, change the subject. Be bubbly and cheerful. You will find that this way, most people around you will be cheerful, too.

☺ When you are focused on reducing your stress levels it is important that you feel happy and positive – so beware the vampires!

It May Not be Personal

Everyone lives in accordance with their own rulebook. Each person has their own complex and multifaceted life, of which some aspects won't relate to you. If you take everything personally it will cause you increased stress. By remembering that you are not the centre of the universe, it will make it easier to realise that a person's bad mood may have nothing to do with you. If you automatically assume it is your fault, it will cause you unnecessary stress.

While it might not be very pleasant if they are taking it out on you, by not personalising it you will be able to keep it in perspective. Likewise, if days or weeks later you find yourself still focusing on a comment made by another that you took to be negative, then the chances are that your self-esteem needs some work. If this is the case you should refer back to the exercises in the previous chapter.

God, give us grace to accept with serenity the things that cannot be changed, Courage to change the things which should be changed, and the Wisdom to distinguish the one from the other.

Extract from the Serenity Prayer by Reinhold Niebuhr

This extract can refer to many aspects of life. When we accept that there are some things in life we cannot change and instead learn to adapt to them, something wonderful can happen in that much of the stress goes away.

My reason for quoting the extract in this chapter is that trying to change other people is often a cause of great stress. When you are raising a child, you can have a significant impact on how their personality develops. But trying to change adults who don't want to change is another matter entirely.

☺ *How many psychiatrists does it take to change a light bulb? Just one, but the light bulb has to want to change.*

Joke

The fact is that you that cannot ever change other people – you can only change how you respond to them. This means adapting your behaviour or taking drastic action and ending the relationship with that person altogether. However, you might find that you don't want to end the relationship. You might even believe that most, or all, of the fault lies with the other person and that it is unfair for you to have to change. In short, you might think that the only way you can improve the relationship is if the other person shows more respect, thoughtfulness, understanding or consideration. Or if they become more exciting and fun to be around, etc. But they are who they are and perhaps they do not want to change. They may even feel *you* should be more thoughtful, understanding and considerate or want *you* to change in some way!

What Do You Want from the Relationship?

Often, problems stem from a person wanting someone to fill a certain role in their lives when the other person does not want to do it. Undoubtedly, the other person will have their own version of how the roles should be filled. As a coach I hear endless complaints about other people not meeting my clients' needs. For example:

- My parents hardly ever babysit for me, yet they often have my sister's children.
- My parents have my son once a week, but I don't feel they really want to do it.
- My parents were never there for me and still aren't; I feel let down.
- My children are grown up now. I looked after them all their lives. How can they be so thoughtless now? I feel let down.
- My son only ever calls when he wants something.
- My daughter is forever asking us to babysit when she should understand that after working all our lives this is our time.
- My husband is always tired at the weekend and never wants to do anything with us.

- My new wife constantly moans about having to look after my children every weekend.

Quite honestly, the list is endless. But they all amount to the same thing: in each case, someone is not doing what the other person wants them to do.

Well, I'm afraid the bad news is that you need to accept the other individual for who they are or you will send your stress levels through the roof trying to shove a square peg into a round hole. That is not to say you should not tell them how you would like them to behave. But at the same time you need to ask them if there is anything they would like you to do differently – and be prepared to take on board what they say. The other person cannot read your mind, so unless you have made your feelings clear, you are not really in a position to complain.

I realise it can be very painful when you love someone and yearn for the relationship to be a certain way, or even for it to go back to how it used to be. After all, you love them and everything would be fine if they treated you the way you want and deserve. However, if you wish to maintain the relationship, sometimes all you can do is change your response – and preferably in a way that maintains the relationship without opening yourself up to pain.

Change your response

Changing your response to people may involve changing how you engage with them. This can mean seeing them less frequently or accepting that not all relationships need to be close and intimate. Another way it could work is if you avoid certain topics or know when to change the subject. You might even have to learn how to:

- take things less personally
- behave in the way you would like them to behave
- learn not feel defensive or guilty
- lower your expectations of their behaviour

Generally, people don't change when other people try to force them to do so. However, people can change and often try when faced with what they might lose if they don't. Recognising the prospect of pain at a possible loss can put the perceived discomfort of doing things differently in perspective. But don't expect them to change overnight and be realistic in your expectations. Like you, the other person doesn't have to be perfect, either, and they, too, have been learning and developing these traits for years.

Focus on being the person you want to be and live within your values. That way, you will keep your stress levels in control, enhance your well-being and honour the most important relationship in your life – your relationship with yourself.

Embrace Differences

We naturally gravitate towards people with similar interests and views, but that does not mean you cannot enjoy a relationship with someone who is very different to you. This is particularly so when it comes to working relationships.

While differences can lead to conflict, they can also greatly enhance the relationship, with both parties bringing very different skills and points of view. When you accept that you both bring different qualities to the relationship that deserve to be respected and valued, there is no need to feel competitive. My business partner and I have very different skills that complement each other beautifully and we are quite happy to admit what our weaker areas are.

One famous, successful relationship was that of Walt Disney and his brother, Roy. Walt was passionate, driven and creative, whereas his brother was financially astute and always focused on balancing the books. Both were happy to admit that without the other's very different approach, attitudes and skills, the Disney Corporation would not have achieved its global success and would probably have failed.

As I explained earlier, things don't have to be perfect to be good and this certainly applies to relationships. I am very fortunate in that I have several people in my life who are perfect for me yet not perfect. However, it is these relationships that are simply amazing.

I also have many other very enjoyable relationships with people with whom I have very little in common. I generally don't agree with their views and in some cases there may even be aspects of their personality I don't like. But even though I might limit the amount of time and restrict how I spend it with them, these relationships can still work.

In my view, the main problem comes when one person has a very strong personality and the other feels intimidated or compelled to change and comply with the other's views. That is not to say there is anything wrong with adapting to the attitudes or opinions of someone you admire. For example, if you have a very positive, proactive, motivated friend and these are qualities you would like to enhance in yourself, then being around this person will be good for you. However, if you spend a great deal of time with someone negative, beware of adopting their attitudes. I therefore actively encourage you to accept the differences of those around you and look at how you can enhance each other's lives.

> *You are the average of the five people you spend the most time with.*
>
> *Jim Rohn*

How Have You Trained People How to Treat You?

From the moment we meet someone new we begin training them how to treat us. For example, are we somebody to be pitied, admired, respected or abused?

If you are allowing someone to treat you in a way you do not like then you have to accept some responsibility for the situation. Tell them how you feel and if they continue to treat you in a way that makes you unhappy, you need to decide if there are sufficient benefits from the relationship to justify continuing with it.

If you remain in a relationship you don't enjoy and are becoming more and more resentful, ultimately it will have a negative effect on both your personality and your well-being.

That said, before you become angry with someone for the way in which they behave, carefully consider the possible reasons for their behaviour. For example, if your best friend is totally focused on their new relationship and you feel let down, it is quite likely that if the situation was reversed they might totally understand. Also, they may not even have realised that it is a problem for you.

Don't Take Everything on Board

- Are you a good listener?

- Do you attract people into your life who like to talk about their problems?
- Do you find your friends ask you for advice on how to deal with their numerous problems?

If you enjoy helping others and you can do so without causing yourself additional stress, that's fine. But when you:

- are taking their issues on board
- find yourself thinking about their problems later
- feel burdened
- hear yourself offering help when you are already overstretched

you need to learn to hold back.

If you know you are taking on other people's problems, consider the following:

1. Offer empathy but recognise that they are responsible for their own lives.
2. If they constantly talk about their situation, showing little interest in your life, are they a true friend?
3. If they appear to go from one problem to the next, consider that the problem may be with them and no matter how hard you try, you will not be able to help them.

The fact remains that if you offer to do something for someone else, they will assume you are happy to do it, so there is no point getting stressed when they accept your help. We all want to be liked, but if someone's friendship or love is conditional on you doing things you don't want to then perhaps now is the time to re-evaluate the relationship.

If you are guilty of regularly getting talked into doing things you don't want to do then practise saying no, particularly if you have someone in your life who is very assertive. It is best to start with something easy or small and then gradually build up to the bigger things.

You may find it easier at first to explain that you are actively aiming to reduce the stress in your life and therefore need to ensure you don't take on too much.

Use the word 'I'. Say, 'I'm afraid I can't go to the cinema today because I want to finish the book I am reading.' Notice that this is not a great lengthy excuse involving something that cannot be put off. It is simply stating your preference on how you spend your time.

Once you have said no, don't keep apologising or worrying if you have upset them. People who care about you will not want you to do things just because you feel pressured.

Why Are You Really Offering Help?

You offer help because you are a lovely person ... right? Well, maybe not ... Absolutely every action you take is to fulfil one of your own needs – covered in detail in Chapter Sixteen. If you frequently do things for others and enjoy it – great. But if on the other hand you are guilty of offering help when you cannot cope with demands in your own life, you need to understand why you do so:

1. Rescuer

If you enjoy the feeling of being needed, charging to the rescue, this is sometimes referred to as adopting the rescuer, superhero or martyr identity. Although it might satisfy the strong need to connect, it can also arouse all of the stress hormones. A lack of self-esteem can result in you seeking relationships and situations where you feel needed and important. As the rescuer you can even feel as if your own self-esteem has taken a knock when there is no one to rescue. Without realising it, you might even launch into another search for the next victim in need of rescue.

2. One for the bank

Another common reason for constantly offering help is the concept of wanting to know people will be there for you when you need them. Not only can this lead to a great deal of resentment if they don't reciprocate, but it is also a sign that you feel you need backup.

3. People pleaser

Low self-esteem and the need to be liked can result in you running yourself ragged because you think by doing things for other people they will like you better.

4. The good girl/boy

Do you feel that you constantly need to do things for others in order to be a good person, even if it makes you unhappy or stressed? Low self-esteem can lead to the feeling that you can only be a worthwhile person if you are behaving in a way that fits in with your idea of being a good person.

5. Avoiding guilt

A naturally empathetic or sensitive child who grows up in an environment with parents and others who cannot be 'wrong' can develop a guilt complex, which they can carry with them throughout their life.

The same applies in situations where the parent blames the child for things they themselves have done or for any unhappiness they feel.

For many people guilt is a frequent visitor to their door. Do you think things like – if I don't do X, Y or Z:

- I am going to have to contend with horrible feelings of guilt later?
- I might be thought of as a bad or selfish person?

If the answer to either of these questions is yes, then you are being emotionally blackmailed by your own guilt. This can become a very destructive habit, leading you to live a life you don't really want to.

Personal assessment through questions can quickly tell you whether or not you are living authentically. Ask yourself:

- What thought or emotion is constantly causing me to offer help and assistance to others?
- What emotion or thought gets me to do things I don't want to do?

The next time you feel the urge to offer help, stop and give yourself some time to think about your reasons for doing so. Consider the implications and impact on your stress levels if your offer is accepted. Then if you genuinely feel offering to help out is the right thing to do, go ahead.

The Bear and the Travellers

A couple of friends were travelling together, when a bear suddenly approached them.

Thinking quickly, the first man climbed up a tree and concealed himself in the branches.

The second, fearing for his life, fell flat on the ground, held his breath and pretended to be dead, for it is said a bear will not touch a dead body.

The bear came up close and pushed him with his snout, smelling him all over. Still the traveller played dead. The bear soon left the 'dead' traveller alone.

When the bear had gone and it was safe to come down, the first traveller descended from the tree and asked his friend why the bear had let him live.

'He did not wish to hurt me. Instead he gave me this advice,' his companion replied. 'Never travel with a friend who deserts you at the approach of danger.'

Notes to Self

- I cannot change other people, only how I react to them.
- From the moment we meet, I am training people how to treat me.
- I don't have to take everything on board.
- I become more like the people I spend most time with.
- I don't depend on others for validation.

Take Action

- Become aware of your body language when communicating.
- Understand others before trying to be understood.
- Don't personalise everything.
- Avoid energy vampires.
- Don't talk about your problems or other people's all the time.
- Embrace differences.
- Think before you offer help.

Chapter Eleven – Healthy, Romantic Relationships

I like not only to be loved, but also to be told I am loved.

George Eliot

Introduction

I believe that the stress of living with someone you don't really want to be with is immense. Not just for you and your partner, but also any children living in the home.

Yet it is a situation many people allow to continue for years, often until one of them meets someone else, which provides sufficient motivation to leave.

Fairy tales and romantic novels and films tend to end once true love has overcome any obstacles and there is a possibility of the couple living happily ever after. But in true life that is just where real relationships begin.

Life expectancy has risen significantly in the last few decades, so making a commitment in your early twenties will hopefully mean spending sixty or so years together. Expecting a commitment of this length to be without issues would be naive, but accepting that challenges are inevitable doesn't make it any less stressful.

When there are relationship problems people often refer to it as going through a bad patch, as they are no longer getting along. When a relationship has completely broken down, either party can usually pinpoint one major event that they believe is the cause of the breakdown.

However, the deterioration generally starts much earlier, stemming back to the significantly smaller events that led to the main event.

Healthy, romantic relationships are based on interdependence. One of the first steps to achieving this wonderful state is identifying any dysfunctional attitudes and beliefs. So if you are:

- hoping a relationship will make you feel better about yourself
- expecting to be looked after
- seeking security
- wanting some other need to be fulfilled

ultimately that will only lead to more stress.

Codependency

The term codependency originally applied to spouses of alcoholics; however, its characteristics are found in all walks of life. A codependent relationship is an unhealthy relationship based on control, where one person is excessively needy and the other is an overly responsible rescuer.

The needy person controls through demands that their needs are met and the rescuer controls through the dependency that is created.

Codependents need other people to like them in order to feel okay about themselves. They are also afraid of being rejected or abandoned. Codependents frequently need to be in a relationship, because they feel lonely, low or even depressed when they are by themselves for too long. This trait makes it hard for them to end a relationship, even when it is painful or abusive, which leaves them feeling trapped.

One of the biggest problems faced by codependent people is a feeling of confusion and hesitancy about what they want in life. Usually, they think the problem is down to someone else or a certain situation. Either that or they stumble from one failed relationship to another, without facing up to the fact that they have a problem. They repeat familiar patterns, by picking untrustworthy people to trust, etc., or by choosing inappropriate people with whom to form a relationship. But by learning to trust themselves and by improving their self-esteem, they can break this pattern.

Interdependency

Not every relationship where one party relies on the other for part of their well-being is unhealthily dependent. In fact, trusting in others is part of a healthy relationship. It is only a problem when the relationship is unhappy and one or both parties remain in the relationship purely because they feel trapped by financial constraints or domestic commitments.

Interdependence is about forming a partnership. In order to live happily we need to be interdependent. We cannot participate in life without giving away some power over our feelings and our welfare, but the healthy approach to interdependence is to be able to see people, situations and, most of all, ourselves clearly.

To me, interdependency means that although someone relies on another for certain things and trusts them implicitly with aspects of their welfare, they equally know they would be okay on their own. However, they choose to be in the relationship because they enjoy sharing their lives and it makes them happy.

You cannot expect one person to meet all of your needs. That is far too much pressure to put on one individual, ultimately leading to an unhealthy relationship.

Having a realistic view of relationships will allow you to work through issues and keep communication going. It will also enable you to form a healthy, interdependent partnership with another human being.

☺ Two people consciously working together can be amazing.

Meaningful Relationships

There are some basic things that are present in healthy, meaningful, fulfilling relationships:

1. Connection

It is easy to develop a peaceful coexistence without communicating other than on mundane matters. But while relationships can appear stable on the surface, unless you are relating to each other, you cannot experience true happiness.

As communication diminishes, isolation and loneliness increases. This can lead to conflict when issues arise that need to be discussed and resolved.

2. External interests

By having friends and interests outside your relationship you are also able to bring new insights, interest and stimulation to the relationship. Having things in common is important, but it is not essential to enjoy the same hobbies. For example, if one of you enjoys playing football and watching motor racing, while the other derives joy from swimming and cake decorating, there is no point trying to inflict your leisure activities on your partner. Instead, ensure that you both have time to indulge whilst leaving time to have fun together.

3. Quality time and common interests

When you first started dating your loved one, everything may have seemed new and exciting. Perhaps you spent hours chatting or coming up with new, exciting things to try.

Unfortunately, many relationships become mundane and ordinary. When coupled with the demands of work, children, outside interests and other obligations, it can become hard to find time to do things together. It is vital for your relationship that you commit to spending quality time together on a regular basis. Even during very busy and stressful times, a few minutes of really sharing and connecting can help keep bonds strong.

It is highly likely you had some things in common that you enjoyed doing together when you met. See if you can go back to pastimes you both enjoyed. Sit down together and make a list of everything you have ever fancied trying and see if you have any of the same things on your list that you could both do together. If not, pick a couple of things from each person's list and give them a go. If you can't think of anything, at the very least find time to enjoy a meal or watch a favourite TV series together.

4. New experiences

New things are often exciting and doing them together is a fun way to connect. It does not have to be elaborate or thrilling and adventurous, like skydiving. Simply trying a new restaurant or going on a day trip to a place you have never been before can bring a closeness derived from the shared pleasure of a new experience.

5. Fun and laughter

Focus on having fun together. Most situations are easier to handle and less stressful when you approach them with humour. Think about playful ways to surprise your partner, like bringing flowers or a favourite bottle of wine home unexpectedly. Laugh together whenever you can. Couples are often more fun and playful in the early stages of a relationship. However as life sends its challenges, stress and resentment start getting in the way. In turn, adopting a playful attitude can sometimes dwindle or disappear. A sense of humour can help you get through tough times. It can also relieve tension and reduce stress.

6. Compromise

It is all right to have strong convictions about something, but your partner deserves to be heard as well. Expecting to get what you want 100 per cent of the time is guaranteed to leave you feeling disappointed and cause stress. Healthy relationships are built on compromise, so both of you need to be prepared to ensure there is a certain amount of give and take. If winning is your goal, it will be difficult to reach a compromise. Sometimes this attitude occurs as a result of accumulated resentment building up in your current relationship. However, it can also come from not having your needs met while you were younger.

☺ But that is no excuse now you are an adult – you can change if you choose to do so.

The most important thing about your personal relationship is that it is loving and happy. If you know you are with the right person it doesn't matter one jot if it doesn't fit the criteria I have outlined. So don't stress yourself out because it doesn't have all or even one of the elements I have explained. Simply rejoice in the fact that you are together and enjoy it. If in your heart you know your relationship is unhappy and adding to your stress, working to improve it should be high on your priority list.

Resolving Conflict

Conflict is inevitable in any relationship, but in order to keep a relationship strong, both parties need to feel they have a voice and that their opinion, feelings and needs matter. The goal is not to win but to resolve any issues without damaging the relationship. Keep the focus on the issue in hand. Don't label – calling someone an idiot or a nag won't help anyone and may severely damage your relationship. Respect the other person's feelings and don't drag old arguments into the mix. If your spouse doesn't buy a carton of milk on the way home from work as you asked them to, find out why and then ask them to rectify the situation, without dragging up all the other things they do that annoy you. There is no point bringing up things they have done in the past that you still feel resentful about. For example, if they have upset you in the past by flirting with your friend, it has nothing to do with forgetting the milk and should not be raised at this time.

Avoid using 'always' and 'never' statements. For example:

- you never do what I ask
- you never help me
- you always let me down

This is because In most cases, it is unlikely to be true – in that it is unlikely that it has never happened or that it always happens.

If you are having a bad day or are stressed, stop and think before you speak. By learning to live more in the present moment, you will become more self-aware and will thereby know how stressed you are feeling at the present time. If you are feeling like a coiled spring, the chances are that you will overreact and as explained earlier, you will not be able to think the situation through rationally. If so, now is not the time to raise issues. Wait until you are feeling more in control.

If a partner is struggling with an issue outside the relationship that causes them stress, as a result they may overreact to small issues. Misunderstandings can then rapidly turn to frustration and anger, while stress can make people short-tempered.

If you are coping with a lot of stress at work and having to keep a lid on your feelings, it might seem easier to snap at your partner than to tackle the real issue.

Often we lash out at the people we are closest to, perhaps because we are more relaxed with them or we feel they will understand. Maybe they will be more understanding than your boss. But in the long term the relationship could be damaged.

Being afraid of conflict is quite common in relationships, especially when trying to resolve problems. But if your fear of conflict results in you bottling things up until you are angry, it may actually provoke the argument you wanted to avoid. I would always advocate discussing things calmly and rationally without resorting to shouting; however, a passionate debate is not always a bad thing.

Working through conflict can actually strengthen relationships. Tempers generally flare when either person is triggered into a knee-jerk reaction that is usually targeted at their partner, who in turn is likely to defend themselves or retreat further into their shell.

By learning what triggers your anger and how it makes you feel physically as well as emotionally, as explained earlier, you will be in a much better position to recognise when this has happened.

Instead of lashing out, you can then tell your partner you have been triggered and take some space to practise a mediation or relaxation technique, before resuming the interaction.

In order for this to work you need to have discussed it with them previously. You will need to have agreed a code word or phrase you can use in advance of any conflict, so that the other person knows you are feeling angry and are about to lose control. The word you use does not matter, as long as you both understand that if in the middle of a heated debate you suddenly say, 'Cabbages,' then leave the room, you are doing so in order to calm down. You can then continue the discussion when you are feeling more in control.

Say What You Want or Mean

Your partner cannot read your mind, so be clear about what you want. If you have been together for a while, you may assume that your partner knows you well and should have a good idea of what you are thinking and your needs. However, while they may have some idea, your partner is not a mind reader.

It is far more sensible to express your needs to avoid any confusion, particularly if you know you have changed and what you needed and wanted five years ago is very different from now. For example, if your priority used to be building a family home and life revolved around the family, but now as you approach forty, you feel time is slipping away and you want to go out and party, you need to explain this to your partner. Ensure they are on board and that they either feel the same way or at least are prepared to support your desire.

Getting in the habit of expressing your needs helps you weather difficult times, which otherwise may lead to increasing resentment, misunderstandings, stress and anger. If you don't state what you want clearly, don't be surprised if you don't get it.

Hinting and hoping that the other person has been able to interpret your needs is not communicating clearly. But remember: if he/she doesn't instinctively know what you want, it does not mean they don't love or care about you.

Don't forget – you can't read their mind, either. Mind reading is a dangerous way of communicating. It is possible to interpret your partner's feelings if you know them really well just by looking at them or even by hearing the tone of their voice. What is not so simple is knowing what they are thinking about. Consider this example:

You have just asked your partner if they want to go on a skiing holiday. You can tell by their face that the idea does not appeal. However, what you cannot know is what they are thinking. Just a few examples of what they might be thinking include:

- That's a good idea, but how will we have enough money?
- What if one of us breaks a leg?
- I don't think my manager will give me the time off.
- Who will check in on my parents while we are away?

Based on what you know about your circumstances, you may be able to guess what is on their mind. But it is much safer to ask what they are thinking before you jump to conclusions. I am sure they will appreciate you actually taking the time to understand how they feel.

Always say what you want, not what you don't want. If your partner loves you, they will want you to be happy. Saying what you want gives them a way to feel like they are pleasing you. If you say what you don't want, that can be seen as being negative and only serves to tell them what makes you unhappy or what displeases you.

Be clear about your expectations from each other. Knowing what is truly important to your partner can go a long way towards building a healthy relationship. Equally, although things may seem obvious to you, your partner may not understand. Alternatively, it is also important for your partner to recognise what you want and for you to state it clearly. As your relationship grows and evolves, this is an ongoing process.

Start by making a list of what you expect from your partner and ask them for a list in return. Go through the lists together and be prepared to be flexible. For example, if you have written down that you expect to be able to play golf every Saturday, whereas on their list they have put that they expect you to go shopping every Saturday, a compromise might be that one of you move your activity to the Sunday.

However, having a hobby or activity that ties up a particular day each week might be too restrictive and thereby have a negative affect on your relationship. Perhaps a better compromise would be that golf and shopping take place on alternate Saturdays and Sundays each week.

Reaffirming Your Love

Make sure you reaffirm your love for one another on a regular basis. If you love them, tell them. Don't wait until they tell you first. Never refuse to give the other affection. It can be extremely hurtful when you go to hug or kiss someone and they refuse your affection.

Touch is a fundamental part of human interaction. Life without physical contact with others is a very lonely life indeed. Studies have shown that affectionate touching actually boosts the body's levels of oxytocin – a hormone that influences bonding and attachment. Studies on infants have shown the importance on brain development of regular, loving touch and holding. These benefits do not end in childhood.

Intimacy

In a committed relationship between two adult partners, physical intercourse is often a cornerstone of the relationship. However, intercourse should not be the only method of physical intimacy in a relationship. Regular, affectionate touching – kissing, holding hands or hugging – are equally vital in order to nurture loving relationships.

A kiss is a lovely trick designed by nature to stop speech when words become superfluous.

Ingrid Bergman

It is important to take some time to find out what your partner really likes. Unwanted touching or inappropriate overtures can make the other person tense up and retreat, which is exactly what you don't want. Perhaps you feel it is acceptable to refuse affection because you are still angry with the other person for something they have done, but it will only damage your relationship. Instead of pushing them away, sit down and talk through your problems until you come up with a suitable resolution. If you say you have forgiven them, mean it.

When you are feeling stressed, your sex life can be adversely affected. Although you might still love your partner, you may lose interest in sex, which they can take as a rejection of them. Also, they will still have physical needs. Everything in this guide is aimed at helping you to feel less stressed, which should allow your interest in sex to return. However, in the meantime, talk to your partner, reassure them and work through the situation together. Sex is a great way to release tension, so the right approach may actually help you to manage your stress levels.

Notice What They do Right

When relationships are great, two people are often so close that they cannot bear to be apart. Then, as they begin to deteriorate – often started by small, insignificant events – gradually, over time, it causes them to drift apart. People forget the things they loved or liked about the other person. They start to focus purely on the negative aspects of the other's personality. Then they become convinced that the problems within the relationship must be the other person's fault entirely.

I have lost count of the number of times a client has said that their partner has changed – and not for the better. However, more often than not they have not really changed, it is more a case of the complainer becoming less tolerant of things they previously accepted. It might be that they even thought it cute or endearing.

If things are not put in check, it can result in a long list of dislikes and irritation. This can result in the discontented party feeling that the relationship is over and in turn, they may become convinced that the perfect person is out there who could sweep them off their feet.

Quite simply, it is possible that you take for granted the good things your partner does – maybe even to the point where you no longer even notice them. Before you dismiss this idea and take comfort in your belief that you are a caring person, so of course you would notice if they did anything right, what I want you to do is put some time aside and really observe them:

1. First, make a list of the things you like or enjoy about your spouse, no matter how small.
2. Make a note of the things you used to love or like about them.
3. For the next week, notice what they do right. Make a note of things they do that are thoughtful or that make you smile, happy or glad to be with them.
4. Are they still doing the things you loved or liked about them in the past?
5. Of the things you have identified, how many did you have on the list at the beginning of the week?
6. Have they surprised you by how often they make you laugh or smile?
7. Had you forgotten about the way they rub your shoulders when you are tired or cook you a Sunday roast even though they never eat one, just because you love it?

If before this exercise you had not noticed the good things they did, you certainly won't have been making them feel appreciated, so make amends and tell them.

☺ If they don't faint from shock, they might just reciprocate and tell you what they enjoy about being with you.

Keep love in your heart. A life without it is like a sunless garden when the flowers are dead.

Oscar Wilde

Work Through Challenges Together

When you are faced with one of life's traumas, such as the death of a loved one, or you are facing a major challenge such as losing your job, it is easy to feel burdened and alone.

It is therefore important to remember that in a relationship, you are part of a team and that by working together you will be stronger. Bouncing ideas off each other, sharing tasks or even having a comforting cuddle can make challenges easier to deal with.

Everyone works through problems and issues in their own way, so be prepared to be flexible. Consider their views and opinions with an open mind. The important thing is to continue moving forward together as one unit, as it can get you through the rough patches.

Serious Relationship Issues

No matter how much you love each other or how long you have been together, problems in a relationship can appear like cracks in a wall. Just like a crack in the wall of your home, if you ignore it, it is likely to get worse and may even be a symptom of a much more sinister problem.

If a certain aspect of the relationship stops working, don't ignore it. Instead, address it together. Things change, so respond to them together as they occur.

Sometimes problems in a relationship may seem too complex or overwhelming for a couple to handle on their own. In cases like these it is important to reach out for help together. There are a number of options available, including:

- couples counselling
- spiritual advice
- individual therapy

Never be afraid to seek professional help. If you cannot sort out your issues alone, seeking help doesn't mean you are inadequate in some way. So don't feel embarrassed or imagine that everyone else can sort out their problems without external help. It is a very true saying that we do not know what goes on behind closed doors and a seemingly good relationship may not be all that it appears. Acknowledging that you have a problem and taking constructive action is a positive step.

Unhappy endings

If a romantic relationship ends, many people feel that they will be regarded as a failure, which isn't the case at all. One of the saddest things I have heard was when someone confessed that during their twenty-five years of marriage, she had only been happy for three of those years! An enduring relationship is not the same as a successful one. It is far better to end a relationship if you no longer feel you can make it work than to stay together making each other unhappy. Where possible, it is best to part on good terms.

A divorce or break-up represents the loss of not just the relationship, but also shared dreams and commitments, causing profound grief, stress and disappointment for both parties. So there is no doubt that ending a long-term, committed relationship is one of the most stressful events in life.

Whatever the reason for the split, and whether you wanted it or not, it can turn your whole world upside down and trigger all sorts of painful emotions. However, you need to remember that everything passes. The difficult times will eventually be over. It *will* get easier and there are plenty of things you can do to learn from the experience in order to grow into a stronger, wiser person.

Break-ups disrupt every part of our home lives, perhaps even where we live and relationships with our children, family and friends. They also often have profound financial implications. Added to this are the long-term questions that spring to mind like:

- What if I am making a mistake?
- Will I end up alone?
- What will life be like without my partner?
- What will people say?

Given our need for certainty (explained in Chapter Sixteen), not knowing the answer to these questions can seem worse than the break-up. Indeed, it is these worries that can keep people in unhappy relationships.

Uncertainty is often so worrying that it can appear more frightening than staying in an unhappy relationship. Accept that recovering from a break-up or divorce is difficult and that healing takes time. Be patient with yourself and focus on moving on with the best possible mindset rather than on winning, being perceived as the innocent party or scoring points against your ex. If it was you who decided to end the relationship, remember: they will be hurting, too. Like you, they will be looking for answers and reassurance that it wasn't their fault.

However tempting, avoid laying blame at your partner's door by listing all the reasons you no longer love them or want to be with them. It will only cause them greater hurt and provide them with the need to lash out.

Your guilt is natural, but if you are truly unhappy you cannot choose their happiness over that of your own life. Even though they may want the relationship to continue, once they are feeling more rational, generally they will realise they would not want you to stay with them out of pity.

Whatever the circumstances, be reasonable when it comes to splitting assets and above all, if you have children, never, ever use them as a weapon. This will be covered in more detail in Chapter Twelve.

How to cope with being dumped

Being 'dumped' is such a horrid word, but that sums up exactly how people feel if they are not the one who chooses to end the relationship. Losing someone you still love is incredibly painful and hard to handle. Not only do you have to deal with the pain of the loss, but there are also a host of other negative thoughts and emotions to deal with:

- feeling worthless – if they don't want you no one will
- no one else will ever be able to fill the huge void they have left in your life
- you will never find love again
- you must be lacking in some way if they don't want you

This type of thought, together with the agony, can keep you hoping against hope that your partner will realise they have made a mistake and come back.

But you can get over the pain and rebuild your life – maybe even improve it. In order to do so you must:

- accept that the relationship is over

- not waste your energies on thoughts of reunion or worse – revenge
- view your single status as an opportunity instead of a punishment
- make a list of all the things about your ex-partner that you did not like and put it somewhere *you* can see it
- write down all your good attributes and all the things you can bring to a new relationship

Occasionally, your ex may get jittery about whether or not they have made the right decision, which can often lead to them suggesting having sex. ALWAYS SAY NO. If you are serious about getting over them this a definite *no-no*. The closeness that comes with sex can set your recovery back months. The most likely outcome is that you will read more into it than they do and will end up feeling lost and lonely again when they leave to carry on with their new life.

Keep in mind the following:

1. They are just one person out of billions on the planet and you deserve to be with someone who truly loves you for who you are.
2. They did not set out all those years or months ago when you first got together with the intention of breaking your heart or leaving you after years of marriage.
3. Just because you no longer fit their criteria for what they want and need out of a partner, it is not a reflection of your worth as a person.
4. You deserve more than for someone to stay with you out of pity or a sense of responsibility.

Many people go on to find greater happiness after a relationship has ended. Whilst I would always advocate working through your difficulties, sometimes all you can do is accept that this aspect of your life has passed and look forward to a brighter tomorrow.

I have found the paradox that if you love until it hurts, there can be no more hurt, only more love.

Mother Teresa

Notes to Self

- Healthy relationships are interdependent.
- No one can read my mind.
- Touch is a fundamental part of human interaction.

Action Steps

- For a week, notice the things your partner does right.
- Be the type of person you want to attract.
- Find common interest.
- Have a plan for resolving conflict.
- Say what you want and mean.
- Reaffirm your love for one another on a regular basis.
- Work through challenges together.
- Make time for each other.

Chapter Twelve – Stressed Parents – Stressed Children

Childhood is a short season.

Helen Hayes

Introduction

Some people say being a parent is the most important job in the world, but I don't think of it as a job. In my experience, as a mother and stepmother, whilst it can be incredibly challenging and a cause of anxiety, it is also the greatest joy of my life.

Let us be clear – not everyone enjoys parenting. But that does not mean that they don't love their children and would not be prepared to lay down their lives for them.

Unlike most decisions, once you become a parent there is no rewind button – you are a parent for life. My advice is to accept that it is a journey of constant learning and enjoy the ride. Parenting is a vast subject, so in this chapter we will only be able to cover some basic concepts that will help you reduce some of the stress involved in parenting.

Children Learn Quickly

Like it or not, children learn from you from a very early age. Although they will look for other role models outside the home in their teenage years, your own beliefs, values and behaviours will have had an effect on how they have developed or turned out. So if you have spent much of their formative years being stressed and negative or carefree and relaxed, they will have learnt these behaviours, too.

☺ Now before you go off and beat yourself up because you feel you have screwed up your kids – read on ...

Children learn very quickly and can adapt to new behaviours far quicker than adults. So you still have the opportunity to help them develop relaxed and happy personalities. By far the easiest way to do this is to lead by example. If they see or hear you reacting negatively to things, or becoming stressed or agitated when things don't go well, they will learn these same behaviours. By learning to manage stress and react differently to situations, indirectly you will be teaching them how to do the same.

Children Learn by Example

Parents often make the mistake of thinking that because they said nothing, their child will not have picked up on how they were feeling. This is simply not the case. Children are experts at picking up on and reacting to body language. Similarly, if your children cause you stress by their behaviour, you need to show them how to behave appropriately.

For example, there is no point complaining to your children to pick up their toys and clothes if you are always leaving your things lying around the house. If you want them to put things away after they have used them, you need to do the same.

Being a Good Parent

It is easy to judge your own parenting skills and those of others – particularly your own parents – negatively. Whilst there are only a few people whose parenting style fits with my personal values and beliefs, I recognise that generally people want to be good parents. Just as with everything else in life, we all have a very different idea of what being a good parent actually means.

No doubt if you ask people to define good parenting, they would say very similar things:

- being loving and supportive
- providing stability
- being financially secure
- giving them opportunities
- caring for them
- spending time with them

But the fact is that those things are concepts within our own heads. What is considered as being a loving and supportive parent to one person might be bordering on neglect to another. In other words, it is about perception. For instance, someone who feels they are very loving and caring might be viewed by others as being overprotective.

Added to these differences in perception is the importance we place on each area. For example, providing financial support might be at the top of the priority list for one parent, whereas another might feel spending quality, one-to-one time with their children is the number one priority. The best approach, therefore, is not to compare yourself to others or to judge. Instead, focus on whether or not you and your child/children are happy with your relationship.

> ☺ God, please help me to be tolerant of other people's attitudes and beliefs – even though *they* are WRONG!

Signs of Stress in Children

Children can become stressed for a vast number of reasons and seeing your child in distress can make you feel guilty. But remember, you are doing the right thing by reading this guide and changing your behaviour, which means you will influence your child in a more positive way in the future. You were also doing what you thought was the right thing with the resources that you had available to you at the time.

As we have discovered, stress is an inevitable part of life and growing up. But parents need to keep a watchful eye on children and intervene when they sense something is undermining a child's psychological or physical well-being. Possible signs of stress in a child include:

- physical symptoms, such as headaches and stomach pains
- restlessness
- feeling tired for no reason
- agitation
- depression, so the child shuts down and won't talk about how they feel
- loss of interest in an activity they once enjoyed

- school work suffering, playing truant or not completing homework
- antisocial behaviour, such as lying, stealing or bullying
- refusal to help out around the home
- appearing to be more dependent on a parent or clingy than in the past

There could be many other reasons for changes in your child's behaviour and talking to them calmly should help you uncover the reasons.

If you believe your child is suffering from stress, as a parent this can certainly increase any feelings of anxiety or stress you already have. Or perhaps you find it difficult to understand how your child can be stressed if you are creating a good home environment and believe childhood is a carefree time. But things like school, their social life, your expectations of them and the home environment can sometimes create pressures that can feel overwhelming for children. As a parent, you cannot protect your children from stress. However, you can help them develop healthy ways to resolve problems, handle life better and cope with stress.

If you constantly fly off the handle or break down in front of your child or if your child senses you are unhappy, they may feel they cannot share their worries with you for fear of making you worse. They may also become stressed and anxious if they are worrying about you. It is important that you do not allow your child to feel the need to become the parent and take care of you. Show them you are in control and that they can rely on you.

Just like adults, children deal with stress in both healthy and unhealthy ways. While they may struggle to articulate their concerns, and may not initiate a conversation about what is bothering them, they do want their parents to help them cope with their troubles. There are things you can do as a parent to help your child by just giving them love and attention:

- give them affection, hugs and cuddles
- distract them with fun things to do together
- go for a walk or a bike ride together
- take an interest in their hobbies, etc.

- watch a movie or play a game
- talk to them – not just about the issue

Whatever you decide, simply being there for them will make a difference. Avoid comforting them with food, as this can lead to emotional eating in later years.

Talking to Your Child

Communicating with others can be tricky, usually because people fail to listen properly. If you have been trying to have a discussion with your child that hasn't gone as well as planned or you want to improve your communication skills, then you need to learn to listen correctly – possibly for the first time in your life. If you feel like you cannot get through to your children, learning to listen is the first step towards building better communication.

When talking to young children, it can be difficult to get them to remain quiet for long enough to listen to you. Wait until they are calm and take things at their pace. If you are thinking of talking to them just before bedtime, you might like to reconsider and address the issue at some other point, as the discussion might make it more difficult for them to sleep. Also, if it has been a difficult discussion, you should ensure that you are around in case they have questions or concerns later.

At other times, they might appear sullen or withdrawn. This can be a sign that they are experiencing feelings of stress or that something is wrong. It can also make it difficult to find out what is wrong or on their mind. Join in with them while they are playing happily or if they are older, when they are chilling out. Wait a while and then raise what it is you need to talk about. However your child appears or is reacting to the conversation, never dismiss their thoughts, feelings or ideas as nonsense or unimportant. You are the parent and therefore should make the decisions, but children need to know that their feelings matter.

Younger children may not have sufficient vocabulary to express their concerns or feelings. This can lead to them acting up or displaying anger, frustration or temper tantrums. When they have calmed down, ask them about how they feel and help them to put words to the feelings. This will help them in the future, as children who are able to identify with their feelings are more likely to communicate with words rather than behaviour.

Instead of talking about what your child could have done differently, focus on what they could do in the future. If there is a specific problem, encourage your child to think of a couple of ideas to resolve it. By allowing them to be involved in coming up with a solution, it will help build confidence in their ability to sort things out for themselves. Support the good ideas and offer suggestions where needed. Once your child feels they have a possible solution, try changing the subject and moving on to something more positive and relaxing. Avoid giving the problem more attention than it deserves.

Accept that your child may not always feel like talking about what is bothering them. Let them know that you will be there when they are ready to do so:

- Ask them in a casual way to tell you what is wrong, ensuring you don't make it into a big deal.
- Listen attentively with interest, patience and a caring attitude.
- Avoid the urge to interrupt, judge, lecture, belittle their feelings, blame them or make it about you.
- Let your child's concerns and feelings be heard.
- Be sympathetic – show you care and that you want to understand.
- Take your time to get the whole story by asking questions like: 'And then what happened?' Or: 'How did you feel?'
- If they are not ready to talk at this point, give them some space and try again later.
- Acknowledge their feelings; for example, you might say: 'That must have been upsetting' or 'I can understand why you felt mad about that'.

Feeling understood and listened to will help your child feel supported by you, which is especially important during times of stress.

It is vital to ensure that you talk to your child at other times as well. If you are a busy parent, you don't want your child to make the unhealthy connection between their being stressed or upset and receiving your attention. If they believe they only get cuddles and chats with you when they are upset, they may actually begin to show signs of stress when there are no problems just to get your attention. By talking to your child regularly, you can avoid this happening.

In my experience, seeing your child unhappy, worried or stressed is far worse than experiencing those feelings yourself. But resist the urge to fix every problem instantly. Instead, focus on helping your child, slowly but surely, grow into an independent person who has developed good coping skills and problem-solving techniques.

Expectations

Most parents want a better life for their child than they had for themselves and if their own life was idyllic, they want the same for their own child. Add to that the desire to see their child achieve their full potential and there can be a strong temptation to have unrealistic expectations. This can lead to stress and unhappiness for both parties.

However well meaning adults are, sometimes they can pile pressure on their child by allowing them to become overcommitted at too young an age by being in a rush to guarantee their child's future. Although well intentioned and generally wanting to provide their child with the best opportunity to succeed, quite often there is no real goal in mind and the child's true talents and interests are not taken into account.

Education

It is generally accepted that children today are smarter and more computer savvy. They also grow up more quickly than in previous generations. But you should never overlook the fact that their childhood is precious. They are blessed with just a few short years of being a child – let them enjoy it.

Of course learning and schoolwork form a vital part of developing into a well-rounded member of society, but not everyone can be an academic. We all have different talents, so help your child to discover what theirs are.

It is important for your child's self-esteem that they recognise they are a worthwhile person regardless of their achievements. Above all, remember: your child is not a way for you to relive your life. They are a person in their own right and deserve the opportunity to be who and what they want to be. Providing of course this means living within the boundaries of the law and they are not harming themselves or others.

Many 15-year-olds from Shanghai, China, easily outperform those of all other nationalities. When compared with societies like China, parents in the Western World are generally not as pushy or focused on ensuring their child achieves the highest educational standard. However, that does not mean that our children are free from educational stress. Some parents are so focused on ensuring that little Adam or Emily are top of the class, that they achieve A grades across all subjects and that they get into the top universities that they fail to notice the negative impact it is having on their child. Sadly, children can feel that their self-worth and their parents' love is dependent on their educational results.

Whilst there is nothing wrong with wanting to achieve great results, if you place too much importance on it, the result will be a stressed-out child. If you have taught your child that it is essential that they achieve academically, once they reach their teenage years the pressure can really pile on.

Teachers quite rightly tell the whole class how important their education is. However, it can be the children who need this message least who take it on board the most. The result is 12 or 13 year olds who are disappointed, distressed and even distraught at having achieved just 98 per cent in an exam. What has happened is that they are solely focused on the 2 per cent of marks they dropped rather than their amazing result.

To avoid stressing your child out and to allow them to develop a love for education, praise them for their efforts rather than their results. Ensure they never feel your love is conditional on their educational results. Most importantly, match your expectations to their ability. This means helping them understand that they can achieve far better results the more they apply themselves. However, focus on what they are good at rather than force them to study physics when they have no aptitude for it and dislike it with a vengeance. Spend time with them and help them to overcome difficulties.

I remember that from a very young age my daughter disliked maths and struggled with it. However, I did not instantly abandon all hope that she would be able to do it. Instead, I developed a times table song that we used to sing together. I also used every opportunity to use maths in everyday life. As a result, she overcame her aversion to the subject, found it easier to do and achieved a very good GCSE grade, which she was very pleased with. Most importantly, she never felt pressured to achieve.

Hobbies and Interests

It is essential for your child to have interests and hobbies, as these activities can help them develop into well-rounded adults. However, issues arise when most evenings and weekends are booked solid with lessons, clubs and associations such Brownies, Cubs, Cadets, sporting activities, dancing and music lessons. What can happen is that the child ends up with few or no occasions when they can have quiet time, or play with a favourite toy or friends.

Younger children in particular may need help balancing their activities and as a parent, you are responsible for ensuring they are not overcommitted. If you yourself are overcommitted by ferrying them around to all their extracurricular activities, this is a good indication that your child might be experiencing the same feelings. In these cases both parent and child can become worn out and stressed. In turn, this can impact negatively on the rest of family, resulting in arguments and additional stress for everyone in the household.

Another common mistake is to project or push your own passion onto your child. Although you may genuinely feel that you are only doing what your child wants, when was the last time you actually checked? Remember, your child will want to please you and receive your praise, so could this be the reason they are so diligent at their piano lessons?

If your child is involved in an activity, be supportive, offer praise and show an interest by attending the activity, but also allow them the freedom to change interests as they desire. Don't forget: your child will have a limited concentration span and so they cannot be expected to focus for long periods of time. If their attention wanders, they have probably had enough.

Letting them be who they want to be can be difficult – after all, they do not have your experience or knowledge. As a parent it is incredibly difficult to stand by and do nothing when you believe they are making a mistake. In these circumstances you should advise and guide them, refraining from forcing your own agenda on them.

Teenagers

Often referred to as the terrible teens, this can be a particularly stressful and challenging time for parents. After all, they may well find that the child they previously had a good relationship with now appears to hate them and that communication has become a minefield. This is certainly not always the case and in my experience, not all teenagers are difficult. However, communicating with this age group needs special consideration, patience and understanding.

Don't worry – the dynamics of your relationship will change as you reach a more equal footing. Many parents find this period challenging, as do the teenagers, so it is important that you keep communicating with each other as they begin to branch out on their own learning, making choices and decisions for themselves.

Whenever you talk to them, address them as a young adult. Ultimately, you may have to set rules and take the role of the parent, but if you can reach an agreement where you are both happy, there will be much less stress all round. It can help to let them take responsibility – providing the mistakes will not result in serious repercussions – knowing they have your support and guidance when needed. After all, we can all learn from our mistakes.

I think it is a shame when parents and their older children are at loggerheads with each other. But it is possible for your relationship with your teenager to be a source of great joy rather than one of constant stress. When they become teenagers, communicating with them is very different to when they were younger. Their thoughts, ideas and opinions are as valid as yours and therefore deserve your respect. If you have a particularly challenging topic to discuss, choose somewhere neutral and a time that is convenient for you both.

Avoid using the parent card by saying things like: 'I don't care what you think, I'm your mother and what I say goes!' Using this type of statement gives the impression that you don't actually have a valid reason for your viewpoint and are simply asserting your authority instead. With teenagers, you are no longer in a position to enforce your rules and beliefs, so before you begin, be prepared to reach some middle ground you can both agree on.

That said, there may be times when as a parent you simply have to state that these are the rules and they have to be adhered to – in which case do so. But don't labour the point or stress about it afterwards. Sometimes being a parent means making tough decisions, but it is worth it.

☺ It is worth remembering that there is no failure – only feedback.

Feedback and Conflict

Sometimes, it can seem as though the only time parents communicate with their children is to criticise or tell them off for doing something wrong or breaking a rule. If you talk to your children all the time then more challenging topics will not be so difficult to discuss.

Receiving feedback can be absolutely crushing, especially for children. Despite how it might appear at times, they do want your approval. Feedback is something you cannot avoid and when delivered correctly, it can be helpful.

If it is delivered in a way that results in your child feeling criticised, they may feel so hurt that they shut down or start defending their position without really listening to what is being said. Fortunately, it is possible to learn how to give feedback in a way that your children don't feel criticised and actually positively take on board what you have to say, using the Feedback Sandwich:

1. Keep calm.
2. Don't wait until you are too fed up or angry.
3. Give your feedback at the appropriate time – not days after the event.
4. Take three deep breaths.
5. Say something positive.
6. Explain what could be done better next time, not what was done wrong.
7. End with a positive comment.

All feedback should deal with the behaviour or task, not the child. And it should always be specific; for example, when your child has not tidied their room to your satisfaction, rather than yelling you could say: 'Thanks for doing your room. If you could also put your laundry in the basket, that would be great.'

Unhappy Home

If your children are living in an unhappy home because of difficulties in their parents' relationship, this can cause tremendous stress for them. Particularly if they are used as messengers, if they are drawn into the argument, where one parent undermines the other or where there is frequently an atmosphere or arguments.

If you are not sufficiently motivated to sort out your relationship for yourself, do it for your children. Apart from the stress that living in an unhappy home can cause them, they are also learning about relationships from you.

The divorced parent

As many of us know, divorce or separation can be incredibly difficult and stressful. When children are involved, the stress felt by everyone can rocket to astronomical proportions. If there are no children, once the financial and other domestic matters are sorted, you can both go your separate ways. However, if you have a child with someone, they are always going to be part of your life.

For the parent with responsibility for care of the child, they now have to cope with doing most things alone, in addition to helping the child who will be missing the absent parent. The absent parent, on the other hand, not only has to cope with their new living arrangements, but they also have to cope with the guilt and trauma at being parted from their child. And this in addition to helping the child adjust to the new situation.

Regardless of their age, divorce can be stressful for children and they may feel confused, angry and upset. As a parent, you can make the process and its effects less painful for your children. This can be achieved by providing stability in your home with a reassuring, positive attitude. If you can maintain a working relationship with your ex, you can help your child avoid the stress that comes with watching parents in conflict.

Avoid creating opportunities for the child to play one parent off against the other, by agreeing on things as much as possible with your ex. Setting ground rules and sticking to them helps. If your ex goes against what was agreed, take it up with them when the child is not around.

Sometimes, no matter how hard you try, your ex will be uncooperative and may appear to overrule you and 'stab you in the back' at every opportunity. It is not easy being the 'bad guy' and although having the same rules and structure in both homes is ideal, if this is not possible, it is not the end of the world. In this situation you can avoid a lot of stress by:

1. Not making assumptions

If you think your ex has broken some previously agreed rule, it is wise to check with the other parent first before blowing your top. You may find there is more to the story than you were initially told.

2. Avoiding comparisons

If your child tells you that Dad lets him spend three hours on the Xbox before doing any homework, avoid the temptation to tell your child what you think of his Dad's parenting skills. Instead, think how you would react if he said his grandparents let him do the same thing when they are babysitting for you. You still might not be pleased, but you would be less likely to explode. Say something simple and to the point like: 'You must enjoy that but it's not happening on my watch. Once your homework is done you can play for an hour.'

3. Looking for compromise

It is unlikely that you will agree with your ex on everything, but hopefully you will both want your children to feel loved and have a good relationship with you both. Keep this in mind and agree compromises where possible. For example, if your 7-year-old daughter tells you your ex-wife has said she can have her ears pierced for Christmas and you think she is too young, talk to your ex and see if you can agree on an alternative. Perhaps she could have them done a few months later or for her eighth birthday.

4. Never undermining your ex

Although it might feel good to join in with your children if they are complaining about their dad, make sure you don't contradict or undermine their authority. Remember: next week it could be you they are complaining about.

If all else fails

If all attempts at cooperation fail, you will need to find a way to minimise the stress for both you and your child. The best way of doing this is to accept the fact that your ex won't behave in the way you wish. Instead, focus on maintaining rules and a stable environment for your child whenever they are with you.

With time, they will come to respect the fact that you only have their best interests at heart and they may even learn to appreciate the sense of security you provide. In addition, whilst your ex may seem to enjoy winding you up, they may actually start to adopt similar rules once they realise you are not biting and when they can see that your way works.

If you can navigate this unsettling time successfully, your child can emerge from it feeling loved, confident and well adjusted. Sadly, you are very much at the mercy of how the other parent is behaving. Because you cannot control the other parent, your only option may be to control your reactions to their behaviour. You can also learn to manage your own behaviour in a way that minimises stress for both you and your child. Their well-being should be your main priority.

Top tips for helping your child and ultimately reducing your own stress:

1. Provide them with a routine they can rely on. They need to know they can count on you for structure, stability and care.
2. Listen to their concerns and feelings in the way explained earlier.
3. Be flexible where possible. You should also be prepared to accommodate their needs, even if you don't particularly want to. For example, if your daughter asks to stay out for an extra hour with her father to go and see a film on a school night, weigh up the benefits of agreeing, perhaps on the condition that homework is completed before she goes.
4. Never, ever fall into the trap of using your child as a weapon against your ex by withholding access. No matter how much you kid yourself that you are doing it for their benefit, you will damage your child and eventually your relationship with them.
5. Ensure your child knows the other parent loves them and that the break-up is nothing to do with them.

6. One of your biggest priorities should be to ensure your child knows it is still okay to love and like the other parent. This means not being critical of the other parent within the child's hearing. Even if you are on the phone to a friend and think they are not listening, they will be.

7. Don't use them as messengers because you don't want to or can't talk to your ex.

8. Never argue in front of the child and particularly not about the child, as this will make them think it is their fault and they will feel guilty and stressed.

9. Allow them to enjoy the time they spend with each of you. It can be difficult if you are the parent providing primary care and you spend all your time making rules and providing meals while your ex breezes in once a week providing treats, gifts and meals out. But believe me – it is not easy being the absent parent. In fact, it is heartbreaking not being able to be there full time with your child.

10. If you are the absent parent, no matter how difficult your ex is making it, never give up on your child – they need both of you in their lives.

If your child is angry and refuses to see you, keep the connection going with telephone calls. If they won't speak to you send them letters, cards, text messages and gifts. Don't wait for birthdays and Christmas to do this.

While it can be incredibly hard, it is possible that they are refusing to see you out of a sense of loyalty to the other parent, despite what they say to the contrary. Of course, they may well be angry, too, if they believe you are the cause of the break-up and have left them. But if you persist, eventually they will come round.

Answering the difficult question

Explaining to your children why your relationship has ended can be incredibly difficult. It can be tempting to lay all the blame at your ex's door; after all, you want your children to love you and not think badly of you. Indeed, you may even believe you are blameless. So while it may be understandable that you want to stick the boot in and make your child side with you – *DON'T DO IT!*

Give your child the benefit of an honest – but child-friendly – explanation of why you split up. While you need to be honest, overly long explanations may confuse them. One-sided views are also unhelpful. For example, don't say: 'We are splitting up because your mum has had an affair/got someone else.' It is difficult in cases of infidelity, but with a little diplomacy you can avoid playing the blame game. Remember: people don't meet someone else if they are completely happy in a relationship – the problem would have started much earlier. Consider something simple like: 'We have drifted apart and don't get along any more. Mum has met someone else and one day I will, too.' Younger children need less detail and will cope better with a simpler explanation.

Let them know that your love for them hasn't changed. Then remind them that no matter what happens, parents and children never get divorced. As much as you can, try to agree in advance with your ex on an explanation for your separation or divorce – and stick to it.

Whatever your access or living arrangements with your child, they can be a great joy and actually help you reduce your stress levels while you are going through it. Ensure that you spend quality time with them. Laughter is great for relieving stress and if you and your child are having difficulties coping with the new situation, having fun together should be a priority.

Step-parenting

Being a step-parent is like walking a tightrope. You move too far in either direction and you will come hurtling towards the floor – usually without a safety net. If parenting is stressful, you can often treble those feelings when it comes to dealing with someone else's children. In fact, it is probably the most difficult role you will ever take on. So how do you get through this potential minefield without any casualties?

A great deal of pain can be avoided if you can agree on some very basic definitions of that role, right at the beginning. If possible, discuss your role with the biological parent. For example, if you are assuming the role of stepdad, talking to the children's real dad will help you to understand his concerns about your involvement – most commonly that you will try to replace him. If this is the case, reassure him that this is not so and respect his position.

Next, ensure you understand what your partner wants from you in the role. Do they want you to become involved? Is disciplining or guiding the child going to come under your jurisdiction? Again, respect their wishes. However, you need to set some ground rules. You should not be expected to look after the child alone if you cannot discipline them, as this could potentially put them in danger.

Disciplining your non-biological children is always difficult and can create resentment on the part of your new partner if you overstep the mark. It can also result in anger from your partner's ex, problems between you and resentment from your stepchildren. However, it is also important that you support their efforts to discipline their own children. That said, if the relationships are in good shape and you genuinely care about your stepchildren, everyone should recognise that you have their best interests at heart.

If you have a child of your own and your new partner's children are allowed to do things your child is not allowed to do, this can cause resentment. These differences in parenting are best sorted out as soon as possible with your new partner. But in many ways, it is no different to them noticing that their friends are allowed to do things they are not permitted to do.

Most importantly, allow your relationship with the stepchild to develop on their terms. If they are old enough, they will be able to tell you what they want, so allow them to do so. In some circumstances, you have to be prepared for them to resent you right from the word go. If this is the case, be patient and understanding. Remember: they are going through a very difficult time and even if they decide they like you, this might be coupled with guilt and feelings of disloyalty towards their biological parent. Indeed, any negative feelings for you may be actively encouraged by the biological parent.

Relationships take time to develop and you have the opportunity to help and guide a child or young person through a difficult time in their life. As you are not one of the biological parents, you can step back and see things from both sides, which should help you to understand any difficulties the child is having. By offering friendship and understanding when it is wanted, you can create a meaningful relationship with your stepchildren.

The step-parent should actively support the child's relationship with the biological mother or father, and appreciate the fact that the children will love the biological parent no matter what they do. As the step-parent, it is not your job to replace the absent parent, simply to provide extra love or care as and when it is needed.

As time goes on and you share life experiences, there will be a levelling of emotions. In the meantime, it can be helpful in the early stages to just accept things as they are without pushing or trying to change or fix relationships.

The Judgement

One day two women sought a ruling from King Solomon.

The first woman said, 'Your Majesty, this woman and I both live in the same house. We both gave birth to a son. My son was fine and healthy. Then while I was sleeping, her son died and she took my son and laid her dead child next to me. In the morning, when I got up to feed my son, I knew he wasn't mine.'

'No! that is not true,' the other woman shouted. 'It was your son who died. My baby is alive!'

'The dead baby is yours,' the first woman yelled.

They continued to argue for some time, until finally King Solomon said, 'Both of you say this live baby is yours. There can be only one answer. I will take my sword and cut the baby in half. That way, each of you can have part of him.'

'Please, Your Majesty, don't kill my son,' screamed the first woman. 'I love him very much. Give him to her. Just don't kill him.'

The second woman shouted, 'Go ahead and cut him in half. That will settle the argument – neither of us will have the baby.'

King Solomon pointed to the first woman and said, 'She is his real mother. Give the baby to her.'

Everyone rejoiced that God gave Solomon the wisdom to judge fairly.

Notes to Self

- My child is a person, not my property.
- I am a parent for life.

- Children learn from a very early age.
- All children are different and should be allowed to excel in different areas.

Take Action

- Listen to your children.
- Learn to give feedback so your children will listen to you.
- If you are involved in a break-up, make your child's well-being your priority.
- Guide your children by example.
- Notice any signs of stress in your children and help them to develop healthy ways to resolve issues, handle life better and cope with stress.
- Encourage your children to take part in activities but don't overcommit them.
- Support and care for your stepchildren without trying to take over.

Chapter Thirteen − Work Stress

*Give your dreams all you've got and you'll be amazed at
the energy that comes out of you.*

William James

Introduction

Work-related stress appears to have taken a back seat in the news as the world tackles bigger issues. However, it remains a big problem both in the UK and in many other countries. It is estimated that employees suffering from stress who remain in work without the support they need cost businesses billions each year. Millions of working days are lost every year owing to mental ill health, with a significant proportion of these attributed to work-related stressed. The cost in staff turnover as a result of stress also runs into billions.

The mental health charity Mind conducted research that highlighted the following:

- 1 in 5 people have claimed to have taken a day off work owing to stress
- 1 in 10 people have resigned from a job owing to stress; 1 in 4 have thought about it
- 19 per cent of staff feel they cannot speak to managers about stress at work
- 25 per cent of people surveyed considered resigning owing to stress
- 56 per cent of employers said they would like to do more to improve staff well-being but don't feel they have the right training or guidance[5]

_5. See <http://www.mind.org.uk/for-business/> [accessed 03.02.14]

Our working life represents a significant proportion of our lives and it is understandable that if we are not happy at work, it can cause us to feel stressed. Indeed, in many organisations stress is accepted as part of the job and people who claim to enjoy the stress are revered. Perhaps if they could see the effects it was having on them outside the workplace they would feel differently ...

It's Tougher Than Ever

In theory, the convenience of working from home, flexible working hours, teleconferencing, etc., mean that working life should be less stressful. Yet lots of working people, and in particular leaders and managers, suffer from anxiety and stress.

Indeed, it is tougher than ever before. Furthermore, with the prospect of having to work longer as retirement looks like a distant dream, it leaves many of us feeling exhausted and overwhelmed.

There are various things that cause stress in the workplace, including:

- working ridiculously long hours
- meeting tight deadlines and targets
- insufficient resources
- too many meetings
- excessive travel
- commuting
- difficult colleagues
- demanding bosses
- managing others

All of the above reasons contribute to massive stress that negatively affects work performance, home life and health. However, the affect these factors have from person to person varies greatly in accordance with their perception, beliefs and values.

Some workers find themselves feeling stressed because they have difficulty saying no. They may even feel that because of their position, salary or personal financial commitments, they have to take on board everything that is thrown at them. In turn, they find themselves saying yes to every request to help another or to take more on, resulting in increased stressed.

When this happens, they tend to react in one of two ways:

1. They push themselves even further, working later while trying to meet new demands.
2. They push the problem onto the shoulders of people working for them, often causing the other person to feel stressed.

Pushing too much work or problems onto others is not the same as delegating, which we will look at later.

☺ The good news is that it is possible to learn how to say no and still be recognised as someone who achieves good results.

When you are asked to take on additional work that you know you will not be able to manage, rather than saying yes or immediately pushing back and saying no, ask questions. Examples of questions to ask include:

- Where you would like me to prioritise this task on my list of jobs to complete?
- Does this task take higher priority than the other ones on my list?
- Doing this will mean X, Y or Z is delayed a week, is that okay?

That way, you are making them aware of your current work commitments and you are allowing your manager the opportunity to re-prioritise or respond.

Questions like this ensure that you are not continuously taking on more than you can handle and pushing yourself harder. It will also ensure you are not constantly pushing back, leading to confrontation. Ensuring that your workload is manageable will reduce the stress you feel. On the other hand, if your line manager insists you take on more than you feel you are able to cope with within the working week and you have advised them of such, you will not have the worry of having to give them a nasty surprise by not meeting deadlines.

We must be free not because we claim freedom, but because we practice it.

William Faulkner

Delegate Correctly

If you hold a managerial or supervisory position, it is essential that you delegate effectively. Some managers and supervisors don't delegate and then complain that they have too much work, an inefficient workforce or insufficient staff. There are many reasons for not delegating, three of the most common being:

1. Lack of trust in the ability or willingness of others to complete tasks to the required standard.
2. Fear that others will become better than them, making their position vulnerable.
3. Insufficient time to train people.

Regardless of how efficient you are, as your career grows, delegating tasks effectively to others who are able to do them as well as, possibly better than you is vital. Delegating allows others to learn and grow. In the beginning, whilst you are unsure of their abilities, ensure you have mechanisms in place for checking their work based on KPIs (Key Performance Indicators – things that performance can be accurately measured by). This is so that you can point out and coach them on any improvements that can be made. As they improve, you will be able to reduce the amount of checking required.

If you delegate effectively you will also have the time to improve and grow your own skills. Therefore, rather than becoming vulnerable, your position will become more secure and your ability to obtain new roles will improve.

If you don't take the time to train people so you can delegate to them, you will never have more time. The amount you can achieve will always be the same. In very simple terms, if your task is to move boxes from one room to another, and you can move 100 boxes per hour, that is all you will ever be able to move.

But if you train two other people to move them as well, even if they are less skilled and can only move 80 boxes per hour, as a team you will still be moving more boxes collectively. Because you are supervising, you may find that you can only actually move 80 boxes, but between you this is still 240 per hour, which is 140 more than you were shifting before.

Delegate and grow

The wider your area of responsibility, the more difficult it will be for you to become an expert at everything within your remit. Delegating allows you to utilise the skills and knowledge of those around you. You might think that delegating will overload team members, but the problem with this thinking is that you might actually be restricting their opportunity for growth. Also, it is rare to hear of someone complaining of feeling overwhelmed if they are carrying out tasks they love.

In my years of managing large teams, I found the best way to delegate was to know my staff. This meant understanding the type of work they enjoyed doing and what their skills were. It was also important to ascertain which team members wanted to be challenged and developed for career advancement. That way, I was able to delegate tasks that they were excited to take on.

It is important that you do not simply push the tasks onto people. Therefore, you need to ensure you are aware of their current workload and can answer the questions about prioritising (given earlier), should they ask you. Better still, tell them how you want the tasks prioritised upfront. If you are unsure if they can manage the additional task with their current workload, ask:

- Can you take on this task and still meet your current commitments?
- How do you think this task is best handled, given your current priorities?
- Can you still meet your other deadlines if you take on this task as well?

In turn, they may delegate some of the tasks to people reporting to them. By training them to ask the same questions, no one in the reporting line should become overloaded and stressed. Eventually, additional work will flow to someone in the business who has no one to delegate to. However, if it is a task they enjoy and is one that makes the most of their skills and talents, they may find ways to improve productivity.

Be prepared to listen to ways your members of staff believe things should be changed in order to achieve more. They will have a different perspective that may allow them to see things you have missed. Also, accept that there is only a finite amount of work they can handle and that additional staff or improvements in technology may be required.

Reduce stress for people reporting to you

Monitoring and measuring both performance and productivity is an important part of running a business. Successful businesses recognise that no matter how great their product is, their success is reliant on the strength and performance of their staff. Fundamental to their performance is their well-being and motivation.

It is well recognised that employees who have a high level of morale and motivation are more productive. There are simple ways to improve the morale of people reporting to you:

- check that their workload matches their skills, abilities and experience
- ensure that they have agreed the deadlines and that the targets are reasonable
- involve them in planning their workload
- ensure that they are given regular reviews and opportunities for career development and learning
- don't save up complaints for review sessions – talk to them about issues as they arise
- wherever possible, create a relaxed atmosphere
- support the working of sensible hours, with regular breaks
- roles and responsibilities should be clearly defined, understood and aligned to business objectives
- people tend to find change stressful, even when it is intended for their benefit – involve them where possible, listen to their views and respond to questions
- empower rather than control or restrict
- give praise and recognition for a job well done
- celebrate success as a team
- always treat employees with respect
- keep the environment suitable for the task required – space, temperature, ergonomics, lighting, etc.

Remember: they are people with personal lives. From time to time they will have difficulties outside work such as financial worries, relationship issues, bereavement, illness, etc. Having policies and training in place to help and support employees through such issues will help them to get back on track much quicker.

Tailor your management style to suit the needs of the individual. One style does not necessarily suit all. You need different personality traits in a highly efficient team and therefore it is logical that these very different personalities need to be managed differently. A good approach is to ask your staff what support they need from you. Develop an atmosphere of trust by regularly asking for feedback. Ask them how they are doing and recognise them as individuals.

Achieving More

If you are stressed about how much you have got to do or if you want to achieve more in less time then time management skills are a vital tool. But before we look at the skills required to manage your time effectively, you need to establish how organised – or disorganised – you are. Perhaps more importantly, you should assess how much time you waste, as this adds to your stress levels.

Take a look at this list of time-wasters and be honest with yourself as to how many of them you are guilty of – and how much time you waste each week because of them. If you are unsure, make yourself a simple timesheet and analyse how you spend your time for a week. It is best to break it down into fifteen-minute segments. Ensure you make a note of when you break off from work to engage in one of the time-wasters. It only takes a few minutes out of your day to complete the sheet and the information it can provide may be invaluable.

Time-wasters

1. Phone calls

Obviously some calls are important. However, some matters can be dealt with more efficiently by a quick email. The main time-waster is prolonging calls. So if you think that everyone keeps you on the phone too long, consider what the common denominator is – you. Because it may just be that the issue is with you, the next time you are on the phone, listen for the clues. Is the person on the other end of the phone saying things like:

- I must go now

- Well, I will speak to you soon
- I will catch up with you again

only to have you carry on talking on the previous subject or even starting another unrelated topic?

How many times do you make a ten-minute phone call when a two-minute email would suffice? I love to talk to people and verbal contact with another human being can provide a sense of connection – one of the emotional needs. But when you have lots of work to do, it can be counterproductive to be picking up the phone for every little thing.

When you are busy, switch your phone over to voicemail until you have finished the task in hand. We live in an instant world and quite often people will expect you to be there to assist them instantly. If they hit a problem, the other person won't know if you are busy and may instantly call you for assistance. Let's be honest – some people won't care if you are busy or not and if you are the type of person who always drops everything to accommodate them, they will come to expect you to do so.

2. Emails

Checking your emails every few minutes is another great time-waster. Unless you are waiting for something urgent, schedule some time twice a day to deal with your incoming mail.

Don't contribute to the tidal wave of emails that flow around most businesses. Copying people in unnecessarily wastes the time of the recipients, who will need to read it to see if it is relevant to them. In addition to this, if you are constantly bombarding them with irrelevant information, they may stop reading your emails thoroughly or may even stop opening them altogether, which could lead to important information being ignored.

3. Not using a planner

Thinking or talking about tasks that are not due yet distracts people from the task in hand as instead they think about things that need to be done tomorrow, next week or even next month, which can be counterproductive. Invest in a planner, either digital or paper-based, put your tasks into it with a start date and deadline then forget about them until they are due to be started.

4. Not completing tasks

Not every task can be finished immediately. There will always be occasions where work needs to be carried over, either because of the sheer volume or because you are waiting for information, reports, etc., from other people. However, it is worth bearing in mind that whenever you go back to a task, there is a certain amount of time wasted as you re-assess where you were up to and then familiarise yourself with the work and what needs to be done. Wherever possible, complete a task in full before moving on to the next one.

5. Instant messaging

Whilst it can be a useful tool, discussions can develop into prolonged chats. Either switch it off completely or at the very least, set your status to busy. If someone insists on interrupting you with matters that aren't work-related, politely but firmly explain that you are too busy to chat during work hours.

6. Open-door policy

We are expected to be approachable in the workplace and open-plan offices are very popular, where there isn't even a door to shut. It is great to be available to people, but the fact is that every time someone comes up to ask you a question it can waste time. The question may only take two minutes to ask and answer, but often the interchange can waste ten minutes or so. It is more efficient if you train people to recognise when you are busy and preferably store up any questions to ask in batches.

Perhaps it is you who is the one constantly interrupting others with questions. Are you responsible for hanging around other people's desks or keeping them on the phone? If so, it is time to change your ways.

Make a note of things you need to ask and save them for an appropriate time. You may find that some questions need to be asked there and then, in which case you won't have a choice. But you should still choose your time carefully and wait until there is an appropriate break. For example, if you can see they are on the phone or typing something, you may need to wait until they have paused from what they are doing. Look for the signs. The same applies to work you have delegated, because the last thing you want is someone being slowed down because they need information.

Follow this simple rule to keep the work flowing:

- only give the information needed – don't waste time going over non-relevant material
- deliver any questions in a precise way
- where possible, offer a solution
- end the conversation quickly once you have the information required

By avoiding the time-wasters you will save both your time and that of your colleagues.

7. Endless meetings

Meetings are an essential part of running a business, but unless they are correctly run, they can be an enormous time waster. Most of us have experienced them at some time or other, where the meeting drags on until you are almost dropping off to sleep, at which point the reason for the meeting appears to have been forgotten.

If you are in any way able to influence what happens in the meeting and how it is run, ensure they are only called if necessary. Once you have determined that a meeting is necessary, issue an agenda in advance, clearly stating the tangible goals of the meeting.

During the meeting, stay focused and keep others on track, following the agenda; you can chat after, if there is time. Ensure the meeting finishes on time. If you have more than one meeting planned for the day, decide in advance what small task you can complete between meetings, so you are not wasting time.

8. Ineffective multitasking

As explained earlier, you are not actually doing two or more tasks at once when so-called multitasking. What you are actually doing is switching your attention from one to the other, effectively wasting time. Stay focused on the task in hand through to completion. This might mean ignoring the 'ping' to tell you emails have arrived and letting your phone go to voicemail for a couple of hours. Most things do not need your immediate attention and ignoring interruptions is a good habit to get in to.

9. Disorganised workspace

Earlier in this guide we covered de-cluttering your home. Your workspace should receive the same treatment. Not only will you feel more relaxed, but you will also be more efficient. Piles of paper on your desk and around your workspace will inevitably lead to wasted time searching for things that could be found in seconds in an organised filing system.

10. Social media

Social media has made it very easy to keep in touch with dozens, indeed hundreds of friends and family members. But if you don't want your work life to encroach on your home life, then you should not expect to be able to do your personal networking during business hours, either. While most employers these days accept that people may want to update their status and check on friends, it is not unreasonable to expect these activities to be kept to lunch breaks. Better still, leave it until you are travelling home if you use public transport, or for when you get home.

11. Surfing the Web

If you are working on a piece of work or project you find boring, it can be very tempting to go online to check out the news, weather or sports results, or to find a bargain. Again, this will lead to time being wasted, which in turn can increase stress when you fall behind. To get yourself through, focus on the end result and how good it will feel to get it out of the way.

12. Cigarette, coffee and moaning breaks

Having a break is essential in order to remain productive, but it is all about balance. Whilst I would advocate stepping away from your computer for five minutes every hour, if you are taking a prolonged break every half-hour or so you will greatly reduce your productivity. And if the breaks are spent moaning or gossiping with negative colleagues, you will find it more difficult to be productive once back at your desk. It will also mean that you are more likely to feel stressed.

Time management techniques

The following strategies may help if you struggle with time management:

1. Plan your week – at the end of your working week, take fifteen minutes to plan for the following week.

2. List all of your objectives for the week. The items on your list will have come from an overall list of things you know you need to do at some point in the future. By adding them to your main list, you can forget about them and then each week, as you plan for the following week, you can decide if it is now time to add it to the to-do list.

3. Categorise tasks according to:

   - most important
   - carried forward (you will not have any of these the first time you perform this task)
   - for completion this week
   - additional tasks if time allows

4. Next, allocate how much time you need to complete each item. Until you become very efficient at estimating the time needed, double it, as it is common to underestimate how long it will take to do things. So if you think it will take an hour, then allocate two hours. If you finish the task quicker, great, move on to the next item.

5. Decide which items can be delegated. Be clear when explaining to the recipient exactly when the item is required for completion. Ensure that they have the knowledge, resources and time to complete the task.

6. Don't put too many things on your list. If you think your week ahead looks too challenging, move some items to the following week.

7. As mentioned earlier, schedule time to attend to emails – either once or twice a day.

8. Allocate an hour a day for urgent unexpected tasks. If nothing unexpected occurs, use the time to work on other items on your list. As you become more efficient at managing your time, the emergencies will happen far less frequently because you will be more on top of things.

9. From an early age, we learn to push ourselves to achieve success. Once our objective is achieved, we immediately move on to the next thing. Barely pausing to acknowledge what has been achieved can lead to feelings of discontentment, self-doubt and stress! So schedule five minutes each day to acknowledge what you have achieved.

The Parato Principle

Most people have heard of the Parato Principle and have some understanding of what it means. However, putting it into place is another matter. Put simply, it means that you will achieve 80 per cent of the results from doing 20 per cent of the tasks. For example, 20 per cent of your sales calls may result in 80 per cent of your sales figure. There are exceptions to every rule, but the Parato Principle holds true for most things. The best way to use this Principle in your workplace to reduce stress is to recognise what tasks you could get away with not doing and still get 80 per cent of the results you desire.

In your diary or planner you may also find it useful to break the tasks down into the following categories:

- activities
- meetings
- remote contact – phone, email, Skype, etc.

This will allow you to assess the type of activities that lie ahead for that day at a glance. At the end of each day, review what you have achieved. Anything you have not managed should be carried over to a column labelled 'carried forward' for the next day.

Simple Tips for Managing Workplace Stress

- avoid drinking excessive amounts of coffee
- don't eat lunch at your desk
- go to the gym on the way home or walk home
- leave work at work – there is nothing you can do until the next day, so thinking about work all evening will only lead to exhaustion and stress
- make stress management techniques a fundamental part of your life; for example, include relaxation techniques and stretching, and practise mindfulness

- de-clutter your workspace
- ensure your seating position is comfortable and your computer screen is positioned strategically, directly in front of you, at eye level

Whatever situation you are facing in your working life, it is essential that you switch off once you leave the workplace. If you are not enjoying the working day, continuing to brood over it when you get home will only make things worse. Use the techniques throughout this guide to unwind and enjoy your free time whenever possible.

The Ass

An ass belonged to an old woman who sold herbs. Though his work was easy, the ass was discontented, believing he had too little food. One day, feeling the need to change his lot, he petitioned Jupiter, saying that he wanted to be given another master.

After warning the ass that he might regret his request, Jupiter decreed it would be so and the ass was sold to a tile-maker.

Before long, the ass was feeling very unhappy. Although he was well fed, he was dissatisfied with the heavy work and so he approached Jupiter to change his master again.

Jupiter warned the ass that this would be the last change but decreed that the ass be sold to the tanner.

Even though his work was now easy and food was plentiful, the ass was still discontented with his lot.

'It would have been better for me to stay with either of the previous masters, for now my present owner will tan my hide and make use of me forever – I will never have rest.'

All our dreams can come true if we have the courage to pursue them.

Walt Disney

Notes to Self

- Managing my time means getting more done in less time.

- I have the power to say no and still be recognised as someone who achieves good results.
- I allow other people to grow and develop.
- As I become more efficient at managing my time, emergencies will happen far less frequently because I will be more on top of things.

Take Action

- Ensure you are delegating correctly.
- Prioritise effectively.
- Ask the right questions.
- Don't take on more than you can realistically handle.
- Take time to train people.
- Utilise other people's skills.
- Recognise and understand other people's needs.
- Make workloads realistic and manageable.
- Become aware of your time-wasters.
- Develop time management techniques and plan effectively.
- Plan ahead.
- Where possible, adopt the Parato Principle.
- Find a way to switch off once you leave the workplace – leave work behind at the office when you go home.

Chapter Fourteen – Study Stress

Opportunity is missed by most people because it is dressed in overalls and looks like work.

Thomas Edison

Introduction

Taking exams or tests is something we all have to do at some point in our lives and for many people it is a period of immense stress. This is because of perceived implications of the results, such as:

- whether or not you are able to move on to the next stage of education
- securing a promotion, career advancement or job
- letting others down; for example: family, a partner, a spouse, teachers, employers, yourself
- how you think you will look to others if you do not achieve your desired or expected results. Will people think you are not good enough or that you have not put in sufficient effort?

Because none of us live in a bubble, in addition to exam stress, often there are other things happening in our lives, adding to pressure. This can make exam pressure seem more intense than we feel able to cope with. However, I know from experience that immersing ourselves in study sessions for a few hours can actually be a distraction from other concerns.

As we have already discussed earlier in this guide, we all have our own unique stress triggers. A situation that is too much for one person to tolerate may be stimulating and exciting to another. When it comes to exams, controlled stress at the right level can work to our advantage, because it can help us to produce our peak performance. Indeed, exams bring out the best in some people and the worst in others.

Keep it in Perspective

Whatever the case, you may find yourself in a situation where you have to sit exams in order to move forward towards your goals or meet the requirements of your employment. If so, bear in mind the following:

- you can only do your best
- you should never compare yourself to others
- having a realistic, thorough study and revision plan will enable you to be well prepared for exams
- depending on your other commitments, you might not be able to do the same amount of study as someone else
- you may not find studying as easy as others
- you might excel better in other areas

Perhaps the most important thing to remember is that what we all strive for is happiness and there is never only one route to happiness. Life has a way of working out. As long as we are:

- enjoying life
- not hurting others
- contributing to the society in which we live
- supporting ourselves and our dependents

then no one has the right to judge our lives. While they may still do so, it is up to us as individuals whether or not we take notice of their opinions. Consider these next three examples:

1. Jane was very stressed about her A-level exams, as she had decided to go to a particular university and become an English teacher. She was panicking as she felt that failure would ruin her future. I pointed out to her that:

   - to become a teacher was not the only way she could be happy in life
   - if she did not achieve the grades she desired there were other universities she could go to where she might also be very happy
   - if she had to re-sit an exam, that would only delay her plans by a year, not destroy them altogether

Don't misunderstand me – I am not suggesting you should not strive for the things you want. But what we often tend to do is get one idea fixed into our heads and become so focused on it that we are oblivious to the alternatives, which might make us equally as happy, if not more so.

In the end she got the results she wanted, went to the university of her choice and achieved a 2:1 in English. She subsequently emigrated to New Zealand immediately afterwards, vowing never to do English again and intending to embark on a career in a totally different direction.

Now whilst I am sure things will turn out very well for her, and that her degree will be of help to her going forward, clearly her desires and aspirations have changed. As you can see in this example, her entire future happiness was therefore not dependent on her becoming an English teacher.

2. Mark was studying biochemistry at university. In addition to being severely dyslexic, he was working full time as a manager of a very busy restaurant. When he took his final exams, his lab work was excellent; however, his written work brought down his final grade significantly, as might be expected with his disability.

   This in no way stood in the way of his career and within three years of leaving university, he was managing a team of lab technicians, all of whom were many years his senior. His employers also recognised how well he had done not only to overcome his learning difficulties, but also to achieve a degree whilst working over forty hours a week in the restaurant.

3. Wayne had wanted to be a sailor from the age of about five and that was all he ever talked about. He planned to see the world, just as his father had before him. Having passed his entrance exams, his family proudly waved him off to training. However, he very quickly discovered that it most definitely was not the life for him.

   Despite being very worried about what people would think, he spoke to his commanding officer, who said he was impressed by the maturity he had shown by admitting that a seafaring life was not for him. His family were completely understanding and welcomed him home – only wanting his happiness. He followed a completely different career path, but never regretted his decision.

Being Organised is Vital

Chaos is very stressful, so the best way to avoid these horrible feelings is to be organised, as this will help you feel more in control. Being organised means you need to have a plan and then stick to it as much as possible. But any plan you make needs to be realistic. It also needs to take into account the fact that you need time to relax and take care of your overall well-being.

Formulating your plan

The first step should be to gather the information you need in order to find out exactly what you have to do and the timescales involved. Once you have these details, you can then begin to formulate a plan. The type of information you will need includes:

- when and where your exams will be held
- what you will be examined on
- a copy of the syllabus
- up-to-date notes
- past exam papers, so you know what to expect
- other resources available to help you study

In order to plan an effective revision timetable you need to:

- compile a list of all the topics you need to cover
- estimate how long you think it will take you to revise each one
- allow extra time for the topics you find most difficult
- add on additional time for flexibility

It is important to remember that you will need breaks, so allow yourself a fifteen-minute break every hour and an hour's break every four hours. It can be tempting to carry on when you are feeling under pressure, but that will sap your concentration. As stated earlier, build in some relaxation time each day and some extra time at least once a week to do something nice, preferably that involves fresh air.

☺ Dad: Why did you get such a low score in that exam?

Son: Absence!

Dad: You were absent on the day of the exam?

Son: No, but the girl who sits next to me was!

Joke

Revision

Revising does not have to be the nightmare it is often envisaged to be. The following will help you to remain calm and focused while revising, which will not only help you avoid feelings of stress, but it will also help you retain more of the information:

1. Start your revision in plenty of time.
2. Identify your best time of day for studying.
3. Where possible, find a comfortable, quiet place to revise.
4. If you are living at home, discuss your revision plan with others at home, to arrange a set time and space where you can work without being disturbed. If this is not feasible, make use of the facilities at school, college or your local library. Likewise, if you are living in halls or shared accommodation at university, where other residents are partying or generally making a noise, take yourself off to the university library.
5. Make a revision timetable that is realistic, flexible and linked to your exam timetable, so you revise subjects in the right order, devoting the most time to the exams that are due first.
6. Balance your revision with other demands on your time, like meals, sleep, other commitments and relaxation.
7. While it may be necessary to cut down your social and sporting activities during exam periods, it is wrong to cut them out altogether. Balancing focused revision periods with periods of relaxation each week is the best option.
8. If you have a problem with concentration, improve it by starting with short bursts of study, adding an extra few minutes to each session.
9. Drink plenty of water to keep you hydrated and have healthy snacks to keep hunger at bay.

10. Have music playing in the background if it helps you to relax and does not distract you – but be honest with yourself about your ability to concentrate while music is playing and what type of music is more conducive to study.

11. If you come to something you don't understand, try reading about it elsewhere. If that doesn't work, then ask someone who knows the subject well.

12. Alternate between methods such as writing notes from textbooks, making mind maps and creating flashcards. This will help to hold your interest and aids absorption of information better.

13. Mix dull subjects with more interesting ones, for the same reason.

14. Take a short break between sessions or if you find things getting on top of you – read a magazine, go for a walk in the fresh air, get some exercise or do anything that gets you away from your desk.

When it comes to revision, there is no perfect formula. There are a wide variety of ways to revise. Explore various methods well in advance to find out what works best for you.

If you find it hard to get started, begin with something easy to get yourself into the flow – starting with something you feel completely unable to grasp will be demotivating. If you are reading notes, skimming over them will result in little or no retention. Actively think about what you are reading then test yourself afterwards. Writing endless notes without any real understanding is probably a waste of time as usually little will be retained. The most effective way to make notes is to reword what you have read. This is because in order to do so it means you have to have a really good understanding of it.

The method I used that always worked really well for me was to reduce the information I was reading into fewer words. This meant I had to think carefully about what I was writing in order to ensure the information was still easy to understand. I would repeat this process several times leading up to the exam, each time reducing the information further. Usually by the day of the exam all I had for each exam was one or two pieces of paper with headings and perhaps four or five words. But by this point the words had become triggers that would allow me to remember all the details relating to the topic.

Often, thinking about your revision before you start can be more stressful than actually doing the work. It can appear totally overwhelming and that is when you may feel the temptation to put it off. This is definitely a mistake. If you find it hard motivating yourself, set yourself measurable goals for each revision session and tick them off when you have reached them. After each session, reward yourself with something nice.

In my opinion, it is very important to complete timed exam questions and papers as part of the revision process. Although it is never the same as the actual exam, it can give you an idea of what the real exam will be like and how best to divide your time between questions.

The Exam Itself

If you have revised sensibly, there will be no need to stay up all night cramming before an exam. Although it is possible to work effectively without sufficient sleep on the odd occasion, eventually it will catch up with you and it is not the best way to work.

If you feel it is necessary to revise in this way, you will ultimately be adding to the stress you are already feeling. So I suggest you regard the night before the exam as the best time to read briefly through your notes and then ensure you get plenty of rest and sleep. The following tips may help:

1. Ensure you are clear about when and where each exam is taking place.
2. Unless you are feeling queasy, have a light meal beforehand, to fuel your mind and body.
3. Ensure you have all the equipment you need, including spares.
4. Set off in plenty of time to reach the examination room.
5. Once in the exam, if you feel you are starting to panic, or your mind is going blank, stop it in its tracks by doing one of the breathing exercises explained earlier or by using your calming anchor, which will help you relax.
6. Read each question three times. It is a common mistake to read the question incorrectly and therefore get the answer wrong.

There are some frequently made blunders that can cost marks, so avoid:

1. Spending too much time on one question or section. If you have two hours to answer four questions, it does not necessarily mean you should spend thirty minutes on each one. Instead, look at how many marks are awarded to each question and allocate time accordingly.
2. Making sweeping statements without supplying evidence to back them up.
3. Giving too much information. It can be very tempting when you really understand a topic to try to show the examiner how much you know by putting everything down. However, this can be a mistake if it is not relevant to the question. Ask yourself what they want to know about this subject and ensure your answer clearly gives that information.

After the exam

Once the exam is over, a new type of stress may begin as you start to go over all of your answers and worry if they were good enough. This stress can be greatly increased by comparing your answers to others.

I remember one particular case in which the young man concerned was very distressed as he was the only person in his study group who had answered a question in a particular way. He was convinced that must mean he had interpreted the case study incorrectly. I do not know if that was the case, but given that he achieved an A*, which was significantly better than all the other members of the group, I think there is a good chance that he was the only one who got it right. He could have given himself weeks of unnecessary worry had he dwelt on the possible mistake.

The best thing to do is:

1. Keep things in perspective.
2. Forget about the last exam and focus on the next one instead.
3. Don't panic – you won't be the only student who is anxious about their answers.
4. Don't compare your answers with those of other students – this can create negative feelings.

5. Don't rush to your textbooks to check your answers. Simply accept that you cannot change anything now – all you can do is move forward.
6. Review your revision plan. Do you need to adjust it?
7. If possible, take the rest of the day off. At the very least, take some time out to relax. Get some fresh air and food before you start to revise again.
8. Refine your exam technique.
9. Think positive. You cannot truly know how you have done, so just wait and see.

Disappointing results

Even if your results are not as desired, bear in mind that we are all unique. We all have different skills and qualities, and achieve at various levels. Exam success does not represent your worth as a person. It is just one aspect of your life, at a particular point in time. You are a whole person, with many aspects to your personality.

Having a contingency plan in case results are not as required can actually relieve some of the stress. For example, perhaps you could re-sit the exam, or consider a different course or university. Maybe there is a less academic career you might also really enjoy doing. If you know what your options are before results day then should the news be bad, you will already know what your next steps are.

Just as there are many routes to happiness, there are also many paths to success. We are not all academic and the world is a wonderful place because we are all so different. Never strive to be someone else, just be a fantastic version of yourself and strive to achieve things because you enjoy doing so.

The Peacock's Complaint to Juno

One day a beautiful but discontented peacock approached the goddess Juno with a complaint. He was greatly aggrieved that when the nightingale sang, everyone rejoiced at his delightful song, yet when he himself sang, people laughed at his poor tune.

The kind goddess consoled him: 'Your beauty is renowned, your plumage exquisite.'

But the peacock persisted: 'What use have I for beauty when another's song surpasses mine by far?'

The goddess merely replied: 'Be content with your lot, assigned by the will of the gods. All must be content with the endowments allotted to them.'

Notes to Self

- There is more than one route to happiness and success.
- I can only do my best.
- Life has a way of working out.
- Revision doesn't have to be a nightmare.
- When it comes to revision, there is no perfect formula – there are lots of different ways to revise.
- Exam success does not represent my worth as a person – it is just one aspect of my life.
- I am a whole person with many aspects to my personality.

Take Action

- Make a revision plan and don't leave revision until the last minute.
- Ensure you are organised and realistic in your expectations.
- Schedule in revision breaks and build in some relaxation time into each day.
- Acknowledge your successes and achievements.
- Alternate between revision methods to build variety into your day.
- If you don't understand something, try researching it elsewhere.
- Mix dull subjects with interesting ones.
- Keep hydrated.
- Condense information.
- Avoid cramming the night before an exam – instead, relax and get a good night's sleep.
- Read the question carefully and not just once.
- Don't spend too long on one question – check how many marks will be awarded for each one and allocate time accordingly.

- Only answer the question – waffle won't add anything. Think about what they really want.
- After the exam, move on – you can't change anything after the event. Instead, focus on the next exam.
- Keep things in perspective.

Chapter Fifteen – Stressless Living

Each morning when I open my eyes I say to myself: I, not events, have the power to make me happy or unhappy today. I can choose which it shall be. Yesterday is dead, tomorrow hasn't arrived yet. I have just one day, today, and I'm going to be happy in it.

Groucho Marx

Introduction

There are events in life that understandably cause periods of unhappiness, like the death of a loved one. But what I am referring to in this chapter is an individual's general underlying level of happiness on a daily basis.

We all strive to find happiness. Unfortunately, for many people there is always something in the way:

- How can I be happy when my love life is a train wreck?
- Work is awful – how can you expect me to be happy?
- It is impossible to be happy when I look like this.
- I'm too busy and stressed to be happy.
- I don't have enough money to be happy.

These are just few of the things that can stand in the way of happiness. But in reality the stress we feel and our happiness is not dependent on what is happening in our lives, or on what we have or don't have in material terms. True happiness comes from our perception of situations, our level of self-esteem and in meeting our emotional needs.

This chapter is designed to help you understand what really makes you happy. It will also provide techniques to help you change the way you feel at any given moment.

Stop Postponing Happiness

Are you postponing happiness? Do you believe that some day, when everything is sorted in your life, you will be magically transformed into a happy, carefree person? Do you think things like: I will be happy when:

- I'm not stressed?
- the mortgage is paid off?
- my husband does more around the house?

There are several problems with this way of thinking:

1. When people who think like this reach their goal or obtain their desire, they usually discover that any happiness or elation they feel only lasts for a very brief time. This is because they instantly look to the next thing they feel they believe will bring them happiness.
2. People miss out on the pleasure they could be feeling right now by only focusing on the future.
3. They are making it harder to achieve their goals or happiness by diverting their energies onto negative things.

One thing that causes a great deal of stress is worrying about possible loss – of a job, home, relationship, etc. Having been in a position myself where I have faced the possibility of losing all of these on more than one occasion, I can understand why your first reaction might be to feel stressed about the prospect of loss. However, the stress related to this comes from two thoughts:

1. That the loss is actually going to occur.
2. Imagined ways in which the prophesied event will make us unhappy.

What we often don't think about is how a much-dreaded event might actually lead to greater happiness in the future if it does occur. There have certainly been several events in my life that although painful at the time, have actually led to greater happiness in the months and years following the event.

No doubt some events do bring only pain and do not lead to a better, happier future. Even so, nothing will be gained by worrying about it for months or even years beforehand. Neither will you be better prepared for it. Given that many things we worry about never occur, all you will have done is stopped yourself from being happy while you could be. The way to do this whilst acknowledging that there are areas you wish to improve is to focus on everything that is good or enjoyable in your life.

A Balanced Life

The phrase 'achieving life balance' is often bandied about, but what does it actually mean? When you have a balanced life it means that many aspects of your life are all fairly evenly balanced and given an appropriate amount of focus. But that doesn't mean that you can devote as many hours to your hobbies as you can to your career or caring for your family.

When life is busy or you are feeling stressed, it is easy for life to get out of balance or sync. While you need to have drive and focus in particular areas of your life if you are going to get things done, taking this too far can lead to frustration and intense stress. A life balance wheel or graph is a great way to enable you to take a look at your life and assess if it is out of balance.

The life balance wheel I like has eight sections, each representing a different area in one's life. I always ask my clients to fill out two wheels. The first is used to score how happy they are with each area of their life, while the second is used to score how much of their focus is devoted to each area. The reason I prefer this approach is because it gives a much clearer picture. It also highlights potential problem areas that may not currently be apparent.

For example, if you score career (work) satisfaction as 9 out of 10 – an almost perfect score – great! However, on the second wheel, if you also score career (work) as 9 out of 10 for focus, this means that most of your focus is also in this area. This can be a problem for several reasons in that people whose work section takes most focus often have issues in other areas such as family, health or socialising, as work leaves little time for anything else.

What this means is that you are neglecting other areas, such as family and health, which could cause problems at a later date in your relationships, in that they may begin to fail if your focus is entirely on career and work. Either that or perhaps because your focus is on your career, worse still you haven't even had time to develop a relationship with anyone. And with regard to your health, not taking care of your body is highly likely to cause issues in later life, both physically and mentally.

If work and career eclipse everything else in your life, you are more likely to suffer from stress should problems arise in that area. This is because you will have made it the most significant area of your life. Likewise, if you should lose your job for any reason, which may not be until you retire, you may find your life feels very empty once you are no longer working, which in itself can cause significant stress.

When some areas of your life are much fuller than others, your life is out of balance. In an ideal world, one might strive to ensure the wheel is completely balanced. This may appear to be unachievable at this stage. Don't be hard on yourself if you score higher in some sections than in others, as this is extremely common and, given time, can be adjusted.

Some things can be fixed Immediately, while others will take longer. All you have to do is to want balance in your life badly enough to take action in order to make changes. I suggest you focus on dealing with the biggest issues first to bring the wheel into a better balance. Once that has been achieved, you can work to improve it further.

> *I know exactly what I want, everything: calm, peace, tranquillity, freedom, fun, happiness. If I could make all that one word, I would – a many-syllabled word.*
>
> *Johnny Depp*

The eight sections of a balanced life

1. career, work, profession, studies
2. money, income, investments, retirement funds, savings, financial security
3. recreation, play, creativity, fun, hobbies
4. personal growth
5. health, fitness and appearance
6. relationships – family, friends
7. romantic relationships, love
8. spirituality and/or contribution to others

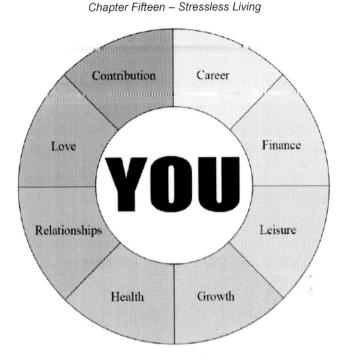

The life areas I have listed are the ones I feel are important for a balanced life. It is these areas that have been highly effective in enabling my clients to assess and improve their life satisfaction.

How balanced is your life?

Not having a balanced life can lead to significant stress, so it is important that you begin to balance your life at the earliest opportunity.

The following exercise will help you assess what areas you need to focus more on. It will also show you what parts of your life are failing to bring you joy or are causing you unhappiness and/or stress:

1. Rank your satisfaction with each section of your life from 1 to 10 – 1 being the least satisfactory and 10 giving the most satisfaction.
2. What stands out to you as you see these different rankings?
3. Now rank them again, to see which areas are getting most of your focus.

4. Which areas are you most motivated to work on that would make you feel more complete, fulfilled, satisfied and happy?

5. Next, focus on the areas that score lowest on your satisfaction scale and write down the three things that would significantly improve your score in that area. I suggest you do this for all areas scoring below 5.

6. Review the areas that are taking most of your focus and list three changes you can make that will reduce the amount of time or focus you give to that area, whilst allowing you to maintain your commitments, if necessary.

For example, if your score for section five 'health, fitness and appearance' is 2 – meaning you are unhappy with it – first you have to be clear what it is about your health, fitness and appearance that resulted in your score. Then you need to decide to take action, for example:

- having a complete change of hairstyle
- joining a gym
- changing your wardrobe

If you score 9 for your focus on section one 'career, work, profession, studies', you may acknowledge that this is because in addition to the hours you work, you never switch off and frequently bring work home. In which case you could commit to reducing your focus on work by:

- using time management tools
- delegating
- applying the 80/20 rule
- learning to switch off using the relaxation techniques in this guide

Don't expect miracles overnight – achieving a balanced life should be an ongoing process and one you should never stop working on. It is essential to recognise that what is important to you in life now will change over time.

Both you and your values will also change. You therefore need to revisit your wheel periodically or whenever there is a significant change in your life.

Recognising Your Values

Most of us live life in accordance with our own values, even though we may not even be consciously aware of what they are. But often we are intolerant of other people's values. In fact, usually we expect those around us to live their lives in accordance with our own values. This can be a major cause of stress when we become angry if people break our rules. Also, our values can be a source of stress if they are adversely affecting our thinking.

The following exercise will help you to recognise what your values are:

1. Begin by listing your values in each area of your life; these are the same areas necessary for life balance, which we have just covered.

2. Taking each one in turn, work out what is important to you in relation to that area of your life. For example, in relation to your work or career, the things that matter most to you (your values) might be:

   - recognition
   - money
   - excitement
   - autonomy
   - power
   - being part of a team
   - winning
   - helping others
   - fame
   - respect
   - honesty
   - integrity
   - freedom
   - appropriate working hours

   Your list may contain completely different values to the ones listed here and that is fine – they are your values and we all live to our own rulebook.

3. Now rate them in order of importance. This will help you identify what is most important to you about your career (work) or whichever area of your life it is that you are looking at. If your current occupation is failing to meet your most important values, this will almost certainly cause you a significant amount of stress.

4. The next step in reducing stress in this area is to understand and accept that others within your work environment or family unit will have their own set of possibly very different values in relation to this particular aspect of life. Therefore, their attitudes and actions will reflect this. So next time you are irritated by someone's attitude, stop and consider what their values might be in relation to the situation. They are not out to annoy you or make your life unpleasant. They are just living to their own rulebook. Not taking things personally will help you to reduce the stress you feel in situations where there is a clash in values.

It's Not Fair

None of us are born equal either physically or socially and like it or not, life is not fair. No matter how much you moan about it, there is nothing you can do about it, so you may as well get on with it and enjoy the things you do have. That might seem like strange advice for a self-help book, but the reality is that life is too short to waste time and effort focusing on things we cannot change.

Instead of comparing yourself to people who you believe have more than you or a better life than you, learn to be genuinely pleased for them and enjoy what you have.

Blame Culture

If life doesn't meet your expectations, blame someone else – sometimes I feel that this way of thinking is becoming an epidemic.

Parents make an easy target. Don't misunderstand me – I truly believe that our childhood experiences can have a profound and long-lasting effect on the personality traits we develop. While there is no doubt that some parents are to a great extent responsible for their children growing up poorly equipped for adult life, that is not to say that these parents have necessarily been cruel or neglectful. In many cases, they have simply parented their children to the best of their ability, often repeating the mistakes made by their own parents.

As a responsible adult it is important to become self-aware and to strive to change any aspects of your personality or beliefs that are no longer helpful to you. You then need to choose to release your parents from any blame you have previously attributed to them for where you are – or aren't – in life.

It is empowering to accept that you are responsible for your own future. So rid yourself of any tendency to blame others or your past for where you are right now. Remember, you do have choices and even not making the decision to make changes in your life is still a choice to maintain the status quo.

Learn to Laugh at Yourself

Seeing the funny side of a situation can help relieve stress. If you have high self-esteem and value yourself as a person, you will find it easier to laugh things off. You will recognise that as a human being you will make mistakes.

☺ Whilst remembering to learn from them, of course.

Stressed people, on the other hand, tend to take everything they do and themselves too seriously. So the next time you do something silly, laugh about it. Every time you laugh you stimulate the release of chemicals that enhance your well-being. If you really can't even begin to laugh at things try this:

1. Turn the event into a movie in your mind.
2. Speed it up so that it looks silly.
3. Add some music like they use in old silent movies.
4. Exaggerate the circumstances so it becomes ridiculous; for example, if you put up a shelf and it falls down, exaggerate it in your movie so that not only does the shelf fall down, but also all the walls of the house like in a cartoon.

Notice How Experiences Affect You

Many people who are stressed become extremely proficient at noticing negative experiences and ignoring positive ones. For the next week I would like you to notice both your positive and your negative experiences. For example, each day make a note of:

- what the experience was
- how you felt, i.e. whether it was a negative or a positive experience
- the thoughts resulting from the experience

The following table may help you:

Monday:

Experience	Type	Thoughts	Emotions	Physical Effects
Missed the train to work	Negative	Typical – now I'll be late	Stressed	Shoulders and chest feel tight
Brother got a new sports car	Negative	Why can't I have a new car?	Envy, fed up	Shoulders and chest feel tight
Got cut up in traffic	Negative	What a dickhead!	Anger	Hands clenched on the steering wheel
Daughter gave me a hug	Positive	She's so cute	Love, happiness	Smiling, feel relaxed and happy

Once you have a good idea of what type of situations you are allowing to affect you negatively, that in turn are causing you to feel stressed, decide to take positive action so you can actively avoid or change particular situations. Alternatively, if it is a situation that cannot be avoided or changed, resolve to use the techniques you have learnt throughout this guide to change the way you feel about and react to the situation.

When the Waters Were Changed

Once upon a time a great god called upon mankind with a warning that all the water in the world would disappear in two weeks, to be renewed with different water, which would drive men mad.

Only one man heeded the warning. He collected water in every vessel he could find and took it up into the hills, where he stored it and waited for the water to change. As the god had warned, all the water disappeared, so the man remained in his cave drinking his preserved water.

When he saw the waterfalls beginning to flow again, the man descended from his cave and walked among the people. He found that they were thinking and speaking in an entirely different way from before, yet they had no memory or recollection of what had happened. When he tried to talk to them, he realised that they thought *he* was the one who was mad and they showed hostility towards him rather than compassion or understanding.

He was dismayed and went back to the hills. Finally, because he could no longer bear the isolation of living alone, behaving and thinking in a different way from everyone else, he drank the new water and became like the rest. He became known as the madman who had regained his sanity.

Notes to Self

- I am responsible for my own happiness.
- I can achieve a balanced life.
- Life is not fair – and that is fine.

Action Steps

- Learn to laugh at yourself.
- Assess how balanced your life is.
- Recognise your values.
- Notice how experiences affect you.

Chapter Sixteen − Better Ways to Live

Worry never robs tomorrow of its sorrow, it only saps today of its joy.

Leo Buscaglia

Introduction

I don't think I will ever be the kind of person who just drifts through life without a care in the world, but I have certainly come a long way. While I still prefer to have a good deal of certainty in my life, I can now handle uncertainty with more ease and I get less stressed when I don't know what is going to happen in the future. I think one of the biggest changes I have made to my life is that I take care of my inner self as well as my physical well-being. In this chapter we are going to explore the best ways to nurture the inner you every day.

Meeting Your Own Needs

Often, we find ourselves looking to others to make us happy, but meeting our own emotional needs is a much surer route to genuine happiness.

1. Certainty

We all need to know that some things are unlikely to change and one of our biggest fears is that of the unknown. But the world is constantly changing − the key is to develop skills to handle any changes and challenges easily.

Fear of death or illness can occur even if you do not have any particular reason to believe your life and health are threatened. If you are experiencing a pause (a period where nothing significant is happening) in your life, your mind can turn to concerns about mortality. This is because what happens after death is uncertain and therefore to some people is to be feared.

It is not always death that we fear. I am sure you have heard the expression: things are going too well; something is bound to go wrong. Sadly, this is part of the culture in which we live, in that people are always ready to expect the worst.

This type of reaction is not uncommon, although incredibly irrational. It comes from the need for certainty and the fear of the unknown. It also comes from a fear of not being able to cope with what we imagine might happen.

People are capable of imagining things will be much worse than they usually are. If negative events occur, they are generally able to apply past experiences to the situation that will help them deal with it. But there is always a first time for everything and this is when it is the most stressful, owing to the element of uncertainty.

Even if the change is positive, like getting married or moving to a new home or job, we may still experience elements of fear as we make fundamental changes to our lifestyle. This is because the consequences of that change are as yet unknown.

2. Variety

How much variety or uncertainty people need depends on many personality factors, such as whether they are an extrovert or an introvert, for instance. Everything becomes boring eventually, especially if there is no variety. Boredom can make us feel discontented and unhappy, which in turn can make us feel stressed.

Become aware of how much variety you need and build some into your day. It does not have to be something dramatic or adventurous, just different from your usual routine.

You probably know people who complain about stress at work and constant pressure caused by changes in the workplace. But then when they reach a situation where it is business as usual and things settle down, they become bored and want to move on. In effect, they are constantly putting themselves in stressful situations.

If this is the case for you, the next time you become bored with work, instead of instantly thinking what next, consider how you can put more of your focus and energies into another area of your life.

3. Significance

Although it varies greatly as to how important significance is to each individual, we all want to feel that we matter. Often we seek recognition from others and many strive to be famous to meet this need. But any feeling of significance that is based purely on what others think is very fragile. Real significance comes from inside you, from knowing that you are good enough and that you are a worthwhile person. Success, wealth and adulation do not matter if inside you feel like you are a failure.

4. Connection with others

Human beings are not solitary animals. We need positive interaction and a sense of connection with others in order to thrive. Loneliness is not necessarily about being alone. It is about the *perception* of being alone and isolated that matters most. For example, a student moving away from home for the first time can feel isolated despite being surrounded by their peers. And some of the loneliest people I know are married.

5. Contribution

Doing things for others without the expectation of something in return is a great feeling and is something that can greatly enhance life. Take care not to cause yourself additional stress by overloading yourself even further by taking on too much.

6. Growth

In order to feel fulfilled we need to feel that we are growing or improving. Growth means stretching yourself and doing more than you are sure you are capable of. This doesn't mean constantly pushing yourself to the limit, which will ultimately just cause you a great deal of stress. The list of ways in which you can grow is endless, including things like:

- learning to play the guitar
- going on a date
- studying a language

- getting fitter
- speaking up in a meeting and expressing your views or ideas

The added bonus is that every time you learn something new or do more than you believed possible, you are expanding your comfort zone. This means you will feel comfortable more of the time and less stressed as a result.

To stretch yourself without causing stress, do one small thing every day that makes you feel slightly uncomfortable. Then acknowledge and celebrate your achievement, even if it is only in a small way.

If you are not sure if you are meeting each of your needs effectively, ask yourself the following:

- How am I meeting each of these needs currently?
- Is the way in which I do so good for me, those close to me and society in general?
- Are there any better ways can I meet my needs in future?

Then plan how you can make changes to ensure all your needs are met in the best way possible. It is even better if you are able to meet more than one need or even all of them in one action. For example, if you do a sponsored run with a group of friends for charity:

- the fact you know how to run provides *certainty*
- *variety* and *growth* are achieved from never having run that far before
- when donating money to charity it is a form of *contribution*
- you are *connecting* with others at the event
- you will achieve *significance* because you know you will have made a difference

Physiology

When you are feeling stressed, even the smallest thing can have you throwing your arms in the air, tutting and punctuating every sentence with an exclamation mark! This is because a stressed state means you are on red alert for problems, which will almost certainly make everything seem worse.

When we are feeling stressed or down it is generally easy to spot from our body language and the tone of our voice. For example, if you speak to someone close to you on the phone it is often possible to tell how they are feeling just by the way they say hello. But did you know that your physiology can affect the way you feel – your emotional state?

If you spend long periods with your shoulders hunched and your fists clenched you will start to feel tense and stressed. Likewise, if you lower your shoulders and release the tension you will feel more relaxed. Smiling can actually make you feel happier – give it a try.

> ☺ Everyone looks better when they smile and people naturally respond and smile back – so give it a go … you will experience your day completely differently.

Many people who are feeling stressed don't even realise that they are holding their stress in their posture. The next few exercises will help you to release the tension from your body.

Snap Out of Your Current Mood

We can't make our problems disappear instantly. However, sometimes simply stopping our current train of thought and shaking ourselves out of our current mood can stop emotions spiralling out of control and our stress levels soaring.

The next time you notice tension in your muscles:

1. Sit up straight and notice the good things around you.
2. Stretch, take several deep breaths and fill yourself with energy.
3. Shake it out and re-energise yourself.
4. Stand and walk around for a couple of minutes.
5. Sing or hum a happy song that makes you feel glad to be alive.

Happy posture exercise

1. Sit up straight and hold your head up high.
2. Focus on your breathing.
3. Take a deep breath and hold it for a count of ten.

4. While counting to ten again, release the breath slowly.

5. Recall all the things in your life that make you happy – from your gratitude list compiled earlier.

6. If you are focused on your happy thoughts, notice how this is affecting your physiology.

7. Allow your gratitude and happiness to be reflected in your smile.

8. Next, allow the good feelings to spread to the other muscles in your face, allowing them to relax.

9. Now let your shoulders relax.

10. Continue in this way as you allow all the feelings of happiness and gratitude to move throughout your body, relaxing all parts of your body to the ends of your fingers and toes.

11. Enjoy how good it feels to be relaxed and happy.

12. Did you feel a change in the way you felt? If not, don't worry. Keep practicing, as you can become an expert at changing your mood no matter what is happening in your life at the time.

Be More Flexible

If you put enough strain on something that is rigid and inflexible, often it will break. By becoming more flexible in your thoughts and plans you will reduce unnecessary stress and may even find that you are more productive and creative. As a result, you might actually achieve more than if you were desperately trying to stick rigidly to your plans.

My natural tendency is to be a perfectionist, but thankfully I have realised that absolute perfection is not always required to achieve the results I want. This means I am far less stressed and I focus on the good things rather than on any slight imperfections.

Another great lesson I have learned is that plans will and do change unexpectedly. Things will go wrong from time to time and deadlines may have to be moved.

☺ Does that make you cringe even thinking about it?

Of course I understand that some things have to happen by a certain time or date and these things should be given priority. But other self-imposed deadlines with no consequences can be moved to ease some of the pressure on yourself.

Tips to becoming more flexible

1. Be realistic and accept that some plans have to change – that way you will be less irritated when they do.

2. If you are faced with changes to your plans or a deadline is placing you under pressure, review your beliefs about the situation with questions like:

   - Is my deadline really important?
   - Are there consequences if it is not met?
   - What is really important about this situation?
   - Are there ways I can change my plans and still achieve my desired outcome?
   - Can these new circumstances lead to an even better result if I am flexible?
   - In what way can I change my desired outcome and still be happy?

The constant battle to achieve everything within tight deadlines can be extremely stressful, without adding self-imposed ones when things could wait a little longer. I am not suggesting that you always leave everything until another time, or that you give up on the things you want to achieve or desire. Just be realistic about the urgency and focus on what is really important. Remember: most of the details we worry about do not really contribute to our overall happiness should they go right.

Big or Important Events

If you have a big or important event to plan it is particularly easy to feel like the whole day/event will be ruined unless everything is perfect. But this rarely is the case and this kind of thinking will send your stress levels through the roof.

But it is fair to say that organising a big event will add more things to your to-do list and can greatly increase the pressure you already feel. Worrying about tasks you haven't completed will also affect your ability to sleep well, in turn reducing how much you achieve the next day, raising stress levels even further. So what can be done about it?

I find the most efficient way to get things done is very simple:

1. Make a written list of everything you think you need to do – trying to retain the list in your head is counterproductive and will lead to mistakes.

2. Prioritise the items in order of importance.

3. Divide the list into:

   • essential
   • important
   • if time allows
   • not necessary

This will help you to see how many items don't really need to be done at all, in which case you can simply cross them off.

☺ You might find this difficult at first, because you would not have put them on the list if they did not need doing – or would you?

The best way to check this is to ask yourself:

• What will happen if this task never gets done?
• Is there another way to achieve the result I want without doing it?

Then look at the normal everyday tasks you have to do:

• Are there any of them that can be left until after the event?
• Can I delegate any of them to someone else?

Take another look at the list:

1. Highlight five or six really important things on your task list that are key to the event's success. In other words, if they go well it will mean you have a great day, even if other things go wrong; this is so that these can be given your focus if time is short.

2. Give yourself time to make decisions calmly and to get the tasks done.

3. Delegate tasks where appropriate.

4. Take as much pressure off yourself as you can; for example, by chopping online for presents or food. This can have double benefits in that it is easy and a lot quicker; it also means you won't waste money on useless impulse buys.

5. Take some time out – regardless of how busy you are, you will perform better if you recharge your batteries.

6. Do whatever it takes so that you can feel relaxed and look forward to the event.

7. Think about what you really want from the day or event and imagine laughing and enjoying yourself.

8. Make sure that all your jobs, or as many as possible, are completed a couple of days beforehand so that you can unwind.

9. Better still, go for a game of golf, book yourself a massage or pamper yourself at home.

10. Accept that events are rarely perfect. Instead, make it as good as you can and enjoy it, no matter what small things go wrong.

11. Keep expenditure under control by remembering that it is rarely the expensive extras that make events special. The most important thing that tends to remain in our hearts and memories is the laughter and emotions.

12. Focus on enjoying yourself rather than the actual details of the event.

13. Savour the experience of being with people you like or care for.

14. Large events can mean being around people you are not so keen on. Be polite and do not allow their opinions or comments to affect you. Only you can control the effect they have on you or your enjoyment.

Unhealthy Vehicles for Relieving Stress

Sometimes people unconsciously turn to unhealthy ways for dealing with stress. If these vehicles bring relief, it is easy to develop a sense of dependence on them as they become a habit. Unhealthy ways for dealing with stress include:

1. Caffeine dependence

Enjoying an occasional coffee is not going to do you any harm, but remember – it is a drug and using caffeine to boost your energy in the long term is not a good idea.

2. Smoking a cigarette

Millions of people instinctively reach for nicotine during times of stress. Unfortunately, cigarettes can come at great cost, both financially and health wise.

3. Drinking to excess

A glass of wine can be a good way to unwind at the end of the day. However, excessive drinking can cause problems in virtually every area of a person's life.

4. Spending to excess

Buying yourself a nice treat once in a while can be a pleasant pick-you-up. However, compulsive shopping to relieve stress or to enable you to feel good about yourself can result in financial stress. This can ultimately lead to feelings of discontentment and even shame if you become surrounded by things you do not need.

Any pleasure or reduction in stress achieved by shopping will be short-lived. All too soon the need to buy something else in order to achieve the same feeling – otherwise known as retail therapy – will surface. As with any addiction, it leads to greater unhappiness.

5. Emotional eating

This has been covered in the chapter on diet and exercise. However, it is worth stating again that frequently eating the wrong things can become a coping mechanism for stress. Like smoking, it can ultimately lead to health, self-esteem and even financial problems that will cause more stress.

If you think you have developed any of these unhealthy ways of combating stress, refer back to the section on methods to nurture your emotional needs earlier in this chapter. Gradually replace bad behaviours with more fulfilling ways to meet your emotional needs, until you have eliminated unwanted habits altogether.

Moving Forward

Be clear about what you want and enjoy the journey in order to live with less stress in your life. Make a conscious decision to decide what is important to you and where you want to be in a month, a year, three years or five years from now. If the answer does not come easily to you, asking the following questions should help you identify what is most important to you:

1. If it was the end of the world and you could only make three calls, who would they be to and what would you say? Why would you choose these people?

2. If you were financially free and rich, how would you want to spend the next twenty years? What would you do? Consider this fully, because it is easy to think that you would travel, give up work or go shopping. But if you are thinking about doing these things for the next twenty years, would these activities truly fulfil your inner needs in the long term? Consider what really matters to you and makes you happy.

3. When you are old, what will you regret not having spent enough time doing?

4. If you were granted another life, who or what would you choose to be?

5. What do you want people to say about you and remember you for at the end of your life?

6. Next, resolve to make living life in a new way your priority. Be confident in the knowledge that when you successfully learn to manage your stress levels by using the methods in this guide, you will also have improved many other areas of your life.

7. Consider writing a journal, into which you make a note of your progress each day, in addition to all the things you feel genuine gratitude or appreciation for.

As with any goal it is important to take action. Commit to doing at least one thing every day to move you towards your goals that embraces your new way of living and thinking. More on this in the next chapter.

Understanding what you want from life is all part of being more self-aware and recognising what makes you truly happy. That way, you are less likely to waste energy and raise stress levels by striving for things that do not fulfil your desires or meet your inner needs.

Alice Meets the Cheshire Cat

The cat only grinned when it saw Alice. It looked good-natured, she thought, but still it had claws and a great many teeth, so she felt it ought to be treated with respect.

'Cheshire Puss,' she began rather timidly, as she did not know at all if it would like the name; however, it only grinned a little wider. Good, it is pleased so far, thought Alice and she continued: 'Would you tell me, please, which way I ought to go from here?!'

'That depends a good deal on where you want to get,' said the cat.

'I don't much care where –' said Alice.

'Then it doesn't matter which way you go,' said the cat.

'– so long as I get somewhere,' Alice added by way of explanation.

'Oh! you're sure to do that,' said the cat. 'If only you walk long enough.'

Alice in Wonderland, Lewis Carol, 1865

Notes to Self

- Meeting my inner needs will help me feel happier and less stressed.
- I accept that plans have to change.
- I am clear about what I want in life and am enjoying the journey.

Take Action

- Review how you are currently meeting your inner needs.
- Make a plan for meeting your inner needs in healthy and appropriate ways.
- Release the tension from your body.
- Learn to be more flexible.
- Let things wait and remove imaginary deadlines.
- Plan for big or important events.
- Remove unhealthy vehicles for relieving stress.
- Decide where you want to be in the future and what you want from it.

Chapter Seventeen – Success without Stress

Shoot for the moon. Even if you miss, you'll land among the stars.

Les Brown

Introduction

I f you have just carried out the exercises in the last chapter you will have a much clearer idea about what makes you happy and how you are meeting or failing to meet your emotional needs. But having an idea of what we want is just the beginning. In order to achieve things, we need to be *really* clear about what we want.

Thinking about what you want in detail is not another task to become stressed about. It should be something pleasant and enjoyable that you do whilst taking a few minutes to unwind, at which point you can allow your thoughts to formulate in detail. In effect what you are doing at this stage is creating a wonderful daydream.

You definitely need to devote time to this. It is not your weekly grocery list we are talking about – it is your future! If you are happy just drifting along then that is great, but as you are reading this book and suffering from stress, then I guess that is not the case.

Benefits and Dangers of Goals

I believe that having goals to improve every area of your life can actually help reduce stress, because it provides a sense of purpose and a distraction for your unconscious mind. However, the desire to improve one's life can for some people become a source of stress, which is definitely not the desired outcome. It is therefore important that you do not:

- set yourself a goal and continuously focus on the fact that you have not yet achieved it

- focus on any setbacks or imperfections along the way

Instead:

- focus on and appreciate the good things you already have in your life
- continually take steps that you enjoy that will lead to your goal; you may have to do some things that are not so pleasant along the way, but try to include as many enjoyable ones as possible
- change your goal if your circumstances or desires change

Natural High

When you are working towards a goal, your brain releases dopamine – the motivation chemical – which increases your ability to focus and motivates you to take action. As you near your goal the levels of dopamine in your bloodstream increase, especially if the goal is one that will meet one of your emotional needs.

When you achieve goals, no matter how small, your brain releases serotonin – the feel-good chemical – which calms and soothes you. Basically, these two chemicals are your drivers, with high levels of dopamine driving you forward and high levels of serotonin providing feelings of satisfaction, safety and comfort.

Setting Goals

Setting a goal and not achieving it can increase feelings of stress and lead to lower self-esteem. In my experience, the reason this happens is because most people don't understand how to set and achieve goals.

For goals to be effective you need to know exactly what you want, why you want it and when you want it. It is not necessary to know how you are going to achieve it. Like any long journey, you get there one step at a time, even if you cannot see the final destination yet. You also need to be prepared to alter your route if you hit roadblocks along the way or if you change your mind.

Setting a goal that is purely based on an end result such as a financial goal that requires you to work continuously doing something you do not enjoy will be very difficult to achieve.

☺ Enjoying what you are doing is essential for getting you through the inevitable tough times and setbacks, so wherever possible set goals that involve doing what you love.

If we set a really powerful goal that is congruent with our beliefs and values, working towards achieving it will be easier than we might think. When we work towards something with absolute conviction, total focus and single-mindedness of purpose, it is possible to become so absorbed in our tasks, to the point that we are oblivious to our immediate environment. In fact, nothing else matters at that exact moment because we have switched off from our environment. This means that we perform without taxing ourselves mentally, physically or psychologically. It is where inspiration and solutions to problems come to us with surprising ease, which means we are in sync with ourselves. In other words, all of our parts are working together, like one perfect unit or a well-oiled machine.

Having faith in your ability to reach your goal, being prepared to trust your instincts and allowing some things to take care of themselves are fundamental to success. However, there are techniques available to make achieving goals easier and less stressful, which we will cover now.

Positive goals

The unconscious mind is constantly working to deliver the things we think about most, because it assumes they are things we desire. Therefore, we must think about what we want, *not* what we don't want.

☺ Don't think about a blue tree.

You did, didn't you?

The fact is you cannot not think about it once the idea is there. You do so automatically. It is impossible not to, even if it is only for a second. What happens is that you have to think about it before you reach a point where you decide that you cannot or shouldn't do so. Consider the following examples of positive and negative thinking:

Wrong:

- I don't want to be fat

- I don't want to be late for work again
- I don't want to be stressed

Correct:

- I want to be slim
- I want to be on time for work every day
- I want to be calm and relaxed

When setting your goals, ensure they are stated in the positive. For example: I have achieved financial independence.

Clarity

Goals need to be really clear. For example, if you set yourself a goal of reducing stress in your life, obviously that is a great goal. But it would be far more powerful if you give it detail:

> It is September of the year 20XX and I am preparing to go on a 5-mile walk. I now feel less stressed. I no longer have stress headaches and I am generally in good health. I am managing my time better and now have one evening a week just for me ...

More and more detail could be added to this, but I think you will have got the general idea. It is well worth investing some time in ensuring you have sufficient detail in your goals.

Being wealthy is a common goal, but what does that really mean? Wealth has a very different meaning to each of us, so if increased wealth is your goal, you need to be far more specific.

For example, do you want to be financially free? How much money will you have in the bank? Keep asking yourself questions like these until you are clear what financial position you are aiming to achieve.

Congruency

One of the pitfalls of setting goals is that we can become very focused on one thing or aspect of our lives. The danger is that we become so overwhelmed with desire for it that we forget about considering certain aspects. For example, would being rich be so great if we did not have our friends and family?

A good example of a goal would be:

> I am fifty, retired, fit, healthy and financially secure. I have both the time and the money to enjoy my retirement with my wife, family and friends.

> ☺ Of course more detail would be better, but this is just to get you thinking the right way.

When you are completely happy with your goal, consider sharing it with your significant other to check if it fits in with their goals. If you intend your futures to be together, you will avoid a great deal of stress that might arise from conflicted goals.

Measurability

It is easy to gauge success if your goal is to:

- make a particular amount of money
- lose a certain amount of weight
- pay off your mortgage
- secure a particular job

This is because goals such as these are very measurable. But often the things that matter most to people are far more intangible. Yet, they can still be measured – however, it is important to know *how* success will be measured. When setting a goal of having a balanced life, thereby reducing stress, you need to decide what your measures will be. For instance:

- What hobbies will you enjoy?
- How much free time will you have?
- How will your free time be spent?

Many people set goals around having better relationships. If this is something you desire, you need to know how that improved relationship would be and how it would feel. This is because if you don't know how you are measuring something, how will you know if you have achieved it?

An example of a good goal:

> It is December of the year 20XX. I have a much better relationship with my sister, where we both contact each other

once a week and we meet to go out shopping or for lunch once a month. We have really enjoyable times together and spend most of our time laughing. We have resolved our past differences and both agree that it was no one's fault – we love each other greatly.

Set a Deadline

The future is just that – always in the future. This is why it is essential that you date your goal and state it in the now. For example, if you are setting a goal in March of the year 20XX to learn to meditate within six months, your goal should state:

It is September of the year 20XX. I am now meditating for fifteen minutes twice a day and find it incredibly enriching. After my sessions I find my days are more productive and enjoyable …

Believe it is Achievable

People around you will judge your goals based on their own limiting beliefs. But who is to say whether or not your goals are achievable? People who live in fear will tell you to be realistic about your goals. This is because their own past experiences and disappointments have caused them to have negative beliefs. Remember: individuals who achieve great things are rarely realistic in their expectations by the standards of most people.

I don't believe anyone should be held back by their own beliefs or by anyone else's beliefs in their abilities, for that matter. Achieving your goals will be more difficult if *you* believe that life is meant to be difficult or that you do not deserve happiness. If this is the case, refer back to the section earlier on limiting beliefs in Chapter Two.

I also don't think success always has to mean a struggle and hard work, but you definitely have to be prepared to take action! And that can be easier said than done. Goals therefore have to be big enough to motivate you to take action and to keep you focused when other things might distract you from achieving them.

Perhaps the most important thing about your goals is that you believe they are achievable. If the goal you have thought of appears too big or too far away and out of reach, it will be difficult to stay motivated. You can overcome this by setting yourself smaller goals that you can achieve along the way to your bigger dream. Working on your limiting beliefs about yourself will also help. For example, if you set a goal to exercise for an hour five times a week, your interim goal could be twenty minutes three times a week.

Achieving goals

Successful people have several things in common. First, they set highly motivating goals and secondly, they tend to follow similar methods in order to achieve them:

1. Write it down

Goals that are written down in black-and-white are far more powerful. This is because a goal that is not written down is just a dream. A dream is very different to a goal:

Dream – something that you would like to happen one day, although you have no idea how it could happen and are not intending to take action to make it happen.

Goal – something you want and are prepared to take action to achieve.

If you have followed the strategy explained earlier in this chapter, you will have set a powerful goal. Remember to write it down.

2. Read it every day

Reading your main goal every day will reinforce it in your unconscious mind. It will also allow you the opportunity to tweak it if what you want changes over time.

3. Take action

a) Write out a master list of tasks, containing everything you think you will have to do in order to achieve your goal.

b) If you think of additional things at a later date, simply add them to the list.

c) From that list, make another list of tasks that you are aiming to achieve in the next month.

d) Next, make a list of weekly tasks.

e) Every evening, make a list of things to do the following day.

By making your list each evening, you are giving your unconscious mind the opportunity to come up with simple creative and imaginative ways to complete your tasks, which your conscious mind might otherwise never come up with.

Visualise the Outcome

Like it or not, it has been proven that our brains cannot tell the difference between something we actually experience and something we imagine vividly. You will therefore greatly improve your chances of managing stress really well by spending time visualising yourself as a relaxed, easy-going person. Mentally going over possible situations that may arise and imagining your strategies for dealing with them can help you become more confident of your success. Note: this is not the same as agonising over things going wrong. The purpose is to acknowledge and take comfort from your ability to manage situations and make positive changes in your life.

Studies on the effects of visualisation in various sports carried out by top universities clearly show that utilising the mind–body connection can significantly improve an athlete's skills.

Vision boards are a useful aid when it comes to visualising, particularly if you find this sort of thing difficult. A vision board is a simple yet powerful tool that increases motivation and assists in making your dreams become reality. In simple terms it is a visual representation or collage of the things that represent your goal.

The idea behind a vision board is to stimulate the reticular activating system (RAS), which is a small, finger-sized control centre at the base of the brainstem. In addition to filtering information received by the brain, it also acts as a receiver for information that is tagged as being important. Think of it like a radio: even though you are surrounded by radio waves from a large number of stations, your radio can only pick up one of these channels at a time. In order to hear your chosen station clearly, you have to tune in to it. Your RAS is similar.

Where it is different is that it does not distinguish between a real event and a contrived reality. We can use this to our advantage in that we can programme it to seek out stimuli in our environment that resonate with our goals. This selective attention filter makes us aware of daily things that can help us achieve our goal and it is our job to take action on those opportunities when they present themselves.

Elements of a good vision board

1. Visual

Because the unconscious mind works in images, your vision board should be as visual as possible, using as many pictures as you can. These can be supplemented with inspiring or motivational words and phrases. Both the pictures and the words should closely represent your desires, so when creating a vision board, use images that clearly illustrate you managing stress well, achieving great health and leading the life you want.

2. Emotional

Just looking at your vision board should fuel your passion to achieve the images. It should also make you feel happy every time you look at it.

Positioning your board

Position your board where you will see it often, giving your unconscious mind maximum exposure to it. This will enable you to achieve your desires far quicker than you might currently imagine. Keep it somewhere private if you prefer or if you are concerned others may be critical of it, thereby affecting your focus.

Beliefs Change

Things that are widely believed as fact are constantly being disproved. Perhaps the best-known one is that the Earth was once believed to be flat. Another great example relates to something that was believed to be physically impossible – for a human to run a mile (1,609 metres) in under four minutes. In fact, for many years it was believed that the four-minute mile was a physical barrier that no man or woman could break without causing significant damage to the runner's health, the belief being that their lungs might explode or their heart would give up.

But while the achievement of a four-minute mile seemed beyond human possibility, on 6 May 1954, during an athletic meeting, Roger Bannister in fact ran a mile in 3 minutes and 59.4 seconds, breaking the 'four-minute mile' psychological barrier.

This was broken yet again fifty-six days later, when John Landy ran the four-minute mile in 3 minutes and 57.9 seconds in Finland. In the coming months and years many others followed their example, breaking their own four-minute miles.

People sometimes change their goals to fit what they believe others think they should have as goals. This means that in effect they are striving for their parents' or spouse's goals, rather than their own. They may even continue trying to achieve goals that they set years or even decades ago, without checking to ensure that they still actually desire the goals with the same passion they previously had. We all change over time and our goals should change with us, whether we have achieved them or not.

Whatever goals you decide to set, remember that they are your goals and no one else's. The whole point of having a goal is that you believe that by achieving it you will in some way be making yourself feel happier and that your life will be enriched in some way. Be prepared to change your goals if what you want from life changes, but never be afraid of taking steps towards things you believe will enhance your life.

The Fox and the Grapes

One hot summer's day a fox was strolling through an orchard, when he came across a vine with a large bunch of grapes ripening in the sun. This will do nicely to quench my thirst, he thought.

Drawing back a few paces, he took a run and a jump at them, but just missed the bunch of grapes.

Turning round again, he ran faster this time and with a 'One, two, three,' he jumped up again, but still did not reach the grapes.

Again and again he tried, but without success.

At last he gave up and walked away with his nose in the air, saying: 'I am sure they are sour.'

Notes to Self

- Without goals I'm just drifting, which is fine if I'm happy, but if not, it is time to decide what I want from life.
- If my beliefs and desires change, so should my goals.
- Goals should enhance my life and never be a source of stress.

Action Steps

- Set goals following the guidelines given in this chapter.
- Plan for the future and be clear about what you want.
- Write goals down.
- Take action towards achieving goals.
- Visualise your outcome.
- Create a vision board.
- Ensure your goals are your goals and not someone else's.

Final Note From the Author

Do what you can, with what you have, where you are.

Theodore Roosevelt

Having read my guide, you will know that it is packed with ways to help you manage and reduce stress that will also help to improve your life in every way. I know these techniques work, but they can only work if you actually use them.

☺ Leaving this book on a shelf collecting dust will not help you
  – otherwise known as shelf-therapy.

Change takes time and patience. Commit to changing one or two things at a time and be prepared to slip back into old habits. Simply start again with renewed resolve.

One of the best ways to master a skill or become proficient at something is to teach it to others. So the next time stress comes up in conversation, instead of telling people how you feel, share the techniques that are working for you. Remember: the more you practise your new way of thinking and behaving, the quicker you will become skilled at managing your stress levels and improving your enjoyment of life.

Here's to the life you deserve …!

Rebecca Richmond

Index

Glossary of Terms

Acute: (of a disease or its symptoms) severe but of short duration.

Adenosine: chemical messenger that plays an important role in biochemical processes, such as energy transfer. It is also an inhibitory neurotransmitter, believed to play a role in promoting sleep and suppressing arousal, with levels increasing with each hour a person is awake.

Adrenaline: hormone secreted by the adrenal glands that increases the body's rates of blood circulation, breathing and carbohydrate metabolism, and prepares muscles for exertion.

Affirmation: action or process of affirming something.

Anchors: stimuli that call forth states of mind, which are thoughts or emotions, and then corresponding actions.

Belief: an acceptance that something exists or is true, especially one without proof.

Brainstem: the central trunk of the mammalian brain, consisting of the medulla oblongata, pons and midbrain.

Calories: unit used to measure the energy value of foods.

CFS: chronic fatigue syndrome. A medical condition of unknown cause with fever, aching, prolonged tiredness and depression, typically occurring after a viral infection.

Cholesterol: waxy substance produced by the liver and found in certain foods, needed to make vitamin D and some hormones.

Chronic: (of an illness) persisting for a long time period or constantly recurring.

Circadian rhythm: any biological process that displays an oscillation of about twenty-four hours.

Circulation: continuous motion by which the blood travels through all parts of the body under the action of the heart.

Condition: illness or other medical problem.

Conviction: firmly held belief or opinion.

Coronary: relating to or denoting the arteries that surround and supply the heart.

Dehydration: loss of a large amount of water from the body.

Diabetes: disorder of the metabolism causing excessive thirst and the production of large amounts of urine.

Dietician: expert on diet and nutrition.

Diuretic: causing increased or excessive production and passing of urine.

Dopamine: compound present in the body as a neurotransmitter and a precursor of other substances, including adrenaline.

EFT (Emotional Freedom Techniques): form of counselling that draws on several areas of alternative therapy. Falls into the category of alternative medicine.

Endorphin: morphine-like painkilling substances occurring naturally that decrease pain sensation.

Fatigue: extreme tiredness often resulting from illness, or mental or physical exertion.

Fibromyalgia: rheumatic condition characterised by muscular or musculoskeletal pain, with stiffness and localised tenderness at specific points on the body.

Fight or flight response: heightened state of arousal to prepare to take action.

Hormones: substances produced to trigger, stimulate or regulate particular body functions into action.

Hydrogenated vegetable oil: widely used manufactured food products.

Hypnosis: trance-like state characterised by extreme suggestibility, relaxation and heightened imagination.

Imagery: use of visual images as part of therapeutic practices.

Immune system: organs and processes of the body that provide resistance to infection and toxins. Organs include the thymus, bone marrow and lymph nodes.

Inner voice: internal monologue, internal speech or verbal conscious thinking in words. Internal dialogue is a conversation one has with oneself at a conscious or semi-conscious level.

Insoluble: (of a substance) incapable of being dissolved.

Intuition: ability to understand something instinctively, without the need for conscious reasoning.

Irritable bowel syndrome: widespread condition involving recurrent abdominal pain and diarrhoea or constipation, often associated with stress, depression, anxiety or previous intestinal infection.

Malignant: virulent or infectious, tending to invade normal tissue or to recur after removal; cancerous.

Malignant melanoma: rare and very serious type of skin cancer.

Meditation: generally an inwardly oriented personal practice that individuals do to achieve a deep sense of inner calm.

Menstrual period: flow of blood and other material from the lining of the uterus (womb), lasting for a few days and occurring in sexually mature women who are not pregnant at intervals of about one lunar month until the menopause.

Metabolism: chemical processes that occur within a living organism in order to maintain life.

Mind–body connection: where the mind and body work together to foster the healing process on a physical level.

Motor skills: learned sequence of movements that combine to produce a smooth, efficient action in order to master a particular task.

MRSA (Methicillin-Resistant Staphylococcus Aureus): skin bacterium responsible for several difficult-to-treat infections in humans, that is resistant to a range of antibiotics.

Nervous system: network of nerve cells and fibres that transmit nerve impulses between parts of the body.

Non-REM sleep: stages of sleep that do not involve dreaming.

Nutrient: substance that provides nourishment essential for the maintenance of life and for growth.

Omega-3 fatty acid: unsaturated fatty acid of a kind occurring chiefly in fish oils.

Osteoporosis: medical condition in which the bones become brittle and fragile from loss of tissue, typically as a result of hormonal changes, or a deficiency of calcium or vitamin D.

PNS (Parasympathetic Nervous System): operates the body's natural rest-and-recuperation process.

Posture: particular position of the body; the characteristic way in which someone holds their body when standing or sitting.

RAS (Reticular Activating System): information-filtering system of the brain that evaluates incoming data.

REM sleep (Rapid Eye Movement): normal stage of sleep characterised by the rapid and random movement of the eyes.

Saturated: denoting fats containing a high proportion of fatty acid molecules, considered to be less healthy in the diet than unsaturated fats.

Selenium: chemical of which trace amounts are necessary for cellular function in many organisms, including all animals.

Serotonin: compound present in blood platelets and serum, which constricts the blood vessels and acts as a neurotransmitter; known as the 'feel-good factor'.

Sleep switch: designed to occupy the mind so it is impossible to focus on negative thoughts, providing a powerful anchor for sleep.

SNS (Sympathetic Nervous System): part of the automatic nervous system, which also includes the PNS.

Soluble: (of a substance) able to be dissolved, especially in water.

Sub-modality: any component that makes up a visualisation or an image; for example, whether it is black-and-white or colour.

Symptom: physical or mental feature that is regarded as indicating a condition of disease, particularly such a feature that is apparent to the patient.

Syndrome: group of symptoms that consistently occur together or a condition characterised by a set of associated symptoms.

Tapping: simple but effective technique used for dealing with emotions and pain, in line with acupuncture pressure points.

Trans-fat: unsaturated fatty acid found in many processed foods.

Tumour: abnormal growth of tissue, whether benign or malignant.

Ulcer: open sore on external or internal surface of the body, caused by a break in the skin or mucous membrane that fails to heal.

Unconscious mind: part of the mind that is inaccessible to the conscious mind but which affects behaviour and emotions.

Vegetarian: person who does not eat meat or fish, and sometimes other animal products, especially for moral, religious or health reasons.

Vision board: simple yet powerful visualisation tool.

Visualisation: when someone forms a mental picture of something.

Zone, the: when you are in 'the zone', you are in a state of relaxation, from which things come about effortlessly and easily.

About the Author

Having experienced a difficult childhood Rebecca suffered from prolonged periods of immense stress. Eventually, she developed the debilitating condition of fibromyalgia until she overcame it by creating a protocol of techniques, which included several methods to overcome stress.

She was also able to use the techniques to ensure she managed it effectively following surgery to remove a pancreatic tumour and a malignant melanoma. For many years she has since lived an active and healthy life.

As a qualified coach and master practitioner of NLP, Timeline Therapy™ and hypnosis, Rebecca is ideally suited to help her readers overcome stress and enjoy life.

Measure Your Stress Levels

Some Blank Tables for Your Notes

Stress Rating	Situations	Thoughts	Stress Symptoms
4	*Just managed to catch the train on time*	*Hope it's not delayed; can't afford to be late for this meeting*	*Shoulders slightly hunched; chest feels tight*

Manage Your Stress Levels
Some Blank Tables for Your Notes

Experience	Type	Thoughts	Emotions	Physical Effects
Missed the train to work	Negative	Typical – now I'll be late	Stressed	Shoulders and chest feel tight

Other Books in the *My Guide* Series

Manage Fibromyalgia/CFS

Overcome Insomnia

Manage Chronic Pain

How to Write a Novel

Market and Sell Books

Coming Soon:

Grammar Rules!

Understanding Your Human Smoothie

Manage Chronic Pain

None of us is
immune to pain. While it is vital to seek medical advice and a
diagnosis – and treatment where possible – the benefits of learning
to manage pain should not be underestimated.

- **Is your chronic pain affecting your ability to enjoy life?**
- **Do you find it difficult to hold down a job or career?**
- **Are you finding you are still in pain despite taking painkillers?**
- **Do you feel it is time to take steps to help yourself?**

Providing comprehensive 360-degree coverage of chronic pain
management, Rebecca Richmond shares the techniques that
she used to win her own personal battle.

Using tools that actually work, you can now reduce pain and
live a better life with these effective pain management solutions.
With all the tools for lasting, positive change, this is an essential
read for sufferers and therapists or trainers looking to add proven
techniques to their repertoire.

Simple and practical, this book is your partner against pain …

Overcome Insomnia

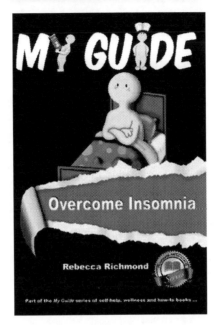

Insomnia does not have to be a life sentence of restless nights – take charge of your sleep and build healthy sleeping habits ...

Written by a former insomnia sufferer, this comprehensive guide draws disparate studies and approaches together under one cover to give you those much-needed eight hours of sleep.

Find out how to:

- **address numerous underlying factors causing insomnia**
- **put your life back on a healthy track**
- **improve overall wellness**
- **change your approach and restore sleep**

With concrete routines and practical exercises, this authoritative guide has all the tools for lasting, positive change ...

Make insomnia a thing of the past with this protocol of powerful techniques that work!

Manage Fibromyalgia/CFS

Explore different techniques and learn to live better with fibromyalgia. Having fibromyalgia doesn't mean the end of your life! Do you want to learn:

- **positive keys to effective management?**
- **to strengthen your resolve to beat this condition?**
- **how to eliminate pain and get back to enjoying life?**

Rebecca Richmond suffered for seven years before she developed a programme of mind–body techniques that enabled her to overcome her symptoms. She then used these same skills to aid her recovery from a malignant melanoma, MRSA and surgery to remove a pancreatic tumour. She now enjoys good health and lives a full life.

Cemented by the author's own experience, Rebecca believes the key to her healing was understanding how to interrupt the pain signal to the brain, overcome the traumas from her past and learn to relax so her brain stopped triggering the fight or flight response. Through these techniques, she has been able to enhance the way she thinks and improve every aspect of her life.

Hands-on hope for winning the battle against fibromyalgia/CFS – all assembled in one book …